Gene Hackman

Gene Hackman

MICHAEL MUNN

ROBERT HALE · LONDON

© Michael Munn 1997
First published in Great Britain 1997

ISBN 0 7090 6041 6

Robert Hale Limited
Clerkenwell House
Clerkenwell Green
London EC1R 0HT

The right of Michael Munn to be identified as
author of this work has been asserted by him
in accordance with the Copyright, Designs and
Patents Act 1988.

2 4 6 8 10 9 7 5 3 1

Photoset in North Wales by
Derek Doyle & Associates, Mold, Flintshire.
Printed in Great Britain by
St Edmundsbury Press Ltd, Bury St Edmunds, Suffolk.
Bound by WBC Book Manufacturers Limited,
Bridgend, Mid-Glamorgan.

Contents

for Kingsley and Marie

List of Illustrations

18   Hackman as the US Cavalry officer out to capture Geronimo
     in *Geronimo* (1994)

Credits

British Film Institute: 1–17.

Foreword

I first met Gene Hackman in the early seventies when I was a junior publicist in Wardour Street and he was here in Britain for reasons I don't recall – he may have been promoting a film, or he may have been here for the British Academy Awards. Whatever the occasion, I had the chance to accompany a PR person who was shepherding him round London. Naturally I took the opportunity, as I always did when meeting stars, to pepper him with questions: did he do his own stunts in *The Poseidon Adventure*? Did he drive the car in *The French Connection* chase scene? How did he get the role of Buck Barrow in *Bonnie and Clyde*? Nothing too in-depth.

In 1978, as a journalist, I interviewed him more extensively. He was in Britain to make *Superman*, and the set at Pinewood was closed to everyone. But as an intrepid journalist I endeavoured to side step the barriers. Talking to Marlon Brando was 'out of the question'. In fact everyone, including Christopher Reeve in his first major starring role, was being kept away from the press. However, one can find ways around these obstacles. For instance, I sneaked in an interview with the executive producer Ilya Salkind in his chauffeur-driven car as he was taken to Pinewood one morning. I saw Susannah York away from the studio. And I was able to speak to Gene Hackman by phone provided I withheld the interview from publication until the film was released.

In 1981 I interviewed Hackman vicariously by putting some questions to *Eureka* publicist Mike Russell – not exactly fulfilling, but an effective way of getting several pages of typed quotes. Finally, in 1986, when he was making *Superman IV* at Elstree Studios, I engineered a face-to-face interview by means of a cunning plan I have no intention of revealing here. None of this means that Hackman and I are old friends by any stretch of the imagination, but it does mean that much of this book is drawn from encounters of the close and not-so-close kind with the man himself.

I have also drawn from other interviews I've conducted over nearly three decades of working in film publicity and journalism, among them with Dustin Hoffman (in 1980 when he was promoting *Kramer Versus Kramer*), Christopher Reeve, Margot Kidder, Ilya Salkind, Sarah Douglas, Gene Wilder, John Sturges, Ronald Neame, James Coburn, Shelley Winters, Arthur Penn, Buzz Kulik, John Frankenheimer, Ernest Borgnine, Stanley Kramer, Ed Lauter, Bud Yorkin, Lee Marvin, Stanley Donen, Richard Brooks and Roy Scheider.

Very special thanks to Kingsley Everett for his invaluable help in the research of this book.

1 The Least Likely to Succeed

Eugene Alda Hackman came from a long line of newspapermen. His father, Eugene Ezra, had been a reporter for almost fifty years, so when Eugene Junior was born on 30 January 1930 it was just assumed that he would one day be looking to get by-lines of his own. In fact, there was nothing to suggest that he would eventually manage to break a long family tradition, reject journalism and become Gene Hackman, the actor.

When Gene was born the Hackman family were living in San Bernardino, California. The Great Depression had cast its pall over the United States, and because of mass unemployment, men had to follow the available work while the women stayed home to look after the family; many fathers were absent for months at a time. It was his talent as a newspaperman that kept Eugene Senior employed – and moving from one town to another, taking his family with him every time he was relocated.

'I must have gone to five different high schools,' Gene Hackman told me.

We never stayed in one place long enough to settle. I never had that feeling of *belonging*, never had any roots. We never owned our own house – always moving in and out of rented accommodation. So I didn't do well at school: I was always behind the others. And I knew that I was expected to go into a career as a journalist: it was just expected of me. But when I found out in school that I couldn't write, I figured that it might hinder any newspaper career! So there wasn't much that made me feel fulfilled in any way, and I kind of gave up trying to catch up.

His one big escape from a somewhat drab life was when his mother took him and his younger brother Richard to the cinema: she was a great film fan, having been in love with movies since her childhood, and her enthusiasm for it rubbed off on Gene.

> I loved the movies even when I was too young to really understand that the stars I loved watching, like Errol Flynn, Tyrone Power and Douglas Fairbanks, were really actors. I simply loved the adventure those men seemed to enjoy. And, like a lot of kids, I used to watch them and think to myself, 'I could do that. That could be me.' I never did any plays at school, mainly because I was terrified. I didn't have the confidence, and I never did things like sing in the choir or join the boy scouts and do all the normal community stuff. I wasn't so much a loner as someone who felt they didn't belong. I wanted to break out. I just became so restless. It wasn't a particularly happy childhood, you could say.

He was made even more miserable by a nagging weight problem; he was a plump little boy, and all through his life he has struggled against his weight. Before he reached his thirteenth birthday, his father moved the family to Danville, a small town in Illinois with a population of just 10,000. Most of the world by then was preoccupied with keeping Germany and Japan at bay, but for the Hackman family it was just a constant battle to keep the wolf from the door. The war was simply something Gene heard about on the radio and saw on the cinema newsreels.

Before long Eugene Senior was working away from home, which came as some relief to Gene, for his father was something of a fearful patriarch. Gene was later to recall, 'Although money was scarce and we never had a place of our own, we never went hungry, so we weren't *that* poor. But I didn't see much of my dad.' Eugene Ezra's long absences from home and the constant worry about money took its toll on the family, and relations between husband and wife became strained. Gene had turned thirteen when his parents finally separated for good, and he and little brother Richard moved with their mother into their grandmother's house.

All this was a lot of baggage for a young adolescent to carry about, and he consequently became withdrawn and rebellious, getting into trouble at home and at school. Restless to get away, he took a summer job at a steel mill. He didn't particularly enjoy the experience, but it served to convince him that he didn't want to get stuck in a dead-end job in Danville for the rest of his life.

My childhood wasn't particularly all I could have hoped it would be, but then I wasn't particularly deprived either. Danville had little going for it, except for a parade every Saturday night down the main street, so it wasn't a great place for a growing adolescent, and there were problems at home. So I ran away, like Huckleberry Finn, when I was sixteen. Only I didn't go down the river. I went round the world with the Marines.

The big break came about because of his growing tendency to lose his temper and lash out at authority figures. One day in 1946 he was playing basketball at school when he managed to get into a shouting match with the coach. He ended up stalking off the field and out of school, headed for home. En route he passed a recruitment centre for the Marines: he must have passed it many times before and thought about escaping Danville for ever. But he knew he needed the consent of his parents, and, figuring they would never give it, had never bothered to enlist. But on this occasion he went into the office and signed on the dotted line. To his surprise, his mother countersigned. 'I figure my mother gave her consent because she'd either had enough of me or thought a spell in the Marines might do me good,' he said. 'Maybe she thought I'd be back in a week after the rigours of boot camp. I sure thought about it, I can tell you! I hated the Marines but loved the freedom and travel. I was in school in the middle of the week, and at the Parris Island Marine base in South Carolina by the end of the week.'

Although he loathed military life, where subjection to authority was more absolute than he'd ever encountered before, the experience toughened him up considerably. Not that he was by any means a weakling to begin with: he may have carried some extra pounds, but he was fit enough to pass the gruelling tests all Marine recruits underwent. In bootcamp the pounds began to drop off him. Once through his training, he spent from 1946 to 1950 serving in China, Japan, Hawaii and the western Pacific island of Okinawa, but he never became what he described as 'the marine stereotype' and remained somewhat intimidated, shy and a little awkward.

While serving in China, and in search of a niche to fill for himself, he answered an appeal from the Armed Forces Radio Service, which needed an extra volunteer to fill in as an all-round disc jockey and broadcaster. It was his first experience of performing, and initially it proved to be a disaster: he dried up while reading the news. 'My nerves got the better of me – classic stage fright, every actor's nightmare,' he recalled. It might have been enough to put most people off the whole idea of performing in any medium, but it just served to make Hackman more determined to succeed. He stuck at it, fighting to overcome his stage fright, until he gradually acquired a taste for the whole thing. 'In the end I figured it didn't matter what I said or how I said it since 90 per cent of my audience was Chinese and couldn't understand a word I said anyway.'

As the Korean War escalated, American troops began pouring into the battle zone. Hackman's battalion received its orders to head for Korea, but by a twist of fate, Gene broke both his legs in a motorcycle accident and was shipped back to the States. Nine out of ten in his battalion never came back.

His left knee held together with plastic and metal joints, Hackman was disabled out of the Marines; forever after he was troubled with discomfort and pain in his leg. Taking advantage of the GI Bill, he enrolled at the University of Illinois to study commercial drawing and journalism. He soon realized that his talents did not lie in the written word, but having had some success with the spoken word, he decided instead to try for a career in radio. So, in 1951, he went to New York to attend the School of Radio Technique.

Feeling considerably older than his twenty-one years, Hackman believed, with some justice, that having travelled with the Marines, he knew more than the average young man. His self-confidence had never been greater. 'I arrived in New York at the Port Authority bus terminal, climbed into a taxi and, with the air of a man who'd seen the world, said, "Take me to Times Square." I didn't really want to go to Times Square, but it sounded good to say it. It turned out it was only one block away.'

Having settled into digs at the YMCA, Hackman began studying to become a professional broadcaster. He also pursued his talent for painting at the Art Student League. The formal training developed his natural flair for art, which was to grow into a lifelong passion. He studied hard, did his painting, and kept running out of money. Inevitably the time came when he was unable to pay his rent, and the YMCA locked him out of his room, confiscating his clothes until he could honour the debt. Determined not to miss that evening's YMCA dance, he turned up in his casual day clothes and was spotted by a young bank secretary. 'I couldn't help but notice him,' she later recalled. 'He wasn't wearing any socks.' Her name was Faye Maltese, a native New Yorker from a large Italian family.

Gene noticed her too, and undaunted by his lack of socks, he asked her to dance. She liked him immediately, and he was 'somewhat swept off my bare feet' by her. They began seeing each other regularly. Hackman recalled, 'I was just a small town hick and she was a big city girl from a big family, so I guess it was a case of opposites attract.'

As the romance grew into a formal courtship Hackman suddenly found himself with a second family, only a much larger one. She encouraged him in all he was doing ('was behind me all the way'); finally, he graduated from the School of Radio Technique. Almost immediately, he landed himself a job as an assistant floor manager in radio and at various local television stations – work which took him around the country but away from Faye. Soon growing bored with the work, and missing Faye, he became restless. Perhaps through nothing more than a lack of ambition to do anything else, Hackman turned instead to acting. After investigating his career prospects, he managed to enrol himself at the Pasadena Playhouse College of Theater Arts, California, whose motto was 'Work with the stars, become a star.' Why acting became his chosen path has always remained what he called 'a mystery I like to leave unsolved,' although it probably had a good deal to do with those childhood trips to the cinema.

The first thing to get sorted out was his love life. He had spent too much time missing Faye during his radio and TV days, and he didn't want to head off to California with the distinct possibility of never seeing her again. So he proposed, she accepted, and they were married on New Year's Day, 1956. Then he let his family know that he was planning to become an actor. To say they were surprised would be to put it mildly: they were in a state of shock. Never before had he shown the slightest interest in acting, and all of a sudden, at the age of twenty-six, he wanted to go on the stage. Hackman recalled, 'Everybody I knew thought that I was crazy when I decided to become an actor.'

With his new wife, he moved out to California. Even though it was the state he had been born in, he hardly felt at home at the college. Most of his fellow students came from the Californian surfing fraternity, so he was something of a misfit. He was also much older than the rest, being twenty-six. 'I was just like a fish out of water – all the others were just kids,' he said. Among the young ones in his class was a nineteen-year-old Californian called Dustin Hoffman, who had only recently dropped out of the Santa Monica City College to attend the Pasadena Playhouse. He looked up to the worldly Hackman, who seemed so much more mature and experienced than the rest of the students. Hoffman, being a drop-out, admired Hackman's anti-establishment attitude. They became firm friends and for a time Gene and Faye lived in the apartment next to the one Hoffman shared with another budding actor, Steve Ihnat.

It seems that Hackman made little impression on his tutors – even then he had something of the hang-up about his looks that would stay with him even through successful times. 'Everything was against me. I was nearly thirty, far from good-looking, and Dustin and I were considered the least likely to succeed.' A minor controversy was sparked by this 'least likely to succeed' quote after the judgement was attributed to their college contemporaries. Although the Pasadena Playhouse went bankrupt in 1969, a group of former students kept the memory of the college alive by forming the *Pasadena Playhouse Alumni and Associates Newsletter*. These former students were not amused by the 'voted least likely to succeed' anecdote, and in April 1989, just after Dustin Hoffman won his Oscar for *Rain Man* and the hackneyed anecdote was again published, the *Pasadena Playhouse Alumni and Associates Newsletter* put out the following disclaimer:

> There has been considerable publicity concerning this year's Academy Award winner for *Rain Man*, Dustin Hoffman, and his fellow nominee, Gene Hackman. The publicity states that these very successful Alumni were both voted the 'least likely to succeed' by their classmates. We wish to state that there was no such vote, nor was there ever in the entire history of the Pasadena Playhouse College of Theater Arts. We believe this puts both the College of Theater Arts and its students and alumni in a very demeaning light. Whoever perpetrated this mythical story should be informed that nothing like this ever happened. We who were there *know*. The good public does not.

* * *

Gene Hackman made his stage debut at the Pasadena Playhouse in *The Curious Miss Carraway* with comedy actress Zasu Pitts. It seems he did not impress the school principal, for whether or not he and Hoffman were ever voted least likely to succeed, Hackman was advised after just four months of study to give up acting. He left the college under a cloud, disagreeing with their assessment of his chances and his talent. He had started to believe in himself, and Faye was still prepared to back him all the way.

When he talked of going to New York to find out once and for all if he could become an actor, she urged him to give it a try. So they left the West Coast for the East, and moved into a sixth-floor cold water apartment in the East 20s, with just one bedroom and a kitchenette, all for $22 a month. Faye, finding work again as a bank secretary, assumed the bread-winner role, while he set about doing the rounds of agents' and producers' offices in search of an acting career. He always maintained that it was through Faye's unfailing support and encouragement that he finally became a success.

By this time Hackman found himself being influenced by Marlon Brando's emergence in the cinema through such films as *The Men* and *A Streetcar Named Desire*. But whereas the majority of America's youth wanted to be like the rebel they saw on screen, Hackman, like a good many other aspiring actors of the time, just wanted to be an actor like Brando. He claimed that seeing Brando in *The Men* made him believe 'that I could maybe do it, that maybe there really was an area for me'.

Acting work was almost impossible to come by, and Gene took on odd jobs to help keep Faye and himself fed and housed. But he kept on pestering agents and producers, and in the process met another struggling young hopeful, Robert Duvall, an admiral's son who had arrived in New York after two years of military service to study acting at the Neighborhood Playhouse. Both Hackman and Duvall had served in the military, both wanted to be actors, and both were out of work – this natural affiliation was the springboard for a good friendship.

Hackman recalled, 'Bobby and I had a lot in common in many respects. We both had our pictures and resumés, making our rounds of agents and producers, and never getting to see any of them. So we'd slide our pictures under the doors: it was ridiculous because we never got jobs that way. But we were kind of paying lip service to the process.'

In 1958 Dustin Hoffman turned up at the Hackmans' apartment, announcing that he had finished his studies at the Pasadena Playhouse, and had come to New York to find work as an actor: he would quickly discover that the Big Apple was full of would-be actors. Hoffman told me in 1980,

I told Gene and Faye I needed a place to stay – you know, just for a few nights. They let me sleep on the kitchen floor, right by the fridge – and they found they couldn't get rid of me. I wanted to go out and find an apartment of my own, but the city was cold and lonely and I was just too scared to leave. I felt safe with Gene and Faye – they were my *friends*, my *family*. So I stayed sleeping on the kitchen floor, and every morning at 2 and 4 o'clock the fridge had a heart attack and woke me up!

Hackman introduced Hoffman to Duvall, and the trio soon became inseparable. Duvall took to calling Hoffman 'Dustbone'; to

Hackman he was always 'Dusty'. They looked out for each other. 'In those days it was a question of who was the more broke, and the other two would help him out,' said Hackman. In the New Year Hoffman finally moved out of Hackman's kitchenette and into a Hell's Kitchen cold-water apartment with Duvall and three other tenants. In later, more successful years, Hoffman would maintain that he was always the shy, awkward one of the trio. He said, 'I really admired Gene and Bobby. If Bobby wanted a girl, he just went right after her. Gene was married so he had to behave himself, but he knew how to talk to people and could have picked up any girl he wanted. But I'd be totally paralysed at the thought of making the right moves.' Robert Duvall told a different story: 'Dustin has had more girls than anyone I've ever known – more even than Joe Namath ever dreamed about!'

Along with a group of other struggling actors – Elliott Gould, James Caan and Jon Voight – they organized playreading parties. Duvall sometimes played guitar while Hoffman sang, and they would also take great delight acting out dirty jokes. Another struggling actor – Robert Redford – joined the group. Hoffman told me,

> My best friends in those early days were Gene Hackman and Robert Duvall. And, I mean, none of us were handsome like Robert Redford who was another friend from those days. We all knocked around New York together for a while trying to become actors, and there was Gene and I with our looks, and I guess if anybody had said to us back in 1958 'You guys are going to make it,' we'd have laughed in their faces.

They all went to as many auditions as possible, and in time began to get small parts in summer stock. In 1958 Hackman landed a supporting role in an off-Broadway production of Irwin Shaw's *Children at Their Games*. Though it played for just one night, it was enough to win Gene the Clarence Derwent Award. Over the next four years they all struggled to get their breaks on Broadway. 'Mostly we just wandered around the streets of New York with Robert Redford and Robert Duvall,' said Hackman.

Those early friendships, founded upon a mutual bid for survival, have lasted. Said Hoffman, 'Robert Redford I hardly see because he spends all his time up in Utah I suppose, but Gene Hackman and Robert Duvall have remained my friends, and we see a lot of each other still.'

*   *   *

'Gene never lost his sense of humour, and in those days that was a feat,' said Dustin Hoffman.

> We were all getting turned down for jobs left and right. There seemed to be no end to our rejections. When we would meet for coffee, we would all crack jokes to keep from crying, but Gene won the award for unflagging good humour. I think that terrific wife he had at home was the reason. He was far ahead of the rest of the world by having her.

Hackman took on a variety of casual jobs to help make ends meet, including stints as a 'soda jerk' and a truck driver. When he heard a big convention was to take place in New York and a doorman was needed at Howard Johnson's restaurant to attract passing delegates, he applied for the job, and got it. Wearing a white uniform with green piping, he stood on duty in front of the restaurant, his main job being to open and close the doors. When a passer-by he recognized as his first sergeant saw him, he snapped to attention and gave a salute. The ex-sergeant looked him over and said, 'Hackman, you're a sorry-looking son of a bitch.' Hackman later recalled, 'After that humiliation I decided I'd become something other than a sorry-looking son of a bitch.'

With what seems to have been a fresh burst of determination, Hackman worked even harder to establish himself as an actor, and managed to land roles in little off-Broadway plays, including John Wulp's *The Saintliness of Margery Kempe* and Valgrem Massey's *Chapparal*. He also worked in an improvisational show in Greenwich Village. Then in April 1959 he made his television debut in the anthology series, *The US Steel Hour*: the episode was called *Little Tin God*. Faye was several months pregnant and would soon have to give up work, so Gene's struggle to make his mark became all the more desperate.

Further television roles followed, giving him just enough work to maintain his often flagging spirits. 'I was really lucky because I'd find that just when I'd get to my lowest ebb, a small job on TV would come along, and that was really encouraging,' he said. 'All I wanted was to be a working actor then; I never thought I could ever become anything more, let alone a star.' He was in a second episode of *The US Steel Hour*, entitled *Big Doc's Girl*, which was aired in November 1959. While Hackman was getting these small breaks, Robert Redford's chance came in 1959 when he played a walk-on part as a basketball player in the Broadway comedy *Tall Story*.

A son, Christopher, was born to Faye and Gene in 1960: thankfully Hackman's career as a television big-part actor was gaining momentum. He notched up another *The US Steel Hour*, called *Bride of the Fox*, in August 1960. The work continued into 1961 when he was cast in the prime-time series *The Defenders*, which starred E.G. Marshall and Robert Reed as father and son lawyers: the episode in question, *Quality of Mercy*, was filmed in New York. Another episode of *The US Steel Hour*, called *Brandenburg Gate*, followed, and then an episode of *Naked City*.

> I would have only five or six lines, and I was so nervous at first; I'd come on and go 'Blaaaaaaghhh!' All I wanted to do was say the lines and go home. Then I realized that it didn't make any sense to put yourself through agonies if you wanted to be an actor, so I learned to relax simply by learning that instead of driving against the lines, you absorb what's there, and that way you relax into it. In acting you have to think and feel; you can't think yourself into a part if you can't relax.

In 1961 he made his film debut in *Mad Dog Coll*: an inauspicious beginning because it was a formula film, chronicling the career of the eponymous gangster. The title role was taken by John Davis Chandler, who had made a decent career playing villains in gangster films and westerns such as *Major Dundee*, *Barquero* and *Capone*.

Naturally for Hackman it was a key moment – his first experience in front of the cameras in the fleeting role of a cop; a youthful Vincent Gardenia and a Telly Savalas with hair also made their screen debuts. Finally, it is also notable as one of a handful of routine films – which included cult B-movie *Murder Inc* – from director Burt Balaban, son of pioneer film exhibitor Barney Balaban.

Towards Christmas 1961 Dustin Hoffman was working at Macey's department store, demonstrating toys. Hackman came by to see him while Faye was shopping. Hoffman remembered,

> There is a strange kind of behaviour pattern to people as Christmas approaches. Seven days before Christmas they run around, picking up shirts and buying them. Two days later they pick up the shirt while looking at the jackets and buy the shoes instead. They'd buy just anything the closer to Christmas. So I bet Gene that I could sell Christopher [Hackman's son], who had this talent of just sitting still and quiet: he looked just like a life-size doll. So I began to demonstrate this new life-size, walking, talking doll, and people gathered round, and finally one lady said, 'I'll take one.' I had to confess that it was a joke, and she wasn't very happy, and neither was Gene because he had to pay me five dollars.

In January 1962 Hackman cropped up in one further *The US Steel Hour*, called *Far From the Shade Tree*, and he continued to feature sporadically in other series. His friend Robert Duvall finally got his big break that year, playing Gregory Peck's feeble-minded neighbour in *To Kill a Mockingbird*, which was released in 1963. It was an excellent film to kickstart his career, and while Hackman was still trying to graduate from television bit parts, Duvall was up and running with a career that would incorporate such highlights as *The Chase, Bullitt, True Grit, M*A*S*H, The Godfather* and *Apocalypse Now*.

In 1963 Hackman landed his second part, in *Lilith*. Starring a young Warren Beatty, who had made a wonderful debut in *Splendour in the Grass* in 1960 but whose next three films had bombed, *Lilith* was a chance to redeem himself. Robert Rossen, the director, had been blacklisted for communist affiliation in 1951, then pardoned by the House Un-American Activities Committee two years later. He had scored a huge success with *The Hustler* (1963), starring Paul Newman: the film re-established Rossen as one of America's most prestigious directors.

Beatty believed that Rossen would be his ticket to stardom. But by the time cameras began turning on *Lilith* in the summer of 1963, the director had fallen terminally ill. Beatty disagreed with Rossen on many aspects of the film, and filming became a battle of wits occasionally interrupted by arguments. Rossen was too weak to fight his corner; Beatty probably didn't know how ill the director was.

The film itself was a fairly faithful adaptation of the controversial J.R. Salamanca novel about a therapist (Beatty), who falls in love with a troubled patient, played by the volatile actress Jean Seberg. Hackman appears briefly as a colleague of Beatty, trying to help cure Seberg.

Seberg, a beautiful and interesting actress who went on to achieve minor cult success in the French cinema, had arrived on the Hollywood scene with much fanfare in Otto Preminger's *St Joan* in 1957. But the film flopped, and she never really managed to get her career more than a few inches off the ground. In the end she took her own life in 1979.

In 1976 Seberg told me

> I went to Europe to work in the end because you just have to fight to be the best in Hollywood all the time. I made several films in Europe after *St Joan* and hoped that *Lilith* might be the film that gave me some recognition in America, but it was such an appalling situation to be in, with the leading actor fighting with the director,

who I thought was wonderful. I also liked Gene Hackman who was then an unknown actor, but I never thought he had a chance of making it as a star because he just didn't look like – well, like Warren Beatty or any of the other handsome men. And I mean 'Hollywood handsome.' To me Gene Hackman was a handsome man because he had such character in that face. That's what makes an actor interesting: it's what his face says about his experiences, not how wonderful he looks. But I knew only too well how everyone in Hollywood who wants to make it has to look their best – that was the pressure I was under, and I suppose while it may be worse for women than men, the men are still expected to convey that 'heart-throb' image. I knew Gene was never going to be a heart-throb, and I doubted that he would ever be successful. But I *knew* he was a really good actor – you could see that just watching him work. He didn't question Robert Rossen about his motivation or ask to have his lines changed or go for any of that method acting. He was just professional, nervous and willing to do his best.

When the film was released in 1964 it was slated by the critics and ignored by the public, meaning that Hackman was to remain relegated to walk-on roles, while Beatty failed to establish himself, and Rossen never worked again, dying in 1966. Beatty later said, 'The best thing about *Lilith* was Gene Hackman.'

Not that Hackman was too disappointed about his failure to make a mark in films. Like most New York stage actors, he considered movie work to be little more than a way of making money, while 'real acting' was to be done on the stage. 'In those days films was just a way to steal money, spend a little time in California, get your hotel expenses paid, and get back home again,' he said. 'Most films were hardly seen because only a handful of films were really successful, so any bad film didn't make a difference to a stage actor. I didn't know anything about the technique of film acting, and didn't really care that much.'

Hackman was intensely proud of his son Christopher, and in 1963 the family swelled when Faye gave birth to a daughter, Elizabeth. Having been raised largely without a father of his own, Gene was determined to do a good job of bringing up his own children. His marriage had been a success, too, unlike his parents': sadly, it would all change with success. But at the time their partnership seemed only to strengthen when the going got tougher. He later said, 'Without Faye life would have been unbearable. To come home every night and find her there made me want to go on. The children gave me the sense of belonging that I think all men need.'

Meanwhile another of his friends, Robert Redford, had been

making a name for himself, starring in a Broadway play, *Sunday in New York*, in 1961. This in turn led to his biggest break, a starring role alongside Elizabeth Ashley in Neil Simon's comedy *Barefoot in the Park*. It opened in October 1963, and Gene Hackman played a supporting role in it for a while. The following month, on 22 November, President Kennedy was assassinated. Hackman was among the millions who felt a sense of immense loss. 'I loved the Kennedy idea and I really don't know why. I just liked the idea that there was a young man who seemed to care about us.'

Redford stayed with *Barefoot in the Park* for four years while Hackman left to land his own starring role on Broadway in 1964 in *Any Wednesday*. This comedy featured a millionaire businessman who spends every Wednesday with his mistress in the company apartment until his young associate, Cass, is accidentally sent to use it. Young Broadway star Sandy Dennis, who had won a Tony for her performance in *A Thousand Clowns*, took the role of the mistress. Directing *Any Wednesday* was Hackman's former tutor from the Pasadena Playhouse, George Morrison; he presumably had been among those who had thought Hackman would never make the grade as an actor. Jason Robards had already been cast as the millionaire when Hackman turned up for his audition.

He couldn't have hoped for a better opportunity, but it almost ended before it began. According to the play's author, Muriel Resnick, George Morrison found it hard to imagine anyone less suited to playing Cass than his former student, who sported a spreading bald patch, a paunch and a face that had not exactly been blessed by the gods. Resnick recalled that during the audition Sandy Dennis found Hackman so 'repulsive' that 'she almost died when he came into the room and she had her first look at him'. Dennis begged Morrison not to cast Hackman. But Gene had a champion in Muriel Resnick, who insisted that he was perfect for the role: 'He was so good and so right.' Morrison told her to wait and hear the other actors who were reading. 'But I knew then that no one could be better no matter how many we read. [He] was exactly the man I meant – warm, funny, mature and very nice.' He got the part.

Twenty years later Sandy Dennis told me,

I was rather snotty-nosed then, I suppose, and behaving like a spoiled *ingénue*. I had become what you would call a 'star' on Broadway but I may not have been completely mature enough to deal with my own neurosis and anxieties. I'm sure that Gene Hackman was feeling even more insecure and anxious. And in the event he was totally professional, not at all unpleasant to work with

and, most important, he was very good in the play. Thank God I was
persuaded I was wrong. I'm embarrassed to think that I refused to
work with an actor who went on to win an Oscar and become a star.
I don't know if he ever forgave me..

Any Wednesday opened on 18 February 1964 at the Music Box
Theater. The generally favourable reviews were peppered with
praise for Hackman. 'The angry young man, who knows what
[Robards] is up to, is expertly and likeably played by Gene
Hackman,' wrote Richard Watts Jr in the *New York Post*. Walter
Kerr observed in the *New Herald Tribune* that Hackman was 'an
exceedingly nimble performer who can put a finger in your eye
before you have quite noticed your eye is open, and he has a wonderfully light-footed habit of stepping off a joke before it begins to
complain.'

Through rehearsals and performances, Hackman had learned a
lot about the craft of comedy acting.

I hadn't really been aware until my last two years in New York how
much more expertise and judgement it takes to do comedy as
opposed to drama. In many ways drama is arbitrary; it's more about
choice, because, for instance, you can choose not to cry when everyone else is crying, and you can defend that choice not to cry to your
death, saying that it's a character who's cut off or whatever. That's
defendable. But in comedy, if the laugh doesn't come, there's no way
you can defend that. If they don't laugh, you did it wrong.

He was disappointed not to be able to reprise the part in the
1966 film version and although Jason Robards repeated his role
Sandy Dennis too was passed over, in favour of Jane Fonda.
Nevertheless, the play earned Sandy Dennis her second Tony
award, and it proved an excellent showcase for Hackman's talents.
Even so he left the play somewhat surprisingly after a single season, having become bored with the grind of repeat performances –
this despite the security a long-running play offered. Having scored
a Broadway success, however, his position was more entrenched,
and this would make it easier to land other parts. After playing
opposite Robert Preston in Jean Kerr's *Poor Richard*, he went on
to act in *The Natural Look*, alongside an up-coming Brenda
Vaccaro. Though the play closed down after just one performance,
Hackman had fortunately been seen by film producer Walter
Mirisch, who was in search of a supporting cast for *Hawaii*.

2 Stealing Money

Walter Mirisch had long planned a film version of the best-selling James A. Michener book, *Hawaii*, or, at least, a third of the massive 964-page saga: there were thoughts that the book might be made into a trilogy. (In the event there was only a second, *The Hawaiians* (1970) which starred Charlton Heston – ironic, as Heston had been offered the first film and had turned it down. The first was the more successful; the sequel proved insignificant.)

The film's director, George Roy Hill, tested Hackman, and agreed with Mirisch that they had found a new and valuable character actor. And that is the direction Hackman supposed his career would head – playing character parts. Not every actor could be a good-looking romantic lead; there was plenty of room in Hollywood for gritty character actors – one thinks of Lee J. Cobb, Robert Ryan, Martin Balsam, Ernest Borgnine, Robert Webber. Hackman could, with luck, join the list. It was mainly a question of getting the breaks, and *Hawaii* seemed to offer one.

The story centred on the early Christian missionaries who travelled across stormy seas from New England to far off Hawaii, bringing the Bible to the natives, and thereby wrecking their ancient culture. The film was going to take six months to shoot in Hawaii, although Hackman's role, that of John Whipple, a doctor-missionary, would not necessitate his presence for the full term. Nevertheless, his part couldn't be shot within one concentrated period as director George Roy Hill intended to shoot the film chronologically.

The film starred Julie Andrews, fresh from *Mary Poppins* and *The Sound of Music*, Max von Sydow, known to American audiences mainly for his role of Christ in *The Greatest Story Ever Told*, and Richard Harris, the Irish actor who at that time was only just beginning to emerge. The key focus, however, was on the teaming of Andrews and von Sydow. As Julie Andrews put it, 'Marvellous publicity –"Mary Poppins marries Jesus!" Gorgeous!'

Filming got under way in February 1965 off Bodo, Norway, under the supervision of the second unit director, Richard Talmadge. These scenes, depicting the missionaries' boat, the *Thetis*, sailing through the Strait of Magellan, did not involve the principals and co-stars. Their work got underway in April in Massachusetts at a permanent historical reconstruction, which served as the town of Walpole, New Hampshire, in 1820. Hackman's first real work in the film kept him in Hollywood for seven weeks for the interiors at the Goldwyn Studio, although he was summoned only sporadically.

Finally, in June, the entire company of actors and crew assembled in Hawaii, where the principals were to spend the rest of the summer. At Maku Beach, on the island of Oahu, a village of 107 buildings was constructed and carefully aged by twenty-eight years as filming progressed. Away from the set Hackman was able to join other members of the unit at gatherings held by Julie Andrews at her house in Kahala, where she showed a 16-mm print of Godard's *Breathless* and, out of loyalty to Walter Mirisch, *The Magnificent Seven*.

Idyllic though it might sound, filming on the Oahu beaches was hot and uncomfortable. Hackman discovered that this was probably the only place in the world where you could go to a roadside burger bar and get a hamburger with fries, mustard and an orchid. As the weeks wore on, the film began to fall behind schedule and drift over the $12 million budget. Tension increased when Mirisch fired Hill and replaced him with Arthur Hiller, a move resulting in a strike among the Polynesian actors, who had come to love Hill. Mirisch had no option but to re-instate him.

Hawaii, $3 million over budget, was finally completed in October, although Hackman had wound up on it some weeks before and had gone back to New York. Even before the film was premiered in New York in 1966, his agent had received several film offers, made purely on the strength of Hackman's participation in the eagerly anticipated film. None of the offers was particularly exciting, but subscribing to the philosophy that film work was a way 'to steal money' – and he needed more now that a third child, Leslie, had arrived in 1966 – he accepted what there was.

The first was *A Covenant with Death*, a dreary melodrama about a man convicted of murder in a town on the American-Mexican border who winds up killing the hangman just as the real murderer confesses. Hackman was way down the cast list – below George

Maharis, Katy Jurado, Earl Holliman, Sidney Blackmear and Laura Devon – in his role as the local police chief. The film sank without trace but the producer, William Conrad, liked Hackman's work enough to put him into his very next picture, *First to Fight*. This tale focuses on a World War Two veteran, played by Chad Everett, who is taken home and feted, then returns to the front only to lose his nerve. Hackman, as the ever-reliable sergeant, saves Everett from certain death at the hands of the Japanese, and gets wounded in the process, leaving a flag-waving Everett to lead the men into battle, announcing he will be 'the first to fight'.

Of those early films, Hackman said,

> I can't say I was any good in those films because I hadn't learned how to do movie acting. But it didn't matter because the films were not much better than my acting. My main function in *A Covenant with Death* was to find a suicide note from the real murderer, so that didn't take much emoting. And in something I did called *First to Fight* I played a sergeant, so I recalled my life as a Marine and pretended I was very brave.

Several more television jobs came his way, with the roles growing in size as he guest-starred in *The Trials of Brian*, *Hawk*, and *The FBI*. Early in 1967 he reported to Universal for a bit part in *Banning*, essentially an opportunity for the studio – which still had something of a stock company of contract players – to show off such home talent as Guy Stockwell, James Farentino and Susan Clark. Hackman, not being one of their prized players, appeared only fleetingly and was probably better off not being noticed in this humdrum soap opera about corruption and infidelity in a swank Los Angeles golf club.

Before *Banning* was released in 1967, a new turn of events saw Hackman having another stab at a good character role in the grade-A picture, *The Graduate*. 'Dusty' Hoffman had had an even tougher time than his friends making it as an actor. He had to wait until 1966 before he landed a starring role on stage, and even then in an off-Broadway production, *The Journey of the Fifth Horse*. As he said, 'Most of my plays were off-off-off-off-off-Broadway.' Nevertheless, for his performance he won an Obie award, which led him to a starring role in the farce *Eh?* Critical acclaim followed, as did an offer from film director Mike Nichols, who was looking for a young actor to star in *The Graduate*.

Nichols brought Hoffman back to Hollywood to make the film that would change his life. Now that he had the chance to repay his friend who had let him sleep on the kitchen floor (by a fridge that had two heart attacks a night), Hoffman persuaded Nichols to cast Hackman in the role of Mr Robinson, husband of the middle-aged seductress played by Anne Bancroft. It was a momentous opportunity for Hackman, but, unfortunately, things did not go well during rehearsal.

Nichols pushed Hackman to do better than he seemed able to, and the actor found himself floundering alongside the experienced and famous Anne Bancroft. Nichols persevered for a while, but he finally lost patience. In the men's toilet Hackman told Hoffman, 'I think I'm going to get fired today.' He was right. On reflection Hackman said, 'That was a painful experience. I think it was my fault. I just wasn't capable then of giving the director what he wanted. I didn't have the right skills as a movie actor – it takes at least ten years to learn that. I'd had maybe five, six years of it. So I figured I'd better get learning. And the only way to learn is to do what you get offered.'

All of a sudden it seemed like the end. It was hard enough to establish yourself as a workmanlike, reliable, always-on-time actor in the film capital – but to be fired for not being up to the job meant almost certain career termination. A call from Warren Beatty saved him from that fate.

* * *

Warren Beatty told Hackman that he wanted him for a vital role in a film he was personally producing called *Bonnie and Clyde*, the story of the bank-robbing lovers of the Depression era. Beatty was going to play Clyde Barrow, and he wanted Hackman to play his brother Buck. The only drawback was that Beatty hadn't yet found a studio prepared to stump up the production money. He had never before produced a film, and even as an actor had not, by 1966, yet conquered Hollywood. He was hoping that *Bonnie and Clyde* would change all that, and he persuaded Hackman what an excellent opportunity it would be for him too – if he could actually get the film made.

French director François Truffaut sent Beatty the original script by David Newman and Robert Benton, two writers who had, in turn been inspired by Truffaut's film *Jules et Jim*. They sent the script to Truffaut because no American studio had shown any interest. The director thought that the film might serve as a possible vehicle for Beatty and his current female companion Leslie Caron to play the legendary outlaws.

Beatty had some doubts about the project, not least the fact that Leslie Caron had a strong French accent that would be impossible

to disguise. Graciously she accepted that this was an insurmount-
able obstacle and encouraged him to find another actress. Caron
persuaded the ambitious Beatty that *Bonnie and Clyde* could be
the film to turn him into both a major star and, in his guise as producer, a powerful force in Hollywood: if this film was successful, he
could become his own man, in control of his future while most
other actors were in the hands of agents and independent producers. This was, after all, shortly after the meltdown of the studio contract system, which had once provided star names with continual
employment. Now it was every actor for him or her self.

Caron also convinced Beatty that the story of Bonnie and Clyde,
while liberally sprinkled with violence and humour, should be char-
acter-driven and not just another gangster film. Moroever Newman
and Benton had touched on Clyde Barrow's bisexuality, and their
original scheme, reminiscent of *Jules et Jim*, involved showing
Bonnie, Clyde and C.W. (Michael J. Pollard) in a *ménage à trois* –
yet another challenge.

Beatty paid a meagre $10,000, all he could afford, for the rights
to the script, and then sent it to Arthur Penn, his director in *Mickey
One*, to read. Although Penn was one of the breed of new-wave
American directors, he counselled against the homosexual angle in
the story, which he felt made it less viable to potential backers: he
knew studios would be looking for a fast-moving action-packed
adventure. So, with Beatty in agreement, Penn got writer Robert
Towne to work with Benton and Newman in honing the screenplay
to make it more mainstream: it was a classic case of commerce versus art. In Hollywood scriptwriters are continually embroiled in
such battles.

Beatty figured that any studio would want a beautiful actress to
co-star, so he asked Natalie Wood to play Bonnie. They had once
been a romantic item, and he had a hunch that this well-known gossip would appeal to the studios. Wood, however, was too busy at the
time to leave Hollywood for the three-month shoot in Texas – not
working, undergoing analysis. Beatty held out in the hope she
would change her mind, but she was a wreck, both emotionally and
mentally, and tried to kill herself with an overdose of barbiturates.
The leading man had no choice but to look elsewhere. He offered
the role to Tuesday Weld, but she was pregnant. Finally he decided
to take a different tack and seek out an exciting unknown. Faye
Dunaway fitted the bill.

Beatty continued to put his package together before approaching the studios. Just how and when Hackman got the call from the
producer is a matter of conjecture. Gene hadn't been completely
idle since Nichols fired him; he'd racked up an episode of *The*

Invaders and the Western series *Iron Horse*, both of which were shown in October 1967. He had not, apparently, been Beatty's first choice to play Buck Barrow; that honour fell to Jack Nicholson. Hackman was an afterthought when Nicholson proved unable or unwilling to play Buck.

In one account Beatty was driving round Hollywood, and spotting Hackman standing on the corner of Hollywood Boulevard and Vine Street, he recalled the quiet newcomer from *Lilith*. Estelle Parsons, cast to play Buck's wife Blanche, remembers suggesting Hackman herself. Arthur Penn said, 'Warren Beatty suggested Gene for the part. He had worked with him on *Lilith* and I had seen Gene in a play in the Berkshires with Estelle Parsons and knew they'd be great together.'

Hackman's own version was that he had actually been ill in hospital for six weeks with blood poisoning. 'Warren popped in to see me. I was not only surprised, but touched. He said he had a film role he wanted to discuss with me. It was Buck Barrow in *Bonnie and Clyde*.'

However it happened, Beatty handed over the script, and with nothing to lose, Hackman accepted, hoping that Beatty had not heard that he had just been fired from *The Graduate*. Another newcomer, Michael J. Pollard, was slated to play C.W. With Arthur Penn's help, Beatty was able to put together a more experienced and distinguished crew, and with his package he went from studio to studio to try and get backing. Said Hackman,

> Considering the enormous success the film became, you'd have thought the studios might have been falling over themselves to back it. But no one but Warren saw the potential he had with that property. I mean, I just hoped it would get made and I'd be paid well enough, and maybe it might be successful enough to bring me more work. It was certainly an excellent script, and Warren's enthusiasm for it was overwhelming. So you had to believe in him. Warren is just amazing. I mean, he has this image of being a playboy, but he's really a shrewd film-maker.

Beatty took the project to Warner Brothers where he had made four of his seven previous pictures. He was well aware that Jack Warner, still head of the studio then, thought little of actors who tried their hand at producing or directing. The mogul made a big point of telling Beatty that not one of his films had made any money for the studio. So Beatty literally got down on the floor and kissed Warner's boots until the ageing studio boss said, 'OK, OK, Warren. You're embarrassing me. I'll do your little picture.

But I warn you, don't go a cent over budget.'

Warner agreed to invest $2 million of the studio's money, so long as Beatty made up the shortfall. The producer would also receive 30 per cent of the profits – which was less an indication of Warner's generosity, than his lack of faith in the project.

So in 1967 Hackman joined the rest of the cast and crew in the rural landscape around Dallas – a Texas that had changed little in appearance since the Bonnie and Clyde days of the 1920s. Never before had Gene been given so much screen time, and he knew this was a heaven-sent opportunity to create an impact. But it was no easy proposition, for he still had much to learn about film acting. His own particular brand of improvisation worked well for the first and second take, but was sorely tried from the third to the fifteenth take. Faye Dunaway later claimed that Beatty would insist Penn shoot everything thirty times. But with Penn's help, Hackman began to learn more about the difference between stage and film acting, and came to appreciate the challenges the medium presented to an actor. The director showed where the adjustments needed to be made – playing with just a little less size, learning to react more internally. He was able to keep his first scene – when Clyde and Buck whoop it up and persuade each other what a wonderful time they are going to have – looking fresh and spontaneous even though it was actually shot around fifteen times.

In fact Hackman grew bored with playing Buck, partly because of the character's lazy drawl. As a budding actor, he had spent years of hard work learning to pronounce every *ing* sound, and here he was having to say *goin'* and *comin'* for the entire film: before long he had really tired of the accent and the character – ironic, in retrospect, since this would be the role that brought him international recognition.

Hackman was full of admiration for the way in which Beatty handled the production work while managing to deliver an exceptional performance. 'The studio was on his back all the time, but he managed to keep them at bay and work closely with Arthur Penn and Robert Towne. And when he started running out of money and Warners wouldn't put up any more, he managed to find it somehow.'

Although Penn was making a film set in the thirties and paying meticulous attention to details of wardrobe, set and props, he felt that his film existed in a timeless limbo. It was how the thirties might have been, a glamorization that was to appeal directly to the young people of the sixties and create a wave of nostalgia for the fashions of the earlier decade. It also helped that the stars of the film, including the 37-year-old Hackman, were young enough to appeal directly to the young audiences that Beatty and Penn were aiming for. The film helped directly to spark off a cycle of youth-orientated movies that became a staple diet of the cinema during the late sixties and early seventies.

*   *   *

After finishing *Bonnie and Clyde*, Hackman guest-starred in *I Spy*, the top action series that made stars of Robert Culp and Bill Cosby. Meanwhile, Jack Warner saw Beatty's finished film – and hated it. Beatty had no fans among the studio's executives, who decided to put out the picture on a limited release in August, the 'graveyard' month. Then came the scathing reviews. Bosley Crowther of the *New York Times* deplored the way the film portrayed the 'hideous depredations of that sleazy moronic pair, as full of fun and frolic as the jazz-age cut-ups in *Thoroughly Modern Millie*.' Joseph Morgenstern, in *Newsweek*, described the film as a 'strange and purposeless mingling of fact and claptrap that teeters uncannily on the brink of burlesque'. *Variety* found the film 'leaves much to be desired' and thought that Beatty was 'believable at times but his characterization lacks any consistency.' It did like Faye Dunaway who was 'a knockout as Bonnie Parker,' but said 'Michael J. Pollard and Gene Hackman are more clowns than baddies.'

There was very limited support from a small circle of critics, including Judith Crist, who wrote, 'Beatty, so often merely a promising performer, fulfils himself as Clyde . . . saturated in time and place we are left with the universality of the theme and its particular contemporary relevance. And this is the triumph of *Bonnie and Clyde*.'

Despite the critical onslaught, audiences were drawn to see the film in the few cinemas it played. Within eight weeks it had become the third most successful film on release. Today the film is regarded as a classic and an artistic triumph. But it is doubtful that audiences of 1967 saw it as anything other than an escapist adventure featuring more blood than probably any other American film up to that time, with two highly attractive stars who were more glamorous than the real Bonnie and Clyde ever were. Yet still Warners seemed reluctant to give the film full rein. After it had finished its four-months general release, Beatty urged studio bosses to reissue it immediately. They refused. Arthur Penn told me:

> Warren was a fighter. Warner Brothers didn't like *Bonnie and Clyde* and released it poorly. But Warren got in there and reorganized the advertising and the release pattern. He became a real pain in the ass

for Warners: they just didn't recognize him as a superior business-man. They do now. He was right behind every decision in how the film was made. He got the cast together and, well, look what's hap-pened to Gene Hackman. Nobody wanted to touch him because he didn't have the right looks. But Beatty knew he was a hell of an actor, and I certainly enjoyed working with him – so much that we worked again on *Night Moves*.

While Beatty was struggling to overcome the misgivings of Jack Warner about his project, Hackman started to reap the benefits of being in a movie that was making headlines. Offers began coming his way, including one from director John Frankenheimer, who was preparing to shoot *The Fall Guys* with Burt Lancaster. But because it wouldn't be ready to roll until the summer of 1968, Hackman accepted a couple of more meagre offers to fill his time. This taste of success Hackman suspected was fleeting, and he wanted to 'steal' as much as he could while the money was on offer. He knew that he was hardly 'leading man' material, and that the road to obscurity in some taped television soap was always a threat. So he felt he couldn't afford to pick and choose what was offered.

Nevertheless the work was available and it paid, offering Hackman the kind of security that unsettled him. Having his life suddenly mapped out was depressing. 'Before I had gone from day to day, not knowing what I was going to do next, and I kind of liked that edge to my life. But after *Bonnie and Clyde* I had three films to do, one with Burt Lancaster, and that was quite tough to adjust to.'

He also had to adjust to being recognized. Once, walking through Greenwich Village, Hackman encountered a group of people calling out 'Buck'. He later said, 'I had never realized the true power of movies until that moment.' If the future was now looking brighter, he was gloomy about one particular thing – his looks. 'I worry about my double chin,' he said in an interview. 'I know I'm not a leading man, but I still worry.'

Eight months after *Bonnie and Clyde* was completed, the film was officially regarded as a genuine smash hit. During this time Hackman got on with the first of the three jobs ready to roll in January 1968: *The Split*, with Jim Brown, Diahann Carroll, Julie Harris and Ernest Borgnine, all of whom were above him in the credits.

Jim Brown was then a star of some significance: a handsome, vir-ile former full-back with the Cleveland Browns American football team who retired from the game in 1967 having been lured to the silver screen. *Rio Conchos* (1964) was his first picture and he went

on to become one of *The Dirty Dozen*. The latter persuaded MGM
to put Brown, perhaps the first bona-fide black male sex symbol of
American cinema, under a short-term contract: he was one of the
last stars to be contracted to that once-great studio. Within a two-
year period he starred in *Ice Station Zebra, The Split, Kenner, Dark
of the Sun* and *Tick . . . Tick . . . Tick.*

The Split featured Brown as a big-time thief bent on committing
his last big robbery – stealing the takings of a football game at the
Los Angeles stadium (an apt setting given his original career). In
the aftermath of the caper everyone goes after the money – robbers, relatives, even cops, none of whom is above killing to get their
hands on it. Among them, Gene Hackman plays a crooked detective. Even while he was making this film, he was being fitted for his
wardrobe for the next, *Riot*.

In January 1968 the American Academy of Motion Picture Arts
and Sciences announced that *Bonnie and Clyde* had been nominated for ten Oscars: for its direction; its costume design; its cine-
matography; its screenplay; for Warren Beatty as Best Actor; Faye
Dunaway for Best Actress; Estelle Parsons for Best Supporting
Actress; both Michael J. Pollard and Gene Hackman for Best
Supporting Actors; and as Best Picture. With this announcement
Warners had no choice but to re-release the film, and it proved
even more successful the second time around, grossing an overall
$30 million in the US market alone, from which Beatty earned
more than $6 million.

The 1968 Academy Awards show took place at the Santa
Monica Civic Auditorium on 8 April. The assassination of Dr
Martin Luther King four days earlier cast a shadow over the glitzy
proceedings. Gene Hackman's defeat to George Kennedy as Best
Supporting Actor in *Cool Hand Luke* was, said columnist Rex
Reed, 'the first upset in an evening filled with weird and totally
unexpected developments'. Arthur Penn, predictably enough, lost
out to Mike Nichols for *The Graduate*. The big surprise came when
The Graduate was *not* voted Best Picture – that award went to *In
The Heat of the Night*: typically the award for Best Film determined
who would win Best Director.

Faye Dunaway had to step aside for Katharine Hepburn in
Guess Who's Coming to Dinner, but Estelle Parsons won. *Bonnie
and Clyde* won only one other award, for Burnett Guffey's cine-
matography. Rex Reed pointed out how amazing it was that
Camelot got the Costume award 'when *Bonnie and Clyde*, which
only started a fashion revolution, got nothing'. Faye Dunaway
put her own disappointment into perspective, saying, 'Martin
Luther King had just been assassinated. It was no time to worry

about a piece of gold statuary.'

America was faced with more tragedy when Robert Kennedy was murdered in Los Angeles in June of that year. Hackman felt the loss deeply. 'I met Bobby Kennedy a couple of months before he was killed and I was so impressed. After he was killed I felt I didn't want to get involved politically any more.'

After the Oscars, *The Split* was rushed out to poor reviews, and Hackman came in for some of the criticism. *Variety* said, 'Hackman lacks authority in a poorly developed role.' Despite this Hackman could feel more than satisfied that, by this time, *Bonnie and Clyde* had pushed him forward into some prominence. To call him a star would be an overstatement, but to describe him as one of the most important supporting actors around was perfectly accurate. The mere fact that he had been nominated for an Oscar gave his agent just cause to demand six-figure fees for future offers.

Paramount executives must have been gleeful to have had the foresight to give the Oscar nominee equal billing with Jim Brown in *Riot*. This violent prison drama found Hackman playing Red Fletcher, a convict who leads thirty-five prisoners to stage what is initially a demonstration of their grievances while the warden is away. Brown played Cully Briston, who is serving only five years, wants nothing to do with Fletcher's plan – a plan that culminates in eight hostages being seized, including the deputy warden. Fletcher tells the gathered news reporters that he wants only to negotiate with the authorities over their grievances, but some of the prisoners, made drunk from moonshine, want to kill the hostages. As the situation grows ever more dangerous, Fletcher tries to stall for time while Cully and some of the other convicts start to dig an escape tunnel.

The warden returns, and as he sets about restoring order, twelve prisoners make their escape attempt. Only three reach the final tower wall: Fletcher, Cully, and Joe, a psychotic killer. Joe tries to put a knife in Cully's back but is himself fatally wounded by Fletcher. While Cully makes it to the outside, Joe, just before dying, cuts the escape rope and sends Fletcher plummeting to his death.

The novel by Frank Elli had sold a quarter of a million hardback copies since its publication in 1966. It was as authentic a novel about prison life as one could hope for: not surprising since Elli had been in and out of prison for some twenty years. It was while taking a correspondence course during a spell in Stillwater Prison that Elli wrote a story in which he recounted a prison riot. Upon reading it, Professor Harold J. Alford of the University of Minnesota urged him to expand it into a full-length novel and helped him to find a literary agent.

The published work won its author the Thomas R. Coward

Memorial Award for Fiction. Paramount bought the film rights and
assigned William Castle to produce and Buzz Kulik to direct. Kulik,
a television veteran, had directed episodes of *The Defenders* and
The Twilight Zone, before going into films with a handful of good
actioners such as *Warning Shot* and *Villa Rides*. He told me,

> I guess so many of the films I did in the sixties depended largely on
> star names more than anything else. I had just made *Villa Rides* with
> Yul Brynner and Robert Mitchum, and then I made *Riot* which had
> Jim Brown who was a big star then, and Gene Hackman who
> nobody had heard of until *Bonnie and Clyde*. Suddenly he was a star,
> although you had to wonder how long that could last because peo-
> ple became big stars quickly and faded quickly. That kinda happened
> to Jim Brown. And you just knew that Hackman was never going to
> be a star like Brown, or any of the handsome leading men. But he
> had something a lot of stars didn't have, and that was versatility. He
> could play anything – good, bad, sympathetic, evil. But at the time
> we made *Riot* they wanted him to be a sort of star heavy, like Ernest
> Borgnine. I guess the thing with Hackman was you knew he was
> probably going to continue working for the rest of his life but you
> couldn't be sure he'd ever become a leading man.

Hackman went on to enjoy greater success and longevity than Jim
Brown. In fact, despite uncertain beginnings, and in spite of what
would later be some disastrous, almost fatal, choices, Hackman has
somehow managed to outlast most of his peers.

Kulik decided to shoot the entire film in an actual prison, complete with inmates. He chose Arizona State Penitentiary, overseen
by warden Frank Eyman, famous for putting the notorious gangster John Dillinger in handcuffs. He accommodated the production
with such enthusiasm that he was even given the role of warden in
the film. Four hundred convicts were interviewed and of them
eighty were chosen to audition in speaking roles. They were put
through a crash course in acting by Paramount's drama coach Bob
McAndrews, and Kulik made his final choice for featured roles.

Generally all the inmates took part as extras, and one even
asked that his parole hearing be postponed so as not to prevent his
participation. To ensure security during production, Hackman and
the rest of the cast and crew had to carry identity cards, producing
them every time they left the compound. Women were completely
prohibited from entering the prison, so associate producer Dona
Holloway was unable to visit the set. But Kulik regarded all the
hassles as worthwhile, and in gratitude to all the inmates for their
good behaviour and unabated enthusiasm, Paramount premiered

the film at the prison in December 1968. Hackman was unable to attend (he was filming *Marooned* in Hollywood), but Jim Brown was there with warden Eyman.

The assembled reporters asked the warden if showing the film to the prisoners might give them ideas. He told them, 'I know the movie depicts a mass escape attempt, but it shows nothing new, nothing that hasn't been used before. In fact so many of them get killed in the process I think it will do them good to see it. It may help get some of that nonsense out of their heads.' The film was shown over five nights to ensure all the inmates got to see it.

The critics attacked it for its extreme violence. The *Time* critic wrote:

> Even in these bloody times, the violence in *Riot* is rather extravagant: when cons are shot in the chest, gore gushes from their mouths, and throats are slit with slashing abandon . . . Although *Riot* aspires to be reformist social criticism, it is about as effective – and moving – as a convict chorus of 'Don't Fence Me in' – Gene Hackman, a fine character actor, deserves better parts than the one he is given here, and audiences deserve better than the careless ease he brings to it.

But *Variety* liked Hackman, who 'gives the best performance as an equivocating, cynical manipulator of crowd psychology'. And the film was greeted with praise in Britain by the *Monthly Film Bulletin*, which called it, 'one of the most striking prison dramas since *Riot in Cell Block Eleven*'.

Before joining John Frankenheimer in July 1968, there was still time to make a television movie, *Shadow on the Land*, which imagined that America is ruled by a ruthless dictator while the underground resistance tries to restore democracy. Gene Hackman received third billing, below Jackie Cooper and John Forsythe, as the Revd Thomas Davis: at least it was a chance to play a good-hearted man for once. Even accepting the limitations of television – a low budget, short shooting schedule – the intriguing scenario failed to take off, mainly due to Nedrick Young's barely adequate script. The film was aired on 4 December 1968.

Before that Hackman set off for Wichita, Kansas, in July 1968 to make the Frankenheimer film, now renamed *The Gypsy Moths*. This seemed to offer his best opportunity for a quality film since *Bonnie and Clyde*, not least because he would be working with a really big star, Burt Lancaster, as well as a distinguished director (who had previously worked with Lancaster on *Seven Days in May* and *The Train*).

The Gypsy Moths are the name of a trio of skydivers – Rettig (Lancaster), Browdy (Hackman) and Webson (Scott Wilson) – who tour small-town America. They arrive in Webson's home town of Bridgeville, Kansas, where his Aunt Elizabeth (Deborah Kerr) and Uncle John (William Windom) still live. The skydivers are given lodgings in Elizabeth and John's home, and before long Rettig becomes romantically involved with Elizabeth. Webson, mean-while, gets involved with a college girl, and Browdy takes up with a topless waitress.

Rettig asks Elizabeth to leave with him, but she is unable to make the difficult break, and at the next show, he jumps to his death. Browdy and Webson perform a memorial show to raise funds for Rettig's funeral. Afterwards Webson tells Browdy that he has made his last jump, and Browdy decides to try his luck as a Hollywood stuntman.

Not surprisingly, experienced sky-divers were drafted in for the aerial work, brilliantly filmed by stunt cameraman Carl Boenisch. Watching the footage of these scenes thrilled Hackman and inspired him to learn to pilot a plane – he even took up stunt-flying as a hobby. In fact flying was to become a great passion in his life, and with the kind of money he found himself making from films, he began to indulge himself in this kind of expensive hobby and, gen-erally, a more affluent life-style. He and Faye bought their own house in Hollywood, the first of many luxury homes.

About Hackman, Burt Lancaster said, 'I noticed that he seemed a little edgy waiting around for the set-ups. He wanted to get on with it. I understood that, because he came from a background in theatre where you rehearsed a great deal, and then you performed. There was none of the waiting about you get on film sets. But when Frankenheimer called for action, he was good, every time.'

Lancaster was the first really big Hollywood name Hackman had worked with, and he saw first hand what it meant to be a living legend. 'I found a lot of people would defer to him, and I wondered, Why don't they argue with him a little bit? Is he gonna punch them out or something? Well, he's not because he's a bright guy. It's just that, as I later realized, you just reach a certain level and people get frightened of your money or your power, or both.'

Fortunately Frankenheimer knew how to handle the star. 'When you work with Burt Lancaster you know there's going to be some fighting. This is because Lancaster cared about the work. It's never because he wants to have the focus on himself. He is very generous to other actors and he works harder than anyone else.' Lancaster let Wilson and Hackman have their space on the screen, and the latter learned a great deal about how an important actor handled himself on the set. Lancaster's selflessness was even noticed by critic Richard Shickel, who wrote in *Life*, 'As he has grown older, Mr Lancaster has developed a capacity, unique in established stars, to "give away" scenes that his status in the movie pecking order entitles him to dominate. He did it in *Castle Keep* and he does it again in *The Gypsy Moths* and he deserves full credit for his shrewd selflessness.'

Most reviews were lukewarm when the film was released in 1969, but *Variety* noted, 'Hackman and Wilson are forceful, both giving excellent accounts of themselves.' *Time* said, 'The interrelationships of the characters make sense but have little emotional resonance, a handicap that only Gene Hackman manages to surmount. His brassy characterization of a free-living skydiver adds a poignant dimension of reality to a film that, like skydiving itself, is an exciting but slightly dubious exercise.' Unhappily, the film bombed in America, and in Britain the distributors put it out as a second feaure to the James Garner thriller *Marlowe*.

If nothing else, Hackman had the reputation of delivering the goods, and he found himself in some demand for further films. Still not yet at the point where he could afford to pick and choose, Hackman went to work for John Sturges as one of three astronauts lost in space in *Marooned*. The film had much going for it. Director Sturges was responsible for two of the most enduring hits of the sixties, *The Magnificent Seven* and *The Great Escape*, as well as some classics from the fifties like *Bad Day at Black Rock* and *Gunfight at the OK Corral*. The film also had a great star in Gregory Peck. And it had a storyline that was to prove all too realistic, despite the subject matter. Three astronauts are embarked on an eight-month mission on board a space laboratory in orbit. But after serving five months the men are suffering from severe fatigue, and it is decided to bring them home. They board their NASA spacecraft and break away from the laboratory, but as they prepare for re-entry their retro rockets fail to fire. With only forty-eight hours of oxygen left, they are marooned. Down at mission control, the chief controller, Charles Keith, played by Gregory Peck, tries to figure out how to save the astronauts from certain death, and after much discussion, argument and experimentation, the astronauts safely return.

Recent spage-age features such as *2001: A Space Odyssey* and *Planet of the Apes* were garnering huge profits, but Sturges' contribution to the genre involved more than just an element of realism. As he told me in 1976, 'It was not so much a science fiction film, but a science *fact* film. I'd never been interested in making the kind of space film where astronauts go up in a rocket and meet space monsters. I wanted *Marooned* to be a film that could happen. The thing is, we didn't know that after we finished filming it and it was on release, it did happen, to Apollo 13.'

With Gregory Peck topping the cast list, Sturges didn't need big stars to fill the rest of the roles.

> I had a formula which I liked to stick to: get a big star and surround him with the best supporting actors around. That's exactly what I did with *The Magnificent Seven*. People forget that when we made that Yul Brynner was the only star in the line-up. Steve McQueen had not yet become really big, and they all became stars because of the film. Sometimes you need two big stars for two big roles, like Kirk Douglas and Burt Lancaster in *Gunfight at the OK Corral*, but the principle's the same – surround them with really good supporting actors. So when I made *Marooned*, I had Greg Peck, and then I took three good supporting actors to play the astronauts – James Franciscus, Richard Crenna and Gene Hackman. It was easier to make the audience believe these men really were in trouble up there, whereas if I'd had someone like Paul Newman, Steve McQueen and Yul Brynner in that spacecraft, everyone would know they'd get back. In fact the studio would have insisted on them surviving. But there's something about an actor like Gene Hackman because he doesn't have an image – not even now he's a star. So an audience believes in him. James Franciscus and Richard Crenna were concessions to the studio's requisite for actors who were not stars but were well known. Hackman was the new boy, and his presence alone gave a greater sense of realism that was essential to the story.

Virtually all Hackman's scenes called for him, Franciscus and Crenna to sit in a claustrophobic set representing the spacecraft, which was constructed at Columbia Studios. Apart from the short time spent on location at Cape Kennedy, the three actors were for the most part cooped up on a hot, cramped set.

Despite the workmanlike performances of all the principals, they all took a back seat to the film's technical aspects. The stunning photography by Daniel Fapp was nominated for an Oscar, while the special visual effects by Robbie Robinson won the Academy Award. Ironically the film, released in 1969 shortly before Apollo 13 found itself stranded in space and brought back on a wing and a prayer, was generally slated by the critics as farfetched. *Variety* said: 'The film is superbly crafted, taut and a technological cliff-hanger. The production's major flaw is a hokey old-fashioned Hollywood Renfrew-to-the rescue climax that is dramatically, logically and technologically unconvincing.' Pauline Kael described it as a 'space epic with a horse and buggy script.' *Time* thought '*Marooned* rates about one half out of a possible 2001.'

It was April 1969 when the film opened in Britain, coinciding with the Apollo 13 crisis: *Marooned* was suddenly not quite so far-fetched after all. No doubt the crisis helped to attract big audiences, who would sit in tense silence knowing that the film they were watching reflected real events that were happening outside of the Earth's atmosphere. Perhaps this made the film seem better than it really was. It meandered at times and could have benefited from some of its 134 minutes being trimmed, and Gregory Peck, in the least interesting role of the man at Mission Control, had little to do in performance terms. Nevertheless it was a tense, sometimes spectacular film that made Hackman's face ever more familiar to audiences. To many who were not avid film fans, he was one of those actors they recognized but whose name they could rarely recall.

3 The Right Connection

By now Gene Hackman had more or less accepted that he would never be cast as a leading man. The emphasis was on glamour and good looks, and around that time two actors more than any others seemed to epitomize those qualities. They were Paul Newman and Robert Redford, the stars of the big hit of 1969, *Butch Cassidy and the Sundance Kid*. Redford had previously made only a handful of films, including *Barefoot in the Park* (1967), an adaptation of the stage version that had made him a success on Broadway a few years before. After that the film offers flooded in, but he allowed himself the luxury of taking his time to choose his next project.

He elected to do an unusual Western, *Tell Them Willie Boy Is Here*. But the film flopped commercially, and he was lucky to be rescued by George Roy Hill, who was planning to direct *Butch Cassidy and the Sundance Kid* with Paul Newman in the role of Butch. While Twentieth Century Fox wanted Marlon Brando, Steve McQueen or Warren Beatty for the role of Sundance, Hill only ever wanted Redford for the part, and he got backing from both Newman and the film's writer William Goldman. The studio capitulated, Redford played the part, the film became the biggest hit of 1969, and the two men became Hollywood's hottest properties.

Now with the muscle to make his own films, Redford set up his own company, Wildwood Productions, and immediately got to work on *Downhill Racer* in 1969. To direct it, he assigned 29-year-old Michael Ritchie, who had episodes from *Dr Kildare* and *The Man from UNCLE* under his belt: this was to be his first film. Along with co-producer Richard Gregson, they assembled their cast. Ritchie complained that the role of the ski-team coach was only 'half formed' and told Redford that 'it needed an extraordinary actor to bring it to life'. Redford agreed, saying they needed 'someone like Gene Hackman'. Not someone *like* Hackman, Ritchie responded; they needed the genuine article. So the director went to meet Gene on the set of *Marooned*. Hackman's confession that he knew nothing about skiing had Ritchie admitting that he didn't either. Having come to an agreement as to how his role should be rewritten, Hackman accepted.

While it may have been slim on plot James Salter's screenplay was filled with action. Eugene Claire (Hackman), the American ski team coach, sends for a replacement after his top skier breaks a leg. David Chappellet (Robert Redford) arrives, brilliant and tough, but arrogant and undisciplined: he refuses to ski in his first big race when he's given eighty-eighth position. Eugene believes David can be a champion, but his assistant, Mayo, urges him to forget the arrogant newcomer aand concentrate on another brilliant team member, Johnny Creech.

When Eugene manages to get David a better starting position in his next race, the skier pulls out an incredible performance. He also finds himself a girlfriend, Carole (Camilla Sparv), who follows the team to the FIS World Championship, where David and Johnny are hailed as America's new hopes for the Olympics.

During the second season, David's seeding rises to 20, but he falls. Later he meets Carole and her boss, Machet, a ski manufacturer doing business with Eugene. When David should be practising, he goes skiing with Carole. Later in the season they spend some time together in Montreux. The American team finishes the season with their sights set on the Olympics, and Eugene spends his time raising funds.

Carole refuses to spend Christmas with David, and when they later meet by chance at St. Anton, he ignores her. He has become completely single-minded about the Olympics, and when Johnny breaks his leg during the last pre-Olympic race, David sees his chance to prove himself. He skis brilliantly during the climactic downhill event and is catapulted into gold medal position. But he is followed by a challenger who seems set to beat him. The rival falls and David becomes the downhill gold medal champion.

Redford and Ritchie had everything to their satisfaction, including a budget of $3 million from Paramount. Then, to everyone's horror, Paramount cancelled the film, deciding that the budget was too high for a film whose commercial appeal was limited. Ritchie and Redford persuaded the studio they could make the picture for just $1.8 million, and the powers-that-be relented. The cast and crew took off for the Alps where filming got underway during spring 1969; this was timed to take advantage of the Winter Olympics in Switzerland where Ritchie secretly filmed the

Olympic skiers in order to save money.

Unfortunately it just so happened that there was an early thaw in Switzerland that year, right in the middle of filming. Nearby the James Bond film *On Her Majesty's Secret Service* was being made on a huge budget: Hackman witnessed crates of champagne being hauled up the mountain for the 007 VIPs. They also had their own fake snow, and when they finished their location and moved on, Ritchie quickly moved his unit on to the artificial slopes.

The picture was little more than a star vehicle for Robert Redford, and Hackman later admitted that during production he often felt like 'a high-priced extra'. Deep down what he really wanted was to land a romantic leading role, one in which he got the girl – even though he knew it was unlikely to ever happen. But for once he wanted to be like Errol Flynn. Ritchie suggested, in 1978, that this frustration is the key to understanding Hackman's career.

Ritchie was full of praise for Hackman, and in writing about the making of the film said, 'Gene quickly breathed life into his character. He brought such strength and authority to the part that the only problems we had were over those scenes where Redford was supposed to leave Hackman bewildered and ploughed under.'

Ritchie couldn't wait to work with Hackman again – he did so later in *Prime Cut* – and felt that he had discovered some of the secrets of Hackman's success as an actor during the making of *Downhill Racer*. At the end of the film Redford believes he has won the race, but Hackman tries to take the credit himself. Then comes news that another skier is on course for taking the championship. Somewhat despondent, Hackman moves away from Redford, until he learns that the challenger falls, at which point he goes back to Redford, slaps him on the back and shouts, 'I knew we could do it.' Ritchie observed, 'That kind of ambiguity and even outright duplicity is seldom found in parts for "leading men". After all, how could such double-dealers deserve the girl? But it is very human, and it's at the core of Gene Hackman's greatest performances.'

The film offered the viewer some of the most exciting ski footage ever filmed. But even with Redford's pulling power it just didn't have enough going for it to make it a commercial success, although it has since become something of a minor classic. Hackman's role was significant enough to give him second billing to Redford, and as usual he received uniformly good notices: 'Hackman's characterization is virile and thoroughly human,' said *Variety*.

Hackman was quickly establishing a reputation among directors, several of whom wanted to work with him again. John

Frankenheimer, for example, had the actor in mind for a leading role in *I Walk the Line*, playing a sheriff whose life is wrecked when he falls in love with a moonshiner's daughter. Hackman, who hankered after a romantic-lead role, regarded it as a heaven-sent opportunity. Such a part, he felt, would be a crucial career move. 'You can't become a really big star unless you have played a romantic hero of some kind. After that you can do anything and the public will play along with you. It was exactly the same in the old days of Hollywood. You didn't have to be good-looking to be a star, but you did have to have a romantic aura.' Columbia Pictures, however, didn't feel the public was ready for Hackman in this new light, and they insisted Frankenheimer cast Gregory Peck.

A leading role finally came his way in *I Never Sang for My Father*, even though top billing was given to Melvyn Douglas in a lesser part; no one, however, doubted that Hackman was the star of the film. He played Gene Garrison, a kindly middle-aged widower who desperately wants his cantankerous old father to know he loves him. Despite his father's continual rejection and scorn, he finds it hard to escape the old man's domination.

Curiously the screenplay by Robert Anderson was based upon a play that was itself adapted from a screenplay, called *The Tiger*, which Anderson had written in 1962. Fred Zinnemann had wanted to film it provided he could get Spencer Tracy to play the father. But Tracy had fallen terminally ill and would not have been able to meet the physical demands of the part.

When Zinnemann lost interest, Elia Kazan urged Anderson to turn his screenplay into a stage play, which he did, and called it *I Never Sang for My Father*. It opened at the Longacre Theater on 25 January 1968 and ran for 124 performances, with Hal Holbrook as Gene Garrison, British actor Alan Webb as his father, Lillian Gish as his mother, Hal Holbrook as their son and Teresa Wright – Mrs Robert Anderson – as his sister. Then Gilbert Cates produced the play on Broadway, and decided that it had potential as a film.

Cates approached a number of American actors to play the father, including Edward G. Robinson, Fredric March and Melvyn Douglas: Douglas had turned down the stage version because of the prospect of repeating the role night after night; but the idea of doing the role on film appealed, and he accepted.

Lillian Gish was unavailable, so Cates cast Margaret Garrison as the mother. Hackman and Estelle Parsons were cast as the brother and sister. Dorothy Strickney played the mother, and Elizabeth Hubbard played Peggy. When Hackman read the screenplay, he was delighted to find that his role was actually the larger one.

The story begins when Gene Garrison visits California and falls in love with Peggy, a divorcee with children. He is faced with the dilemma of whether to marry Peggy and move to the west coast, or finish the relationship and stay east to be near to his parents. He can't bring himself to consult his father, Tom, a domineering, demanding and irascible old man.

When Gene's mother suddenly dies, his sister Alice arrives from Chicago for the funeral. Till now banished from the family for marrying a Jew, she advises Gene to settle down with Peggy and be happy in California. Gene hopes that his father might also come round to the idea, but Tom rejects any suggestion of being left to rely on a full-time housekeeper or being placed in a nursing home.

Peggy arrives for a convention and Gene introduces her to his father. Tom behaves himself and she is charmed by his manners, but when Gene suggests he might come and live in California with them, Tom becomes rude and obnoxious. Gene is hurt by his father's continual rejection of his love, but finally accepts that he must leave his father and marry Peggy.

Directing the film himself, Gilbert Cates put the actors through a week of rehearsals, then began filming on location at Kennedy Airport. Much of the movie was shot at the old Biograph Studio in the Bronx, and at a house owned by the mayor of White Plains, New York. The film's storyline must have reminded Hackman of the fact that he'd been raised by his mother alone, and here he was playing a grown man saddled with an ageing father. He said, 'Making the film wasn't gratifying; the script was tight and the material depressing. It only worked because of what people brought to it.'

But the finished product delighted him. 'I loved that film. I loved working with Melvyn Douglas. What a beautiful film. But it didn't have the kind of shoot-outs and fist fights that draw the public to theatres. They didn't want to see a film that worked on an entirely different level, looking into people's emotions and having to deal with old age and dying.'

He was right: people couldn't be persuaded to come and see it in the cinema, despite the favourable critical response. 'Gene Hackman has his best screen role thus far,' announced Pauline Kael in the *New Yorker*. 'He's a fine, naturalistic actor, and though he isn't particularly handsome, he has an interestingly expressive face. He's believable and compelling in what could have been a drag of a role.' He is, wrote Gavin Millar in *The Listener*, 'emerging as one of the current screen's great character actors.'

The Hollywood fraternity also approved of Hackman's work in the film, so much so that the Academy of Motion Picture Arts and Sciences nominated him for an Oscar – but not as Best Actor, because that honour fell to Melvyn Douglas, who had had top billing. So for the second time in three years Hackman found himself nominated Best Supporting Actor, and he told Michael Ritchie, 'I think the Academy is trying to tell me something.' Robert Anderson was also nominated for his screenplay.

With his 'major supporting actor' status, Hackman began to wonder if this was to be the peak of his career. 'When things are going well, you just don't know when it's all going to end. So you start getting reckless, doing what comes your way, just in case it's suddenly all over.' That could be the only rational explanation for his decision to make *Doctors' Wives*.

This sex drama was presumably hatched in the wake of the success of *Bob and Carol and Ted and Alice*, and even featured one of that film's stars, Dyan Cannon, as leading lady. Competing as the male leads were Richard Crenna and Gene Hackman; the former won out because of his conventional male-lead looks. Nevertheless, only a careless actor would boast that he was the star of *Doctors' Wives*, and Hackman has certainly dismissed it with a curt 'I never saw it.'

In this salacious glimpse behind the modern façade of an American clinic, doctors are sleeping with nurses, and the doctors' wives are betting on which of them will seduce which man on the clinic staff. When the wife of a brilliant brain surgeon and her medic lover are found shot dead in bed, the surgeon is arrested for the double murder. However, his skills are later needed to save the life of a nurse's injured son. Hackman's own little subplot focuses on his attempts to cope with the psychiatric problems of his wife (Rachel Roberts). When she confesses that her troubles stem from a lesbian affair in her past, the two become reconciled.

The film's dire quality is surprising given it came from the pen of Daniel Taradash, screenwriter of *Golden Boy*, *From Here to Eternity* and *Hawaii*. But responsibility fell to a director inexperienced in the movie medium: George Schaefer had been very successful in television, winning eight Emmy Awards, before making a handful of forgettable films in the sixties. After *Doctors' Wives* he returned to the small screen.

Had the film's success depended on critical favour, it would have died a death. Christopher Hudson wrote in the *Spectator*, 'In appealing unashamedly to vicious morons the film will no doubt find a permanent place in the affections of its makers.' *Time* said, 'By most standards this is a terrible movie. This does not, however, prevent it from being fun . . . it is an example of assembly line, bit-studio movie-making at its grotesque best.' Fortunately, the film had just enough sex, plus a grisly heart operation, to draw an audience.

As Hackman's face gradually became more familiar to movie-goers, so too did his name. But he was still hardly an actor who could be expected to draw large audiences. Nevertheless, when B-picture director Don Medford was given a grade-A budget to shoot a western called *The Hunting Party* he considered himself very fortunate to acquire the services of Gene Hackman. The main star was Oliver Reed, who had graduated from the Hammer horror school of acting to become a big name after his performance of Bill Sykes in the British musical film *Oliver*. In *The Hunting Party* he played an illiterate outlaw, Frank Calder, who kidnaps schoolteacher Melissa Ruger (Candice Bergen), because he wants her to teach him to read and write. Unhappily for him, she turns out to be the wife of a local rancher, Brandt Ruger (Hackman), who proves to be far more sadistic than even Calder. A fanatical hunter, Ruger rounds up a posse to track down Calder and bring Melissa home. However, as they cross deserts and plains, Melissa finds herself increasingly drawn to her captor. Meanwhile, Ruger's men decide to abandon the chase, so the obsessive husband goes on alone, finally killing Calder, then his wife, before dying of thirst.

One has to question why the actors got involved with such an appalling film. Oliver Reed said, 'I wanted to do a western, so when this came along I did it.' Bergen's stance was lighthearted: 'All I do in this film is get raped and have orgasms. But I've got the orgasms down pat now! It's your token ten seconds of heavy breathing followed by my baroque expression, eyes heavenward.' Hackman had no good reason to sign up other than the fear that his run of gainful employment would suddenly dry up. An ultra-violent film, it was made in Spain in just eleven weeks over the summer of 1970, using cheap sets and props available from all the Italian westerns that had already been shot there.

During production a magazine managed to find someone who resembled Gene Hackman, rounded up a few half-naked girls, and photographed them draped over the lookalike. When the pictures appeared in print and Faye saw them, she thought it really was Gene, and hit the roof. Hackman had to convince her that it was a set-up.

If this seemed like a storm in a marital tea-cup, there was a whole lot more brewing. Hackman was making films virtually back to back, and, like his own father had done, was spending a great deal of time away from his family. Most actors try to compensate for this by making one film a year, and then spending concentrated periods with their families in between work. But Hackman was to some extent running scared. Having struggled for so many years, he never wanted to repeat the experience, and while he was still employable, he wanted to carry on working, no matter how lousy the films were. But there was a price to pay, and it was his marriage: relations between him and Faye had become strained.

Faye was unable just to pack up the family and follow her husband to each new far-flung location. Christopher was now ten, Elizabeth seven and Leslie only four: the last thing Faye wanted was to disrupt their schooling. Gene felt the same, having himself been moved around so much as a child, and never having been able to settle in school. Now with his career really starting to pick up, the time away from home was becoming detrimental to his marriage. It was no wonder Faye blew up when she apparently saw her husband cavorting with half-naked Spanish beauties.

Essentially the film jumped on the spaghetti western bandwagon, with director Medford trying to compete with both the Italian westerns and Sam Peckinpah, whose *Wild Bunch* had set new standards of high-profile blood letting. Hackman hated the whole thing, vowing to avoid getting involved in any more gratuitously violent films. It was an honourable intention, but as he was to discover violence had become an integral part of action movies. It was a stark choice: either do the work that was offered to him or starve.

In the autumn of 1970 he appeared in *Cisco Pike* as a corrupt cop: the main performer was rock star Kris Kristofferson as Cisco Pike, an over-the-hill rock star who is busted on a drugs offence for the second time. Detective Leo Holland, played by Hackman, has a heart ailment that threatens to end his career prematurely. He decides to compensate for what will be a pitiful pension by hijacking a consignment of marijuana, and tells Pike that he will use his contacts to have the court show clemency if he will sell the drugs. Pike accepts the proposition, and the film thereafter traces his attempts to shift the dope to customers that range from rich executives, lawyers, junkies and musicians.

UCLA film graduate Bill Norton both directed and wrote the screenplay, which was based on his own experiences. He was as surprised as anyone when Columbia agreed not only to finance the film but to give him the chance to debut as a director. For Hackman this was a chance to work from home: Faye and he were growing apart, and he hoped to patch things up before they got any worse.

The finished film managed to find some admirers, but generally it was a critical and commercial failure. Hackman must have been wondering if he would ever get to play a substantial role in a sure-fire success. Trying to juggle the priorities of having a great career and an enduring marriage was proving far from easy.

                        *   *   *

Eddie Egan was a real-life cop, a narcotics officer in New York who liked to break a few rules. In 1961 he and his partner Sonny Grosso uncovered a drug-smuggling ring whose route originated in Turkey, passed through the South of France and ended up in New York. After four months of surveillance, officers seized $32 million-worth of heroin, enough to supply New York's addicts for two years. Author Robin Moore decided to write a book inspired by Egan's and Grosso's exploits, and called it *The French Connection*.

Philip D'Antoni, the producer of *Bullitt*, bought the film rights to Moore's book, sensing it had all the ingredients for a first-rate cop film, and persuaded Ernest Tidyman to write the screenplay. However, when the script was completed it was turned down by every studio. D'Antoni and Tidyman reckoned that one key element was missing – a great chase to rival the one that became the highlight of *Bullitt*. Puzzling over how to concoct a chase with a difference, the two men walked along Lexington Avenue, New York, and inspiration came to them: a sniper takes a pot shot at their anti-hero, Popeye Doyle, based on Eddie Egan, then gets on board the elevated train while Doyle gives hot pursuit in his car.

They now had their story. Jimmy 'Popeye' Doyle is a hard-drinking, mean, weather-beaten, uncouth, New York Irish cop with strong-arm tactics and a history of shooting his fellow officers by mistake. He and his partner Buddy Russo corner a drugs pusher in Brooklyn. The pusher manages to cut Russo's arm, but Doyle brutally beats him up before arresting him. Later Doyle persuades Russo, his arm bandaged, to accompany him to a club on the East Side for a drink, and they end up following a couple with known drug connections who are spending piles of money. The trail leads through Manhattan, across the bridge into Brooklyn, and to a candy store. In the ensuing days Doyle and Russo put the store under surveillance and discover that the gangster Sal Boca owns it.

From France sails in a television star, Henri Devereaux, along with a companion, Nicoli. Disembarking with them are businessman Alain Charnier and his wife Marie who later meet Boca at a hotel, witnessed by two narcotics policemen under assignment to Doyle and Russo. Several days later Doyle is shot at by a roof-top sniper, and a passer-by is killed. Doyle sets off in pursuit and, seeing Nicoli heading for the subway and boarding a train, commandeers a passing car. Zigzagging through the traffic beneath the elevated subway, he reaches the next station before the train, and is waiting for Nicoli when he arrives.

The Lincoln that Devereaux has brought with him from

Marseilles is secretly searched by police, who discover heroin hidden inside. They leave the car to be collected by Charnier who drives it to Ward's Island where he rendezvouses with Boca, Joel Weinstock, a known narcotics importer, and some other men. The police spring their trap. Weinstock surrenders, but Boca is killed by Russo in a shoot-out. Boca's brother Lou joins Charnier in hiding in the old abandoned asylum. Doyle follows, and when he is fired upon, shoots back, mistakenly hitting a narcotics officer. Charnier escapes and returns to Marseilles.

D'Antoni thought William Friedkin would be an interesting director to approach for this unconventional story about unconventional cops. Friedkin got his start on television; made his big screen debut with *Good Times*, starring Sonny and Cher; then directed a British film, Harold Pinter's *The Birthday Party*; the offbeat musical comedy *The Night They Raided Minsky's;* and the first mainstream gay film *The Boys in the Band*. He seemed a most unlikely choice of director to Twentieth Century Fox for what they thought would be a regular cops'n'robbers actioner. But for D'Antoni that was just the appeal: his unusual pedigree meant he was unlikely to make a predictable and conventional thriller.

Friedkin read the finished script and agreed that the chase was 'the most important element in the film,' at least from a commercial standpoint. Finally Twentieth Century Fox agreed. All they needed now was a high-calibre star to play the part of Popeye Doyle. D'Antoni showed the script to Steve McQueen, but he declined; perhaps the part wasn't quite glamorous enough for the superstar. Larger-than-lifesize comedian Jackie Gleason was considered, but he would never have been able to cope with all the running. At one point it was decided that the film required a complete unknown, and Jimmy Breslin, the New York columnist, was put through some rehearsals with Roy Scheider, slated to play Doyle's sidekick. Breslin was, said Scheider, great in action scenes but had trouble being convincing when he had lines to say. Then they gave Eddie Egan himself a shot at it; that didn't work. Egan's own preference was for Rod Taylor.

Finally the name of Gene Hackman was put forward. Studio executives were nonplussed, and the accountants worked out that he had never single-handedly created a box-office success. But Friedkin thought he would be ideal, called him in California and invited him to come to New York to discuss the part. Hackman flew over, read the script, and saw his chance 'to be like James Cagney. I loved it.' Friedkin told him to wait at his hotel while he and D'Antoni set about persuading the east coast Fox executives that Hackman was perfect for the part. Having lived in New York, he would be at home there, and while not a star, he was a respected actor who would not be trying to mould the part to suit himself. In the end Fox could find no suitable rival either available or willing to play the part.

Hackman spent an anxious weekend before finally receiving the good news. He was, he admitted, as surprised as anyone. 'It was certainly a departure from anything I'd done before. I was not known for playing heroes of any kind, and was usually cast as the heavy. I'm not sure I'd have cast myself in the part, but I'm damned glad somebody did.' He was also delighted to receive a fee of $200,000.

To some degree, the amount of money Hackman was earning helped make the required absence from home more bearable. The whole film would be shot on location in New York, and it would be three months before he could return to Hollywood. Free time would be hard to come by, but throughout filming, when Friedkin was concentrating on scenes involving Charnier, Hackman hopped on a plane and flew home. He was there, at least, for Christmas of 1970.

For once Hackman was in the position of having good character actors giving *him* support. Roy Scheider, for example, had notched up some solid but minor roles in movies such as *Klute*, but he would have to wait a couple more years – until *Jaws* – before becoming a major star. Fernando Rey, distinguished Spanish character actor and star of several Luis Buñuel films, was cast as Henri Charnier.

To prepare for the role, Hackman accompanied Eddie Egan on a tour of Harlem. Hackman recalled,

That was the scariest thing, to burst into a crowded bar and watch the way Egan dealt with things. He had this way of talking like a drill instructor – flat and unemotional, and very authoritative. If anyone talked back, his voice would go a pitch higher. No one got the better of him. You couldn't go in there and be Mr Nice Guy. You have to get their attention if you're a cop, and I found that being around cops made me realize what a tremendously difficult job they've got. I found I had a lot more respect for cops after being with them, because they've got so much to contend with, and they're just trying to do their job in sometimes dangerous circumstances.

So I was able to watch all this and learn the man's style. There's actually a certain kind of New York street guy – the way he walks, the way he talks, the way he carries himself. That was Egan, and I tried to copy all that. Men like that have all this violence inside of them, and that would scare the hell out of me. But that's not the way I am at all, even though people think I am.

Playing Doyle presented Hackman, despite his admiration for the cops of New York, with some tough challenges, not the least of them being his own grim perception of the character. 'I didn't have any sympathy for him at all,' he said. 'I'm sure his sort of violent cop does exist. Some people'll see this movie and see some social significance in it. The only social significance as far as I can see is that we have allowed tough cops like the one I play to grow up.'

Filming commenced in December 1970, in a New York winter that turned out to be particularly harsh: Hackman had to work in rain, sleet, snow, and in temperatures so cold that the film equipment sometimes froze. The locations triggered a good deal of anxiety – many of the scenes were shot in authentic hard-core drug locations in Manhattan and Brooklyn, all superbly captured in colour by cinematographer Owen Roizman. Friedkin's unofficial location manager was one 'Fat Thomas', a wheelman for local drug gangs who had been arrested fifty-two times.

The film's featured violence became a real problem for Hackman, especially the opening scene which called for Doyle to beat up a drug pusher. Hackman remembers the scene was shot more than twenty-seven times, 'and I really had to hit him. Between takes he kept saying it was all right and he'd smile and we'd do it again. I felt horrible.' So horrible, in fact, that he announced he was quitting the film. Fox quickly pointed out to him the contract he had signed; the studio would not hesitate to sue him for all he was worth. Faced with this ultimatum, he went back to work, coming to terms with the violence by approaching it as 'a simple acting problem, but one that has to be resolved anew each film I do.'

The car/subway chase was the most complicated scene to film. Friedkin got permission to use the Stillwell Avenue Line between 10.00 a.m. and 3.00 p.m. each day for five weeks. Stunt specialist Bill Hickman did the most dangerous driving, but for much of the time Hackman insisted on handling the Pontiac sedan himself, often reaching speeds of up to ninety miles an hour. He thoroughly relished the thrill of high-speed driving. Fortunately he was not at the wheel when, on the first day of shooting the chase, a stunt driver in another car mistimed his cue and crashed into the Pontiac, stoving in the driver's side. No one was hurt.

Filming continued through to March when, on the last day of shooting, Friedkin wanted one long uninterrupted shot of the chase taken from Doyle's point of view. A 50 mm lens was placed inside the Pontiac to shoot through the front windscreen, and a 25 mm lens was mounted on the bumper. No special arrangements had been made to ensure the roads would be clear and traffic lights controlled. It was simply a sheer piece of audacious filming: Bill

Hickman got in the car and drove at high speed for some twenty-six blocks, swerving down wrong lanes and gunning through red lights. All the public could see was a speeding police car with a flashing light. The scene was completed and the film wrapped.

Hackman was at the Oscar ceremony in April 1971 to find out if he had won an award as Best Supporting Actor for *I Never Sang for My Father*. Many were surprised when he lost out to John Mills for *Ryan's Daughter*. But the evening's biggest shock came when Melvyn Douglas was overlooked for Best Actor in favour of George C. Scott as *Patton*. Scott had told the Academy he didn't want the award and would not be there to collect if he won.

After its release in 1971 *The French Connection* failed to pull in big crowds straightaway; but critics quickly took it to their hearts. *Variety* said, 'Gene Hackman and Roy Scheider are very believable as two hard-nosed narcotics officers.' Alexander Walker of the London *Evening Standard* wrote, 'Just as it happened with Lee Marvin [in *Cat Ballou*], the film makes a star out of a character actor who is no beauty but a force of flesh, bone and blood who takes over a role and lives it.' Dilys Powell, writing in the *Sunday Times*, felt that Hackman 'gives a performance of devoted, inexorable vindictiveness'. When released years later on video, *Empire* called it 'an opportunity to see America's most underrated actor do some of his finest work'.

Gradually the film gained momentum at the box office, and went on to become one of the studio's most successful films of the year. Hackman, though hailed as a major new star, modestly never took any credit for the film's success. 'I really don't think I had anything to do with the quality of the film,' he said. 'That was a director's film. Anybody would have been good in my role. Even Jimmy Breslin would have been fine because of Billy Friedkin's direction. He could probably have won the Oscar.'

He also felt the film's success owed a lot to the fact that he is not the archetypal good-looking leading man. 'I guess audiences see me as the working guy who's doing vicariously what they'd like to be doing. And I think that's what made *The French Connection* work.' The only problem was, immediately after finishing *The French Connection* the offers of work dried up.

4   More Juice, More Power

The film industry in the early 1970s was undergoing one of its worst slumps; as audiences dropped away so fewer films were being made. Hackman seriously wondered if he might ever work again. Momentum was slow to build for *The French Connection* at the box office, much as it had been with *Bonnie and Clyde*, and the economic climate in Hollywood was at an all-time low. He made use of the enforced hiatus to spend time with his family and indulge himself in his hobbies. He still enjoyed painting, and for greater thrills he went dirt-track racing, or took to the skies, having qualified as a pilot. But life seemed tough: being at home helped to heal some of the rifts in his marriage, but unemployment made him restless.

Michael Ritchie (the director of *Downhill Racer*) called. He had been given the green light on a film starring Lee Marvin and desperately wanted Gene to play the secondary role – a role for which he would receive equal billing. Hackman respected Ritchie's skills behind the camera, and figuring he might not get a better offer for months, he accepted. The downside was more time spent away from home, as some of the scenes were to be shot on location in Kansas.

In *Prime Cut*, a thriller that followed the contemporary trend for anti-heroes, the principal characters are criminals or prostitutes. Hackman was to play 'Mary Ann', a gangster who manages a slaughterhouse as a front for drug-running and prostitution. His barns and cattle pens are filled with drugged, naked teenage girls. Lee Marvin played Nick Devlin, an underworld enforcer who goes to Kansas to collect a million dollars that 'Mary Ann' owes to Chicago mob boss, Jake: a previous debt-collector sent on the same mission had been sent back as hot dogs.

Devlin arrives in Kansas with three hired hands and a sub-

machine gun. When 'Mary Ann' invites him to join his organiza-
tion, Devlin rejects the offer and kidnaps one of the girls, Poppy
(Sissy Spacek), to use as a hostage. Eventually Devlin kills 'Mary
Ann', frees the girls and takes Poppy back with him to Chicago.

Making the film in the late summer of 1971 proved miserable for
everyone. Marvin and Ritchie were at each other's throats half the
time, and the atmosphere was poisonous. Hackman steered clear.
In December 1972 Lee Marvin said, 'I've made some mistakes I
wish I hadn't. One of them was working with Michael Ritchie on
Prime Cut. Oh, I hate that son of a bitch. He likes to use amateurs
because he can totally dominate them. Nothing worked with that
guy, and the whole picture fell apart.'

Presumably the 'amateurs' dig was aimed at Eddie Egan, the
real 'Popeye Doyle', who made his acting debut playing Jake, the
Chicago mobster who sends Marvin to get his money from
Hackman. Ritchie, incensed by Marvin's outburst, made his feelings clear to Donald Zec: 'I am prepared to talk about, say, Burt
Reynolds, Robert Redford, Walter Matthau or any other pleasurable subject. But not about Lee Marvin. He said some wicked
things about me and I am not disposed to reply in kind. Nor, on the
other hand, am I disposed to say anything favourable either.'

Some years later Lee Marvin told me,

> I'd probably had a little too much booze inside of me when I said
> those things. Okay, so I didn't hit it off with Michael Ritchie, and I
> got pissed off about some things, but if I said anything out of order,
> which I probably did, I shouldn't have done. And I'm very sorry.
> Maybe I felt a little left out of the Gene Hackman Appreciation
> Society. I mean, Gene, God knows, is a great actor and a great guy,
> but he wasn't the only actor in the film, for crissakes.

Presumably Marvin and Ritchie never did patch things up
before the actor died in 1987. *Prime Cut* was released in the summer of 1972 in a version Ritchie insisted was not his final cut; his
version was shown in Minneapolis, Minnesota, where it met with
great success. Elsewhere it fared moderately at a time when many
movies were sinking without trace. *Variety* declared, 'There are no
serious dramatic demands made of the players. Marvin and
Hackman do this sort of thing all the time.' Alexander Walker
wrote in the *Evening Standard*, 'It is the outstanding achievement
of this film to smooth over Lee Marvin's rough edges and to make
Gene Hackman's well-rounded gutsiness perfectly flat.'

Hackman recalls the film as 'not especially rewarding. It works
on a certain level. I didn't expect it to work in any other way. It's

just that sometimes your working experiences are very exciting, sometimes they are not.' Nevertheless, the result was a dark and gritty study of the American underworld, violent, often disturbing, and in its way quite compelling. Marvin was strong as a good-bad guy, and Hackman even better as the thoroughly bad-bad guy. Ritchie's flair in blending tense build-ups with explosive action set-pieces made for a slick pulp thriller.

Before the release of *Prime Cut* Hackman had the pleasurable duty of collecting numerous awards for his performance as Popeye Doyle. Early in 1972 he was named Best Actor by the National Board of Review; this was swiftly followed by a Golden Globe. Paulette Goddard presented him with the New York Film Critics award: the vote was a close-run thing between him and Peter Finch (for *Sunday Bloody Sunday*) – so much so that a second count had to be conducted. Then came the Oscars in April. He was facing considerable competition as Best Actor of 1971: Peter Finch, Walter Matthau as *Kotch*, George C. Scott in *The Hospital* and Topol for *Fiddler on the Roof*. The Golden Globe winner was usually expected to win the Oscar, but there were no guarantees.

Hackman, after helping Raquel Welch present the Best Supporting Actress award, returned to his seat by Faye – they were still together but far from happy. Perhaps he hoped this evening might make it all seem worthwhile. Liza Minnelli stepped up to read out the winner for Best Actor. 'Are you as nervous as I am?' she asked the audience as she opened the envelope. 'The winner is Gene Hackman for *The French Connection*.'

He went up to the podium, and taking the envelope from Minnelli's hand, read it and confirmed, 'This is what it says.' He took his Oscar from Minnelli, thanked Faye, William Friedkin and many others. It was a gracious acceptance speech that gave the audience cause to applaud warmly after the débâcle of the previous year, when George C. Scott snubbed the ceremony by not turning up.

The French Connection also won Best Director, Best Screenplay and Best Picture of 1971. Cinematographer Owen Roizman lost out to Oswald Morris for *Fiddler on the Roof*, and Roy Scheider was pipped at the post for Best Supporting Actor by Ben Johnson in *The Last Picture Show*. Twentieth Century Fox were already contemplating a sequel to *The French Connection*.

In 1982 Hackman summed up his feelings about winning the Oscar by telling publicist Mike Russell,

The Oscars as such – the evening itself – is a tremendously high evening; at least it was for me. But since then the Oscar *per se* doesn't mean that much to me. What does mean a great deal after the Oscar is your career. And sometimes it can affect it adversely, especially in supporting categories. An actor will immediately try and move up several notches, or beyond where they're saleable, and that's a real detriment to them.

He said he found the whole business of competing for an Oscar 'fairly ugly'. To have been nominated was 'a nice thing,' but only one test would show who was the very best actor: 'we'd all have to play the same role'. No special niche has been reserved for his Oscar on the mantelpiece. But he did concede, 'Yeah, it's nice to have. It's kind of special.'

As well as an Oscar, Hackman's fee shot up automatically from the typical $200,000 to $500,000. Suddenly everything changed. Offers came flooding in, and he was being sought for starring roles for which a few years earlier he would never even have been considered. To avoid being overwhelmed by it all, he braced himself. 'In this business you are made so many promises,' he said, 'that you tend to hold back your hopes. You keep a little of yourself in reserve so you are not hurt too much.'

More than ever before he found himself in control of his own career. But he was aware of the pitfalls, and of the many conmen and back-stabbers in the business. 'After the Oscar, I found suddenly I had the juice to pick what I wanted to do and have a say over scripts and casting. The first thing about so-called stardom is that you become a little paranoid. Do people want you for yourself or what they can get from you?'

*   *   *

In 1972 Gene Hackman was at the top of his profession – or very near it. But a tumble into obscurity was always possible, and the Oscar winner proceeded with caution. Hoping still to reach the very top, Hackman instructed his agent not to start demanding exorbitant fees. He was well aware of those he called 'greedy agents', who priced their clients out of business. 'The bubble then bursts,' he said, 'and actors find themselves on the "resting" lists.'

He soon discovered another unhappy facet to becoming a star, or what he called 'a hot item'. Friends he hadn't seen for years began coming out of the woodwork, some asking for money, some wanting him to read their scripts. Some had turned their backs on him during tough times. He had to learn to cope with all this, what they called the 'price of fame'. He said, some years later,

I wasn't really properly prepared for the success I suddenly had. I thought I was. What happens is, no matter how much you prepare yourself, you just get swept along with it. All of a sudden you're living this fantasy, but it doesn't last. You have to deal with the reality of it all, and the reality is that you have to continue to do the work that got you there in the first place.

His new-found power made him uncomfortable.

I had changed, and people's attitude towards me had changed. People feel they have to defer to you. You find yourself with more juice, more power, the handling of which is always a fascinating process. You use power for a number of reasons, to get what you want, to feed your ego, or to become a prick or whatever. It's a dangerous situation because one never knows quite how to read what is happening with you.

He could remember how people deferred to Burt Lancaster, and although he saw clearly then how detrimental that could be, he would increasingly find it difficult to resist flexing his own star muscle.

Latent aspirations began to reveal themselves – to direct films, to return to the stage. But since the Oscar he had become in demand as a film actor, and that was hard to ignore. For the first time in his career he had the power to say no to work he didn't like, instead of cherry-picking the best projects. He soon learnt that not everything you chose to do came to fruition just because you had won an Oscar. David Foster and Mitch Brower, the producers of *McCabe and Mrs Miller*, announced that Hackman would star in their forthcoming film *The Big Wild Red*. A film was mooted about dirt-track racing, one of Hackman's pastimes, called *Dunn*. But just a month after the Oscar, both films were shelved.

Then along came a script Hackman grasped with both hands and refused to let go, like a man clinging on for life, which is pretty much what the script called for him to do. *The Poseidon Adventure* launched a cycle of epic 'disaster' movies that dominated the early to mid seventies. Produced by the king of the 'disasters', Irwin Allen, the screenplay had to convince the cinema-going public that a liner would be knocked upside down by a tidal wave, and then the surviving passengers and crew would make their way up through the overturned ship to the hull, where they could escape.

To help him accomplish this Allen brought on board Ronald Neame to direct, and a gallery of stars led by Gene Hackman. After a succession of gangster roles and tough cops, Hackman was playing a reverend, 'a really good man' who would become the film's number one hero; ultimately, he even sacrifices his own life. On reading the script, Hackman knew he couldn't refuse. 'This one I liked because of the project, not the character so much,' he said. 'This was a different challenge – combining theatricality with honesty, trying to convince people that what you are doing is real but giving it just enough theatricality to make it larger than life, which is what was important in making the film work.'

Hackman and the other stars, including Shelley Winters, Ernest Borgnine, Roddy McDowall, Carol Lynley and Stella Stevens, spent a short time aboard the *Queen Mary*, on which some of the opening scenes were filmed. Then the whole crew decamped to the Twentieth Century Fox studio for the interior shots that comprised the bulk of the movie. Sets were created to replicate upside-down cabins and even a ballroom.

Physical demands were made of every member of the cast, for Neame needed his actors to do as much of the dangerous climbing and underwater swimming as possible. 'I had a method that generally worked,' he said.

> I'd tell an actor, 'We can use a double for this scene, but I'd have to shoot it from behind, whereas if you did it yourself, I could shoot you in close-up.' And the actor would say, 'No, no, you don't need a double. I can do that. I'll do the shots you need.' In fact they all did the shots I needed. Gene Hackman didn't need any kind of convincing. He was up there jumping and climbing, and he just refused to have a double if he could do it himself. Same with Ernie Borgnine. He's a tough guy who'll do anything, and once those two had said they'd do it, the next one just sort of followed on, and then the next. Then there was Carol Lynley who was so brave and so terrified when she had to climb that Christmas tree. When she got to the top and I got a shot of her face, that wasn't acting, that was real terror.

Shelley Winters wasn't going to be the exception. She said, 'Of course that was me swimming underwater. I was like Esther Williams only bigger! And as for some of the men, talk about testosterone. Gene Hackman said,"If anyone's gonna jump into a tank of water surrounded by flame, it's gonna be me." '

Hackman knew, of course, that this kind of fantasy adventure, complete with cardboard characters, had but one purpose – to thrill audiences. This was something he wanted to do just for a change.

> I didn't so much have to act as be plausible. I also liked the fact that I was more involved because there were stunts to work out, and so

much of the work was purely physical with just a bit of dialogue. I really don't want to sit around all day waiting for a dialogue scene. When the juices begin to flow and the adrenaline pours into your system there's a feeling of wanting to do the stunts so the director can get the close-ups, and the audience knows you are up there on the screen.

He liked the chance to face a little danger when working; he usually only got to do that off set when he could race cars or fly his stunt plane, activities he was forbidden to do when filming.

As he was making the film at Fox, the studio took the opportunity to talk to him about their planned sequel to *The French Connection*. 'As they say, it seemed like a good idea at the time,' was his later comment. He was even given a choice of cast approval or director approval, a prospect irresistible to anyone flexing their new film muscle. He chose to have director approval.

Another old friend popped up from nowhere on the set of *The Poseidon Adventure*, saying, 'I need $8,000 right away.' Hackman replied, 'Don't we all.' He never saw that 'friend' again.

He also took seriously his unofficial role of the team leader. 'Although there are a lot of stars,' he said, 'the picture kind of depends on whether you like my character. I've always played roles where I didn't have the responsibility of the picture, or anything else, other than doing my part as well as possible and going on to the next job.' This means that if *The Poseidon Adventure* had flopped he would have had to share the responsibility. As it happened, it became a massive hit on its 1972 release, earning $160 million worldwide, and Hackman can certainly take his share of the laurels. But then, like all those disaster films, it was pretty much a team effort.

Irwin Allen outlined the reasons why the film became the biggest money-spinner in America that year: 'I think the appeal of the disaster movies is the vicarious thrill the public get from seeing others in deep trouble. It's true, isn't it? We all stop to look at a fire or a road accident or some tragedy. You have to make your characters so ordinary that the public can identify with them. It's no use making them brain surgeons because there aren't too many brain surgeons.'

The Poseidon Adventure remains the definitive disaster film, full of wooden characters and tinny dialogue, but all assembled with such flair by Ronald Neame that the overall effect is endearing. Incessant repetition of the formula through successive films, many made by Irwin Allen himself, prevents us from remembering the movie's qualities – a unique and slick piece of sheer entertainment that requires nothing from the audience but to sit on the edge of their seats. As predicted, the film went on to be Oscar-nominated for its special effects, and for its song 'The Morning After'.

Variety found it 'highly imaginative and lustily-produced,' while the *New Yorker* rightly asserted, 'the script is the only cataclysm in this waterlogged *Grand Hotel.*' The script came in for more berating in *Time*: 'Gene Hackman, who seems to have the lion's share of the bad lines, nevertheless acquits himself very nicely indeed. There is one scene in which he is required to pray to God, pleading with him and admonishing him, that Hackman, against all odds, manages to make believable.' Hackman would have been well satisfied if he'd ever read that review; but it is more likely that he didn't, making it a rule to ignore the opinions of the critics. In a blunt admission of what makes Hollywood tick, he once said,

> In the final analysis you have to trust the box office grosses. A film only works if the public likes it. I don't trust a critic's view of what a film is, and there are only a few film critics who know what they're talking about. Many times people's careers are changed by what someone says about them, and that's why I choose not to read reviews.

He must, therefore, have been pleased to find himself third on the list of top box-office stars in the United States for 1972, coming behind only George C. Scott and, at number one, Clint Eastwood. Scripts continued to flood in, most of them offering him roles as violent cops or even more violent gangsters. He turned them all down, saying, 'I don't want to go on playing violent parts. I don't want to be the Bogart of the 70s.' He was seeking unconventional films that moved beyond stereotypes, and one – *Scarecrow* – seemed to fit the bill. It was, he thought, an off-beat buddy-cum-road movie: 'a mixture of *Midnight Cowboy* and *Of Mice and Men'*. Hackman relished the kind of humour promised by the script. 'It's a kind of marvellous complement of a comedy and a look at life through the eyes of a couple of bums,' he said. 'It's a very exciting role for me: it deals with comedic elements and they are always a challenge.'

Al Pacino, his co-star, was at that time riding high on the success of *The Godfather*. Together they played two misfits: Hackman is tough, quick-tempered Max, just out of prison after a stretch for assault, and Pacino is peace-seeking Lion, home after six years at sea, returning to the wife and child he'd abandoned. They meet up on a deserted highway in northern California, trying individually to hitch a ride. Finally they laugh at the absurdity of the situation, and begin travelling together towards Detroit.

The fact that Warner Brothers were prepared to approve director Jerry Schatzberg's choice of actors – Hackman and Pacino –
without an argument spoke volumes for the actors' box-office credentials. 'I was expecting the studio to want totally wrong actors,'
said Schatzberg, who had directed Pacino in *Panic in Needle Park*
in 1971.

It was, as some observers put it, a pedestrian *Easy Rider*. Filming
actually took the cast and crew on a trek across America, beginning
at Bakersfield, on to Reno, then to Denver, and finally to Detroit.
Hackman had a whale of a time. 'It was the only film that I made
totally in sequence. Any actor will tell you how helpful that is in
understanding character development.' He also secured employment for his brother Richard, who became his stand-in as well as
playing a corrupt prison guard.

Hackman, Pacino and Schatzberg, not to mention Warner
Brothers, had high hopes for the film's success, but while boasting
some wonderful photography, its uneven, and all-too-predictable
script kept the action from taking off. This film would have to rely
on its star power to do well.

Inevitably the time away from home took its toll on his marriage, and Gene and Faye separated. After winning the Oscar, he
had undergone what he called a 'whole metamorphosis', an
attempt to come to terms with the way sudden success was affect-
ing both his professional and his private life. By the end of 1972 he
had maturely reflected on, and faced up to, his new life – to grasp-
ing 'friends' and intense professional demands. Ultimately he came
through the metamorphosis unscathed, and he persuaded Faye to
give their marriage another chance.

Hackman attended the 1973 Oscars ceremony in order to
announce the award for Best Actress, which was won by Liza
Minnelli for *Cabaret*. *The Poseidon Adventure* walked off with only
one of its eight nominations – for its song 'The Morning After',
composed by Al Kasha and Joel Hirschhorn. The evening was ren-
dered unforgettable when Marlon Brando, winning Best Actor for
The Godfather, failed to show and sent in his place an actress
dressed in traditional Native American garb. Announcing herself
as Sacheen Littlefeather, she read aloud part of a letter from
Brando, in which he refused to accept the Oscar as a gesture of
protest at the way Indians had been portrayed in films.

Hackman received a British Academy Award for Best Actor of
1973 – although in the curious way that the British Film Academy
used to function, he won for both *The French Connection* and *The
Poseidon Adventure*. This confusing state of affairs has since been
rectified, so that only one film can win such an award. At the 1973

Cannes Film Festival, *Scarecrow* was awarded the Palme d'Or as best film. Hackman could have expected this success to bode well for the film on its American release, but it failed to endear itself to the critics.

American critic Stanley Kaufmann stated bluntly, 'Here's a picture that manages to abuse two American myths at once – the Road and the Male Pair.' *Variety* was more lenient: '*Scarecrow* is a periodically interesting but ultimately unsatisfying character study of two modern drifters . . . Gene Hackman is excellent as a paroled crook with determined plans for the future, but Al Pacino is shot down by the script which never provides him with much beyond the freaky second-banana status.' Hackman dominated the film, reckoned *Time*, but not to good effect.

> Scruffy and bespectacled, Hackman has a good time hunkering down into his characterization of the snarling Max. But he gets in so far that no other actor can reach him. Pacino's characterization of Lion therefore remains unresolved. Hackman remains too self-absorbed. The tension between the two actors is tangled and interesting, at least initially, but it eventually hobbles what small humanity the movie might have had.

The subsequent box-office failure never dampened Hackman's spirits. As he told *Premiere* magazine in 1986, 'It just worked so well. A lot of people come up to me still and say it was one of their favourite films.'

*   *   *

In 1973 Hackman refused to be driven by commercial demands, and even before *Scarecrow* had flunked at the box office, he was already at work on another thoughtful film that shunned the usual conventions.

The Conversation was Francis Ford Coppola's first film after the phenomenal success of his *The Godfather*. One of the rare genuine *auteurs* of American cinema, he had not only written the screenplay of *The Conversation*, but would also direct and co-produce it. When a director of his stature offered you a role, it was, as Don Corleone might have said, an offer you can't refuse. Hackman had no intention of turning him down when he read the script, which told the unusual story of a surveillance expert – 'the best bugger in the business' as his character Caul was described.

Caul's job is simply to bug people's private conversations for money – no questions asked. He remains completely detached about his work, lives alone and guards his privacy with a vengeance – even his lover thinks he is a professional musician. One day he is assigned by a large corporation (whose purpose is unknown to him) to listen in on a young couple, Mark and Ann. He will receive $15,000 on delivery.

With his small team, he records the couple in a San Francisco park. Later on playing back the tapes in his apartment, he becomes unusually concerned and intrigued by the conversation. At the corporation's headquarters he is met by Martin Street but refuses to hand over the tapes. Then he sees the young couple in the building and, growing ever more obsessed by the situation, he returns to his apartment and replays the tapes over and over, gradually coming to the realization that some kind of conspiracy is being planned. He hears Mark say, 'He'd kill us if he got the chance,' and also learns that some kind of meeting will take place in a room at the Jack Tar Hotel.

Plagued by guilt about what might happen to the couple, Caul goes to confession for the first time in months, and tells the priest that two people might be hurt because of his work. He decides to destroy the tapes but discovers them stolen. The company director insists on paying Caul his fee.

He tries to forget about the couple, but becomes so tormented that he books into the Jack Tar Hotel where he overhears an argument and sees a body lying on his terrace. Trying desperately to shut out the incident, he closes the curtains and turns on the television. Sleep proves impossible, so he decides to investigate. He breaks into the next room which seems undisturbed. Then he flushes the toilet and sees the bowl fill with blood.

At the corporation building Caul sees Mark and Ann there, surrounded by reporters who are pumping her with questions about the sudden death of the company director – her father. Street later phones Caul and tells him not to get involved, and that he is being observed. Caul takes his flat apart, searching in vain for bugging devices. He finally gives up, and overcome with feelings of guilt and confusion, he begins to play his saxophone.

Coppola began writing the script in 1966. 'I had been terrified by the whole Orwellian dimension of electronic spying and the invasion of privacy when I started it. I realized that a bugging expert was a special breed of man, not just a private eye playing with gadgets, and I thought it would be fascinating to get inside the mind and experience of such a man.' He completed the script three years later, having been diverted by directing *Finian's Rainbow*. After that musical débâcle he wanted to ensure that he only ever directed his own screenplays. Moreover with *The Godfather* he was per-

ceived by many to be the most important film-maker working in
Hollywood, so it was not difficult, therefore, to persuade
Paramount, then filling their coffers with the takings from his gang-
ster epic, to back *The Conversation*.

Hackman was Coppola's first choice for the role of Caul. 'He's
ideal because he's so ordinary, so unexceptional in appearance,'
said the director. But he was also an actor who brought tremendous
dedication to his craft, getting every facet of his character exactly
right, even down to learning how to play a saxophone convincingly.

The role was stimulating: an anti-hero who didn't need to resort
to violence. With San Francisco being the most distant location, he
was able to work from home. There was the additional pleasure of
getting to work for the first time on screen with his old friend,
Robert Duvall, who appeared briefly and uncredited as the company director. The film marked an early appearance of Harrison
Ford as Martin Street. All three actors became favourites of
Coppola, and he would try to entice them all with future projects.

Perhaps after this film Hackman should have slowed down a bit.
Work dominated his life and his marriage continued to fray around
the edges. He said, 'I worry that one morning the whole bubble will
simply disappear."Gene who?" Yes, I'm a worrier.'

Fear of bursting bubbles led him in 1973 to work on *Zandy's
Bride*, a slow-moving western in which he played a pioneer who
acquires a mail-order bride (Liv Ullmann), because he considers
the local women unworthy. Hackman relished the challenge of
playing a 'stubborn, egocentric mountain man and a real loner,' an
apparently shallow character who undergoes a major change.
When his wife arrives, he sees her as merely a provider of sons and
a glorified servant. Gradually, however, he falls in love with her.
Change of character became a notable feature of the roles he
would later choose.

Swedish director Jan Troell had a few years earlier made *The
Emigrants* and its sequel *The New Land*, both with Max Von Sydow
and Liv Ullmann. *The Emigrants* was a contender for a Best Film
Oscar – most unusual for a foreign language film – as well as Best
Foreign Film, while Troell found himself nominated for his direction and the script he co-wrote with Bengt Forslund, and a nomination for Liv Ullmann. With these credentials, Warner Brothers
were happy to green-light a budget of $3.5 million for *Zandy's
Bride*. Hackman found himself spending three months' total filming at Big Sur and Carmel in California, which again meant he
could work close to home.

In the event the schedule seemed interminable, his temper
began to fray and unpleasant exchanges broke out between him

and Troell. These were sparked, reportedly, when Hackman killed a snake and Troell voiced his disapproval. Eileen Heckart, who played Hackman's mother, said that Hackman was suffering personal problems and that as a way of releasing tension he was throwing his star's weight around.

Gene played down the conflict in interviews; difficulties arose, he felt, because Troell had 'a tunnelized vision of what it is he wants, and when you are working in someone else's country, it's sometimes hard to communicate that.' This was a coded reference to the director's poor command of English; but, said Gene, 'we finally got to a place where we worked quite well together, where we kind of respected each other.' Certainly he had no reservations about Troell's potential and gifts: 'All in all,' he said, 'I think he's very talented.'

Troell was frustrated by American union rules that forbade him from operating the camera, as he did in Sweden. Indeed so efficient were his Hollywood crew that he felt underused and actually fell asleep during one set-up that needed the attention of the stunt director rather than him. It was only when he heard someone say, 'We're just waiting for your"Action!" ' that he woke up to watch the scene being played.

With filming over, Hackman might have considered taking a break, but he couldn't resist the temptation to do a guest spot as the blind man in Mel Brooks's brilliant horror spoof *Young Frankenstein*. After a two-day stint of work he was home for Christmas.

* * *

In 1974 Dustin Hoffman approached Hackman for help in financing a production he wanted to direct on Broadway. *All Over Town* by Murray Shisgal would be Hoffman's directorial debut, and he was tired of trying to get established entrepreneurs to back him. He needed around $300,000: Hackman went into partnership with him by giving him some of the money as an investment. The play was a small success, though neither Hoffman nor Hackman got rich in the process: but then Hackman's involvement had more to do with his fondness for his long-time friend than any desire to become a theatre producer.

While Hoffman was taking a stab at directing, Hackman was eagerly awaiting the reaction to *The Conversation*, which was due to open in 1974. By pure chance the film's release coincided with the Watergate scandal, an irony Coppola felt diverted attention away from his main theme, which was the questionable responsibility any organisation had for carrying out actions such as bugging.

The critics loved it. Michael Billington in the *Illustrated London News* called it, 'Alert, truthful, unarty and absolutely essential viewing.' *Sight and Sound* found it to be 'a private, hallucinatory study in technical expertise and lonely guilt.' The *New Yorker* found the film, and Hackman's portrayal, to be 'a terrifying depiction of a ransacked spirit'. *Variety* noted the clever use of sound, which made 'voices come in and out of aural focus in a superb tease'. 'For Hackman', said *Time*, 'Caul presents a substantial challenge. It is a largely interiorized role in contrast to the action parts in which he has recently built his career. He responds with the most substantial screen performance he has done.'

The film, shown at the Cannes Film festival in 1974, was awarded the Palme d'Or. For both his screenplay and direction Coppola was Oscar-nominated, but didn't win. However, the National Board of Review named him Best Director, Hackman Best Actor and the picture Best Film. Despite the low audience figures, this highly regarded film remains one of Hackman's best.

Hackman and Coppola were disappointed by the poor box-office returns, although the director said, 'It was not a film that I set out to earn a great fortune on. I do think that a very awkward distribution made the difference between a picture that might have made a profit and a picture that had a loss.' Hackman said of the film's financial failure, 'My biggest disappointment was not for myself or for my performance not being seen but because I thought we had a really valuable film. I thought people would enjoy it.' Perhaps he can take heart in hindsight, knowing the film has come to be regarded as a classic, and joining the long list of other movies that failed on release then were later discovered, such as *It's a Wonderful Life*, *Ace in the Hole*, *The Beguiled* and a host of others.

The depression that descended on Hackman after the failure of yet another film he believed in so much was compounded by a growing drinking problem. 'Not that I was an alcoholic,' he told Robert Ward in 1982. 'But I was at the point where I was having two vodka and tonics to start the night and just to quench my thirst. Then a couple more later.'

Further grim news beckoned. *Zandy's Bride* was released in 1974 to generally fair reviews but virtually no business. *Variety* called it, 'a good period frontier romantic melodrama,' and noted 'the plot line is thin but sufficient.' It felt the performances of Hackman and Ullmann 'sustain Jan Troell's delicate but placid direction.' The *Hollywood Reporter* thought the first quarter of the film the best, being 'subtle, humorous and even breathtaking.'

If the director had a habit of falling asleep during shooting, one should not be surprised that the audience nodded off while watching it. Warners, it seems, were pretty much in sympathy. They regarded the film as a waste of time and money: rather than spend any more finance on promoting, printing and exhibiting it in Great Britain, the studio shelved it. Unlike *The Conversation* it was not destined to be rediscovered.

5 A Four-Star Pain in the——!

The juice Hackman had acquired was leaking away fast. He was suddenly in dire need of a box-office hit if he was to retain his all-too-slippery star quality. Twentieth Century Fox appeared to have the answer with *French Connection II*, whose storyline took Popeye Doyle to France in search of his elusive prey. But Hackman was unhappy at the prospect. 'In the two years that the sequel took to set up, all sorts of interesting things were offered to me. In the long run I began to dread going back and doing that character again. I didn't want to go to France and I knew enough about myself to realize that I wasn't going to be very docile about it.'

Perhaps aware of his lukewarm feelings about the film, the studio granted him certain additional privileges, such as consulting him about storyline developments. His contract gave him director approval, and he made sure he used it, approving John Frankenheimer with whom he'd enjoyed working on *The Gypsy Moths*.

With Frankenheimer busy doing pre-shoot development, Hackman had the time to reunite with Arthur Penn for a film originally called *The Dark Tower* – ultimately released as *Night Moves*. Hackman would play private detective Harry Moseby, assigned by former Hollywood starlett Arlene Iverson to find her wayward daughter, Delly. Complicating his own life is the discovery that his own wife Ellen is having an affair.

He eventually finds Delly living with her former stepfather, Tom Iverson, in Florida. To continue collecting maintenance from her father, Delly says, is the only reason her mother wants her back. Harry finds himself in no hurry to leave Florida, and becomes attracted to Paula, Tom's girlfriend. While Harry is on a boat trip with Delly and Paula, they discover a crashed plane and the skeleton of the pilot.

Harry and Paula make love before he returns to Los Angeles with Delly. Once home he tries to mend his marriage. Then he hears news that Delly has been killed in a car driven by film director Joey Ziegler. Visiting one of Delly's old boyfriends, Quentin, he learns that the dead pilot in Florida had been one of Delly's lovers, a stuntman called Marv Ellman. Believing that Quentin had murdered Ellman and then arranged for Delly's death, Harry follows him to Florida. But there Quentin is murdered by Tom, who has been smuggling archaeological treasures out of Yucatan.

Paula confesses that she had allowed him to seduce her to distract him from Tom's activities, but now helps him to try to find where the submarine treasures are hidden. As Paula dives from their boat, they come under fire from a plane, and Harry is shot. The plane crashes into the sea, killing Paula. Harry recognizes the pilot as film director Joey Ziegler. Wounded and disillusioned, the detective attempts to pilot the boat, but it just goes round in circles.

The film had some early appearances by two up-and-coming stars: Melanie Griffith as Delly and James Woods as Quentin. A good cast also included Susan Clark as Hackman's wife, Janet Ward as Arlene Iversen, John Crawford as Tom Iverson and Jennifer Warren as Paula.

During the pre-production stage Penn and his screenwriter Alan Sharp disagreed on several aspects of the story, as directors and screenwriters are apt to do. While they managed to maintain an uneasy spirit of compromise – Penn gave way to Sharp on a number of points – the screenwriter later criticized Penn for this apparent failing. They met halfway on the final ambiguous scene: Penn had wanted Harry to be offered a glimmer of a chance to reunite with his wife, while Sharp thought Paula should survive to start a new life with Harry.

They did agree wholeheartedly on the choice of Gene Hackman for their hero. Penn knew that Hackman preferred to work intuitively rather than intellectually. Hackman's usual method was to read a script twice, then put it down for a while, so he could absorb the words and allow ideas to filter up. He could memorize pages of dialogue before going on the set, and when he arrived he did so without a strong preconceived notion of how the performance would evolve. But on this film Penn rehearsed his actors for ten days prior to filming, during which time dialogue was reworked, after much input from the actors themselves.

Sharp found that Hackman was 'a wonderfully skilled actor who seemed able to make very complex perceptions without having to verbalize or intellectualize them.' There was, perhaps, a note of personal conviction when Hackman says in a scene in which he comforts a tearful Melanie Griffith, 'It's bad when you're sixteen but when you're forty, it's no better.' Sharp observed, 'When I saw that rendition I was so astonished. There was that personal content which I found worked successfully.'

The rehearsal period allowed Penn to indulge his personal method of digging into the personal life of whichever actor he's working with, and seeing if he could unearth something there for the actor to draw on. The director was aware that Hackman was undergoing personal problems and that this mirrored the plight of his role. Like the fictional private eye, Hackman was torn between the demands of his job and the demands of his family.

After it was finished, at a cost of $4 million, Warner Brothers seemed to be unsure of quite how to market the film. Penn had produced a dark and complex *film noir*, full of fine performances, murky atmosphere and a gripping climax. At the same time the picture seemed to up-end many of the standard detective genre conventions. They just didn't understand it, and Arthur Penn, recalling *Bonnie and Clyde*, must have been thinking, Here we go again.

Sharp blamed Penn for what he perceived as the ambiguous structure, which, he said, 'stemmed from Arthur's uncertainty about the kind of film he was going to make'. During their disagreements over the script he expected Penn to put his foot down and stick to his own ideas, 'which I felt was not only his right,' said Sharp, 'but his duty as an *auteur* director.'

Warners decided to shelve it for a while, bringing full circle a poor year for Hackman. In October 1974 he told Bart Mills of the *Guardian*, 'I've been doing too many films. I'm trying to think who I'd go and see at the pictures four or five times a year. I can't think of one.' He said he needed six months' break, and felt that after a prolonged spate of continual working he felt he was just making one long film. 'You start drying up after that.'

* * *

Hackman's gloom over the prospect of making *French Connection II* had not lifted by the end of 1974, and he found a way of delaying it further when he insisted on making a western for Richard Brooks, *Bite the Bullet*.

Between the late 1880s and early 1890s a series of endurance races on horseback were held in what was still the wild west. Brooks had written a screenplay recounting such a race which covered 600 miles. Like his classic western *The Professionals* the scenario was tough and spectacular, but a lot less violent, a fact that would have appealed strongly to Hackman. Gunning down bandits and Indians at every turn was not on the menu; rather, the hero was called upon to stop en route to assist his troubled challengers. The race itself supplied the action and violence was manifested solely in the ruthless determination to drive both humans and animals to compete for the winning prize of $2,000.

This western relied on the exploration of character. Hackman played Sam Clayton, a one-time Rough Rider with Theodore Roosevelt, who is more concerned with the welfare of horses and riders than with winning. James Coburn played Luke Matthews, Sam's long-time friend and rival. Candice Bergen supplies the one touch of glamour, as the sole female rider in the race who wants the prize money to help spring her husband from prison. Jan-Michael Vincent serves as a variation on that western cliche, the young hot-head: he seeks fame and fortune, not as a gunslinger, but as the win-ner of this race, and in the process runs his horse to death. Ian Bannen played Norfolk, a titled Englishman who has come out west in search of adventure. Ben Johnson, the laconic veteran horseman known only as Mister, dies en route. The race, and the movie, ends with Sam holding back from the finishing line so Luke can join him in a tie.

Richard Brooks was used to working with a star cast: Burt Lancaster and Lee Marvin had been far bigger headaches on *The Professionals*, 'so to work with Gene Hackman, Jim Coburn, Ben Johnson, Candice and Ian Bannen was a joyride,' he told me. 'Each has their own foibles, but as a director you have to cope with that. It was interesting to see how different Hackman and Coburn were in their approach. Hackman could walk through the scene and he found what he needed almost intuitively. But Jim Coburn likes to talk about it, to find his way round it, to know what his motivation is. I can work with them both.' Brooks emphasized that the film was

an attempt to do something different with the genre. *The Professionals* had been a tremendous success for me and for every-one else concerned with it, but for me it was something that I felt was very much in the tradition of the western but it also had three-dimensional characters and some interesting developments. I wanted to do that again with *Bite the Bullet* but by that time you couldn't do just another film about guns blazing and the good guys and the bad guys because things had changed so much. You had to do something different, so I wrote a story of an endurance horse race and tried to bring in all the elements that had made *The Professionals* successful. So I was careful in who I cast, like Gene Hackman. He was just coming to the fore then, and so he was a star name *and* a really good actor with insight, intuition even. He wasn't going to just ride a horse: he was showing there was something going on inside his head. He reminded me a lot of Lee Marvin, but without the hellraising.

Variety described the film as 'an excellent, literate action drama ... After a leisurely though intriguing build-up, the race begins, and during the daily ordeals of mountain, desert, rain, sun, cold and heat, the pressures and the secrets of the characters emerge plausibly and rationally.' The only problem, as Brooks had been aware, was that the genre had been catapulted forward by Sam Peckinpah's *The Wild Bunch* (1969), which dealt the old-time western a fatal blow. Many tried to overcome it – few succeeded. Clint Eastwood triumphed with his apocalyptic *The Outlaw Josey Wales*, in which his usual lone gunman became the centre of a small community before returning to the desert at the end. John Wayne failed commercially (but excelled critically) with his last and best film, *The Shootist*, which saw him go out in one last classic gunfight at the turn of the century. *Bite the Bullet* also ploughed a different furrow and is now deemed one of the best Westerns of the seventies, though audiences of the time could not be convinced.

Its failure came in the wake of the long-awaited release of *Night Moves*, which Warners had finally distributed in a last-ditch attempt to find an audience. It didn't. Sharp believed that Hackman was part of the reason for the film's poor return. 'It's hard for me to imagine who'd be better than Gene Hackman, although he was, in the end, one of the liabilities in the film. People don't go to see Gene Hackman movies, although sometimes they go to see movies that Gene Hackman is in. His gift is that he's not a star.'

Hackman reached the end of 1975 with a new philosophy: if the public wanted to see only commercial films, then commercial films he would make. The problem with that approach is that film producers and studios have trouble creating a straightforward formula, the right blend of ingredients. If it were easy, the industry would not have been faring so badly then. Universal, for instance, churned out one 'disaster movie' after another, most of them with all-star casts headed by Charlton Heston. When the last one, *Two Minute Warning*, flopped in 1976, Universal pulled the plug on the whole genre.

Other studios were struggling. MGM was virtually dormant, and although Universal enjoyed some successes with Clint Eastwood, he soon switched over to Warner Brothers to become their biggest money-spinner for the rest of the decade. Paramount, Columbia, United Artists, and Twentieth Century Fox were all trying to figure out how to reel in the dwindling crowds. Fox's answer was to get *French Connection II* up and running. While Hackman both knew he needed a hit and never doubted this would be it, he nevertheless agreed kicking and screaming all the way.

In the original film Doyle's quarry Charnier had escaped, so in the sequel Popeye Doyle is sent to France to try and lure the big boss out of hiding. Characteristically the New York cop fails to endear himself to the French police and breaks all the rules they impose on him. During a drugs raid Doyle, who is under orders not to interfere, pursues a suspect. When he is informed that the suspect is actually working undercover for the police, Doyle gives up the chase. The undercover cop, his cover blown, is murdered.

Charnier, again played by Fernando Rey, manages to kidnap Doyle, and repeatedly drugs him with heroin until he has become an addict. Only then is Doyle released. After enduring 'cold turkey', Doyle recovers sufficiently to pursue Charnier, leading to a long sequence in which he chases Charnier on foot through Paris all the way to his yacht, continuing to run even when Charnier boards a bus. Reaching his boat Charnier sets sail and Doyle keeps running, despite exhaustion. Just before Charnier can sail out of range, Doyle shoots him.

Hackman had always suffered painful discomfort in his left knee when called upon to run, and the first *French Connection* had called for considerable physical exertion. The climax to the sequel needed to be shot in short spurts as Hackman's leg would seize up. His aching limb symbolized his whole attitude to making this movie: it was something to endure. Instinctively repelled by the studio's attempt to repeat a successful formula, Hackman just couldn't enjoy his work knowing the film was being done purely for money. His scruples and creative integrity were still intact; he would soon learn to lose those, or at least put them on hold. On the set he was a 'four-star, homogenized, all-American pain in the ass,' as one crew member put it.

Hackman was heard to moan quite a bit, even though he tried to hold his tongue. 'I don't mean to do a poor-mouth job on the sequel,' he said. 'This one may very well be as good as the first one.' He later conceded, 'Although the whole experience was appalling to me, I was pleasantly surprised by the way it turned out.' John Frankenheimer had succeeded in making a sequel that stood up on its own.

Released in 1975, the film was an immediate hit, with both public and critics alike. Hackman's volatile grumpiness throughout filming may well have helped his performance; as *Variety* noted, 'Hackman's performance is another career highlight, ranging from cocky narc, ugly American, helpless addict, humbled ego and relentless avenger.' The *Listener*'s reviewer wrote, 'I haven't enjoyed an American thriller as much since *The Conversation* – which also starred Gene Hackman. The man will soon be a walking guarantee.'

The guarantee the critic mentioned couldn't have referred to his general box-office pull, although perhaps no actor could have turned this Popeye Doyle series of films into any more of a smash hit. No one knew the answer to that, least of all Hackman, which is why he decided that scruples and creative integrity would now go out the window in favour of whatever paid well and looked like a sure bet. He never denied the fact, telling Robert Ward, 'I started to say,"Hell, I'll do movies that will definitely make money and then I'll have plenty of dough." ' He described it as 'real establishment thinking' that was ultimately self-defeating. But at the time he thought he was 'playing safe.'

*　　*　　*

Certainly everything about *Lucky Lady* suggested the phrase: 'playing safe'. Stanley Donen, the director, had produced films for Twentieth Century Fox since 1973, and had found the script by husband-and-wife team Willard Huyck and Gloria Katz, 'funny, touching, romantic, different'. During Prohibition a ménage à trois are running rum and generally enjoying their adventures in breaking the law, fooling the revenue men and fighting off gangsters who try to take over their business. The climax of the story features a sea battle between the trio and the mobsters.

Donen said, 'I'm always intrigued when a screenplay has a truly strong leading lady's part,' and agreed with producer Michael Gruskoff that they ought to approach Liza Minnelli. Two years earlier she had told Donen, 'Let's find a movie to do together,' so he sent her the *Lucky Lady* script. She read it and the same day called him to say she'd do it. It was her first film since her Oscar triumph in *Cabaret*. Perhaps fate had been at work: one year she was announcing Hackman as Best Actor only to be receiving the award for Best Actress from him the next. But Hackman's name didn't spring to Donen's mind just yet.

Burt Reynolds and George Segal both signed up. Filming was scheduled to begin in February 1975 in Guaymas, Mexico and last for twelve weeks; but Segal failed to turn up. Ill health, it seems, was the cause, and in the end he resigned while Donen's cast and crew waited on the sidelines. The film began to seem ill-starred. Donen went in search of an immediate replacement, and called agent Sue

Mengers to ask if Steve McQueen would accept a considerable financial reward for stepping in. McQueen, then in semi-retirement, declined. Mengers also represented Warren Beatty, and Donen enquired after him. He also turned down the project. Michael Gruskoff, having recently wound up work as producer of *Young Frankenstein*, advanced the name of Gene Hackman – also represented by Mengers.

Hackman, around that time, was approached by Michael Douglas, who at that time was known for little else than his famous father and a central role in the television series *The Streets of San Francisco*. But he was now setting himself up as a producer and his first picture would be *One Flew Over the Cuckoo's Nest*. He offered the leading role to Hackman. Whether or not his fee was too paltry, or whether he thought the film didn't sound like the much-needed money-spinner, he turned it down. The rest is history. Jack Nicholson said yes and won an Oscar – justice, perhaps, considering Nicholson turned down the role of Buck Barrow in *Bonnie and Clyde*.

Hackman was also sought by Sidney Lumet for *Network* to play the passé evening news anchorman who finally goes off the rails. Incredibly Hackman gave this the thumbs-down, too, allowing Peter Finch to snap up the part and win a Best Actor Oscar in the process.

Then along came Stanley Donen and, in Gene's words, 'I was seduced.'

He at last found himself in a strong position to haggle, and succeeded in getting Fox to charter his own King Air twin-engine plane for ferrying supplies to and from the Hollywood set: he and his plane amounted to $1.35 million. Burt Reynolds was netting a mere $500,000 and Liza Minnelli $350,000. The budget rose from $10 million to $12.6 million.

Donen was hoping to achieve something of the charm of a Clark Gable/Spencer Tracy film, with a touch of Jean Harlow or Hedy Lamarr thrown in for good measure. The director, now that they were up and running, crossed his fingers that his luck would hold out. But it was not to be.

Shooting commenced in the spring, much of the action taking place at sea off the Mexican coast. The unusually rough water meant that cast and crew were laid low with seasickness. There was even dysentery. Filming proceeded haltingly, and gradually the original twelve-week schedule began to extend. Fox wanted the film finished so they could release it in time for Christmas. Donen told them they'd have to wait.

Shooting at sea was a nightmare. Beside the seasickness, Donen faced the sheer logistical problem of trying to get usable footage of a large number of boats. 'You can't make a camera or boats or actors stay still on water,' he said. 'So when you shoot, most often there's nothing in view – boats are nowhere to be seen. They are impossible to anchor. Even if they swing two degrees it's too much.'

After managing to complete a scene, one of the cameras toppled into the sea, taking all the footage with it. One boat crashed into a Mexican coast guard cutter. All of this led to severe tension, frayed tempers and arguments: producer Michael Gruskoff stormed off the film.

Hackman was boiling over with frustration and anger. 'I can hardly stand it another day,' he said on the set. 'The work isn't satisfying. It's not acting – it's trying to remember what went on before.'

He seemed to be growing disillusioned with the whole process of film-acting, and in particular frustrated by the hold-ups caused by technical hitches. 'I get really weary of waiting to be called for a scene. As an adult I ask myself, why am I sitting my life out on the sidelines? All an actor is concerned with is himself and his performance. He really isn't involved with the rest of the picture.' He reiterated his determination to become a director. 'While the actors are idle on the set the director is busy setting up scenes, checking the cameras, interpreting the script.' But this film really *did* spell trouble. The director, with producer Gruskoff gone, said, 'There are times that I feel like committing suicide.' Everyone involved seemed to feel they were heading for some kind of monumental disaster.

Burt Reynolds grimly persevered through the calamities, but then he had had three flops in a row, and badly needed *Lucky Lady* to be a success. Liza Minnelli grew ill, suffering rapid weight loss, while Hackman felt he was going crazy.

With filming completed at the end of August, and the cast breathing a collective sigh of relief, everyone was recalled. Towards the end of 1975 Donen had first decided that the film's denouement, in which Hackman and Reynolds are killed by federal agents, was too downbeat for what was supposed to be a jolly romp, and he wanted to shoot a new ending. The final scene showed them made up to look aged, all sharing a bed together. Then another alternative ending was shot, in which the three simply continued their reckless rum-running ways.

News of the troubled film was leaked, and a press conference called. Hackman kept quiet while Minnelli supported the director, saying, 'The changes made in the film mark the difference between a work of art and a commercial movie.' Reynolds also defended

Donen's right to make the final choice of ending. Not even the actors, it seemed, knew what ending was going to be used. Very possibly, Donen didn't either. The final choice was the happy ending, with the three of them leading their flotilla of ships.

The final budget had rocketed to around $22 million. Fox knew they were in trouble, and all concerned braced themselves for the critical backlash. 'They're all rumrunners in the early 30s, and they're meant to be adorable,' wrote Pauline Kael in the *New Yorker*. 'This is a big expensive movie for people who don't mind being treated like hicks: the audience is expected to shudder with delight every time it hears an obscenity or sees a big movie star grin.' *Sight and Sound* gave it short shrift. 'It sports its calculations on its sleeve like rhinestones.' *Variety* wrote that 'what appears to have been conceived as a madcap Prohibition-era action comedy, combined with an amusing romantic menage, emerges as forced hokum.'

It had its admirers, such as Susan D'Arcy of *Films Illustrated*: 'The combination of Reynolds, Minnelli and Hackman works perfectly: Reynolds' likeable fall-guy is all charm and confusion; Minnelli's easy showgirl wants to be respectable; the multi-talented Hackman is the one with the know-how. Only the churlish could dislike such a winning combination.'

Tom Vallance of *Focus on Film* felt the film finally displayed something that Hackman had long possessed and needed only the right film to display. 'Far from being the sort of tour-de-force showcase role in which he tends to be cast, it is a part calling instead for *star* charisma, that mysterious blend of presence, personality and instinctive skill that separates the great movie actors from the merely accomplished. Hackman passes the test with flying colours.'

Despite all the hoo-ha, *Lucky Lady* did not fare too badly, reaching sixth place in the American box-office chart for 1975, although it was unlikely to have done much more than break even. It certainly put its acting trio into the list of top box-office stars for that year. Hackman could be forgiven for thinking that he was right to 'play safe'.

He came out of the experience richer in dollars, but poorer in enthusiasm for his craft. Having, it seems, grown disillusioned with acting, he turned his thoughts to directing. 'I have no idea if I have the credentials to be a director, but I want to try,' he said. In partnership with Irwin Allen, he purchased the screen rights to a mystery book by Richard Neely, *Walter*; but the project fizzled out.

Hackman unwound from his Mexican experience by painting: he desperately needed to relax. On those days when he craved a burst of adrenalin, he would get into one of his stunt planes and take to the skies. Taking a longer break from filming than was usual for him, he took the opportunity to plough through scripts and offers.

Hackman began to make the most of his now immense wealth, buying property in the United States and Europe. In the South of France, one of his favourite spots, he purchased a luxury home, but in fact it was no more opulent than the main family home, which had a staggering nine bathrooms. 'It's funny, but having been poor you do all the classic poor things when you suddenly become rich; you get *nine* of everything.' Space could also be found for three floors, twenty rooms, an elevator, a thirty-foot playroom, a pantry complete with soda fountain and a croquet court. 'I had all the aeroplanes, all the cars, all the houses. I don't know that I was terribly well prepared for success. I thought I was. I got swept along. It was like a fantasy come true. But the reality is, the fantasy is fleeting: you have to keep doing the work that got you there. You can't live a myth.'

Perhaps to maintain that lifestyle he embarked on the busiest phase of his career; and it was the one that nearly ruined him. He chose to do three pictures in quick succession; *The Domino Principle*, *A Bridge Too Far* and *March or Die*; in each case the prime motivation, as he admitted, was the cash.

* * *

Hackman's price for *The Domino Principle* amounted to $700,000. Controlling the purse strings was Lew Grade, the British entrepreneur who ran ITC, the television company responsible for such series as *The Saint* and *The Persuaders*, as well as biblical miniseries *Jesus of Nazareth* and *Moses the Lawgiver*. Grade was now making inroads as a film producer.

Written for the screen by Adam Kennedy from his own book, *The Domino Principle* was directed by a tough Hollywood veteran, Stanley Kramer. He had produced and directed classics like *The Defiant Ones*, *Inherit the Wind*, *Judgment at Nuremberg* and the last Spencer Tracy/Katharine Hepburn picture *Guess Who's Coming to Dinner? The Domino Principle* saw Hackman playing a Vietnam veteran in prison for the murder of his wife's first husband. Two representatives of the unnamed organization, played by Richard Widmark and Eddie Albert, propose that he work for them in return for his release, a new identity and passport, plus $200,000 in a bank account. He accepts and immediately finds himself reunited with his wife, played by Candice Bergen. When he learns that his mission is to assassinate the president of the United States, he tries to get out of his contract, but he is forced into the task when his wife is held as a hostage.

The president is killed but Hackman realizes that the assassins' bullets were fired by two other marksmen. Though Hackman manages to fly out of America with his wife, he finds his false passport is missing, and the lump sum has vanished from his bank account. When his wife is killed by a hit-and-run truck, Hackman finally catches up with and kills the men who have set him up.

Although lacking an explicit reference, the film clearly hinged on the theory that Lee Harvey Oswald was a fall guy in the Kennedy assassination. In 1973 *Executive Action*, starring Burt Lancaster, had followed the same theory but had been more open about its inspiration; audiences steered clear of it. This time Kramer maintained the movie was a pure piece of fiction, cannily sensing that America was not then ready for its message. Twenty more years would pass before that was possible, with Oliver Stone's *JFK*. So, ducking the Kennedy – Oswald connection, Kramer said his film was 'a human document of a man trying to survive the jungle'.

A short period of rehearsals prefaced the cameras turning on 12 April 1976. A relaxed and happy Hackman was enjoying working with Richard Widmark, Eddie Albert, Candice Bergen, Eli Wallach and Mickey Rooney. Hackman recalled,

> We started with Mickey in rehearsal and he was flying in and out doing the Cavett show and going back to Chicago doing whatever it is he does in Chicago, and it was a mile a minute with him. He has more energy than anyone I have ever worked with and it's all just like a giant machine. He's five feet tall and he seems like he's nine feet.

Filming kicked off with a week at San Quentin gaol, where Rooney was playing one of the inmates. One of the real prisoners received a knife wound on the first day of filming. The unit then moved on to Puerta Vallarta, north of Hollywood, where it was so hot and humid that by the third day the whole unit was suffering from heat exhaustion and clouds of insects.

Hackman had begun the work enthusiastically, attracted by both the character he was playing and the director's considerable reputation. But before long Hackman grew irritable and argumentative. At some point during filming he had begun to perceive that things weren't working, and he took the matter up with Kramer. In a series of arguments none of the problems was solved, but Hackman's reputation for being difficult was certainly perpetuated. He later said:

> You reach a certain level where people get frightened of your
> money or your power, or both, and I found myself getting my way
> without somebody really pushing against me. That's one of the really
> dangerous things, when you get in a certain position of being able to
> say just anything, and people say, 'Yeah, right, bring it in.' That's bad.

It was some time later that he realized what he was doing: 'When I found myself doing that, I really started getting worried.'

Kramer later said, 'It came as a surprise because he had been so professional, but he just became unreasonably argumentative. Maybe it was the heat!' It turned out that Kramer kept a daily journal and was jotting down each day's events. Hackman's problematic behaviour was recorded in detail, so when Kramer later related the experiences to a magazine, he was able to give an accurate, if inevitably one-sided, account. Later Hackman said, 'Most people didn't seem to understand the film. I'm not surprised. I didn't understand it either. I had lots of arguments with Stanley Kramer.' He later read the article, and said, 'It was embarrassing to read it, but I have to say it was accurate. The truth was I knew we were in trouble on the film, and I got scared.'

Candice Bergen, aware of the disharmony, spoke on set of her personal admiration for Hackman, with whom she was now working for the third time. She said that he had been able to communicate 'his love of acting' to her. 'He always puts himself in jeopardy. He always takes the risk of failing.' She obviously did not know his true feelings at that time, and was praising a younger, more idealistic actor.

The talented Bergen was wasted in her role, and somehow their reunion scenes fail to convince. The confused screenplay seems to have prevented the excellent cast from doing their best, and the film fell far short of the powerful dramas with which Kramer had made his reputation.

Hackman finished the film depressed and troubled. His mood found a reflection in his private life, deep cracks were appearing in a marriage that for some time had been strained. Drastic change was needed, and soon. 'I found my personality was changing,' he said. 'I was becoming mean and arrogant. I didn't slap my wife or three children at home as I did people on the screen, but they noticed the difference in me.'

6   If It's Good Enough for Brando

Hackman was able to wring a little more out of his star status by accepting a small role for a large fee in Joseph Levine's epic war film, *A Bridge Too Far*. In commercial terms the picture attempted to re-create the success of *The Longest Day*, which, like this one, had been based on a book by Cornelius Ryan, and which, like this one, had featured a mammoth all-star cast. The only difference was, apart from the fact that *The Longest Day* was shot in black and white to save costs, that the earlier film had been about a massive and vital victory for the Allies. *A Bridge Too Far* focused on one of the most humiliating and terrible defeats for the Allies. In September 1944 35,000 Allied troops were parachuted into the Netherlands behind German lines in an effort to capture bridges along the Rhine. After nine days of fighting the Allies, having suffered terrible loss of life, retreated. The attempt to capture the bridge at Arnhem was, said Lieutenant-General Browning, 'one bridge too far'.

Levine handed the directorial task to Richard Attenborough, one of Britain's finest screen actors, who had recently made a good account of himself as the director of *Oh What a Lovely War* and *Young Winston*. To reconstruct the great battle he was given a huge budget of $25 million, and fourteen stars from both the United States and Europe. The cast list read like a who's who of cinema: James Caan, Robert Redford, Sean Connery, Michael Caine, Liv Ullmann, Laurence Olivier, Dirk Bogarde, Anthony Hopkins, Ryan O'Neal, Maximilian Schell, Hardy Kruger, Edward Fox, Elliott Gould and Gene Hackman. It was, said Attenborough, 'a cast list rarely, if ever, equalled in any other film.' Though something of an overstatement – consider the casts of films like *The Longest Day* and *How the West Was Won* – it was nevertheless an impressive roster.

Hackman portrayed Major-General Stanislaw Sosabowski, leader of a Polish parachute brigade whose entry into the battle was fatally delayed by bad weather: it all ended in slaughter. Hackman accepted the role for more than just financial reward, though this was the main motive.

> I chose to play Sosabowski because he was a strong individual with a questioning mind. He was fifty-two when the operation was proposed by Montgomery as a means of quickly ending the war. Sosabowski thought his excellently trained troops were likely to be sacrificed to Montgomery's ambitions, and he wasn't afraid to tell his British associates as much. He was my kind of hero despite his outspoken criticism which made him unpopular with his fellow officers. But what happened to his men was truly tragic.

Putting the noble sentiments to one side, Hackman was also being paid a cool million dollars for ten days' work, as were the other stars (except Redford who got twice that). He admitted, 'I did it for the money. But it was all good company and it was a worthwhile role in a worthwhile film.' He admitted that many actors could have played the role as well, if not better, than he, but, he said, 'what they were using was my name for whatever that's worth, just like they used Robert Redford, James Caan and the others. You don't get paid for the number of days you work on a film: you get paid because they need you.'

Filming got underway on 26 April 1976, while Hackman was still away making *The Domino Principle*. Attenborough faced a nightmare schedule of just twenty-three weeks, during which actors had to be able to arrive, do their work and leave, all with clockwork precision. If anyone came late or left early, everything would fall apart. That was one reason why the stars were paid so well; they had no excuse for letting Attenborough down. Under his leadership, and with every star giving their utmost, the picture finished under budget and half a day ahead of schedule.

Hackman could not concede that his obsession with stardom and financial success was wrecking not only his personal life but also his career. Lew Grade was adamant that he needed Hackman in another film – any film – and sent him a variety of scripts and books from which to choose. *March or Die* stood out – a French Foreign Legion adventure story that director Dick Richards had been developing. If the publicity is to be believed, Richards had first conceived of making such a film in 1973 and wanted Hackman to star even then. With a handful of films to his credit, including *The Culpepper Cattle Company* and a good remake of the 1944 *Farewell My Lovely*, Richards was given a generous budget by Grade to make what he envisaged would be a classic adventure film in the *Beau Geste* and *Gunga Din* vein.

Set in Morocco in 1918, *March or Die* was based on a factual story. Major Foster, an American West Pointer-turned-Legionnaire, is assigned to protect a group of French archaeologists who are seeking the tomb of the Angel of the Desert at Erfoud. France desperately needs the treasures to help boost recovery in the aftermath of World War I. The local Arab chieftain, El Krim, refuses permission and eventually a full-scale battle breaks out between Arabs and Legionnaires.

Richards wanted Hackman to play the pivotal role of Major Foster, and at first he turned it down; he was tired of long, hot locations. He was also toying with an offer from Steven Spielberg to star in *Close Encounters of the Third Kind*. Donner and Grade finally succeeded in seducing him, and leaving Richard Dreyfuss to make *Close Encounters*, he spent the autumn months of 1976 makming a film he knew was flawed. Having briefly researched the Foreign Legion, he read the script twice, put it aside, and thought no more about the project until he was on the set in Spain. Richards did location work in Madrid and Almeria, before moving on to Morocco, North Africa.

Once again Hackman sensed they were in trouble early on, and he began arguing with the director. His irritation and foul temper were aggravated by a bad back although, to his credit, no pain can be detected in his face or movements on the screen. Part of the problem was the casting of Marco Segrain, a new recruit to the Legion who was meant to be a handsome hero. Grade gave the part to Terence Hill, formerly Mario Girotti, an Italian lead of numerous sword-and-sandal epics who changed his name when he became a star of spaghetti westerns like the successful *They Call Me Trinity* and Sergio Leone's *My Name is Nobody*. Many believed he was an American actor because his heavily accented voice was so cleverly overdubbed. *March or Die* was his bid for international stardom, but he just wasn't up to it – and because the film relied so heavily on him, neither was the film.

Another glaring fault was the bizarre seventies setting; had it been located in time thirty or forty years earlier it might have succeeded as an old-fashioned yarn. Sadly the impressive scale of the film could not disguise the many substandard ingredients.

* * *

The Hackman bubble was getting dangerously close to bursting towards the end of 1976. Having made three as yet unreleased films, he was being sought for another, *Superman – The Movie*, to play the part of arch-enemy Lex Luthor. 'I was doing far too many pictures just for the money – and it showed,' he said. 'People began to say I was getting difficult to work with, which was maybe true.'

Superman – The Movie, while harking back to the popular film serials of the forties and fifties, sought to take advantage of the latest in special-effects wizardry. As the posters proclaimed on its release, 'You'll believe a man can fly.'

Back in 1975 producer Ilya Salkind and his father Alexander Salkind were looking for a new direction after their enormous success with twin movies *The Three Musketeers* and *The Four Musketeers*. It was Salkind junior who came up with the idea of doing *Superman*. He told me,

> My father, who never read comics, didn't know who Superman was. I said, 'It's this guy who has incredible powers like being able to fly, and he's a good guy.' My father got excited about the idea so we then had to set about getting the rights from DC Comics. After about six or eight weeks of negotiating, DC Comics, which is part of Warner Publishing, called someone at Warners who was in a high position and said, 'These guys want to buy the rights to Superman,' and this top guy just said, 'Then sell it to them.' So we had the concept of a comic book-type science-fiction movie before anyone else.

They assigned Mario Puzo to write the screenplay, 'which was terrific,' said Salkind. 'He really did the basic story. Then Robert Benton and David and Leslie Newman reworded some of the script, and at the end Tom Mankiewicz revised it. Each writer brought something special to the script.' Next the Salkinds needed a director.

> There were three categories of directors. There were the directors who were very excited but were busy like Coppola, Friedkin, even George Lucas and Spielberg. Then there was the second category that just didn't like it. Franklin Schaffner turned it down and so did Robert Aldrich. Then there was the category of guys who would have killed to do the film but they weren't names so the backers didn't want them.

Finally Guy Hamilton was chosen: he'd directed a good many British film successes, including a couple of James Bond films. Then it transpired that Hamilton had some tax problems and couldn't remain in Britain where much of the film was to be made. Fortunately Richard Donner, now regarded as a top-flight director after the success of *The Omen*, eagerly accepted the assignment.

The biggest nightmare was casting. Said Salkind,

The main drama was the casting of Superman himself. I was under incredible pressure from my father who said we needed a name. I argued with him about that, but he was adamant. So I made an offer to Robert Redford. I knew it wouldn't work out because everyone would say, 'That's Robert Redford flying,' and it would have been a joke. He turned it down because he didn't think it was right for him, so I was really pleased.

Then started a whole thing with Paul Newman. Now, he would have been all right for Luthor, but not very good for Jor-El, I thought. We tried him for Superman, but he turned it down, and then turned down every other role we offered him. At that point we had to forget about Superman for a while because after that I got a call from an agent who said, 'I might get Marlon Brando for you.'

This agent was one of the biggest in the business but now he's an old friend and you can't really believe he'll be able to get you a big break like this. But something told me to follow it up. He said, 'How much can you offer him?' So I gave him a figure. He came back and said, 'He'll do it, but he wants more than you offered.'

At this point I'd been in Hollywood for five months [in 1976] trying to get everything together and I was going bananas, so I told him, 'You sort out what you can,' and I left for Cannes. In the morning I saw my father and I said, 'We don't have Brando.' He said, 'What do you mean?' He wasn't pleased. I said, 'He wanted X amount and I only offered him Z amount.' Now I was really feeling sick about the whole thing, but my father said, 'We'll call him up – just to make sure.' My father came back and said, 'Don't worry, he'll do it.'

The moment we got Brando to play Jor-el (Superman's father) everything started moving really fast. We got Gene Hackman the next day practically, because just about every actor wants to play opposite Brando. Then because we had both Brando and Hackman, we were able to get other actors interested. They all realized that if Marlon Brando *and* Gene Hackman were doing this film, then maybe they ought to be in it too. And I guess everyone wants to act with Brando and Hackman, who are two of the greatest actors in America.

Hackman said, 'I had read the script – it was good – but I didn't particularly want to do it, and I probably wouldn't have done the film if Brando had not been in it. If it was good enough for Marlon Brando, who am I to hold back? The money was a big inducement, I won't deny that.'

Around 300 to 400 actors were interviewed for the role of Superman. 'Then one day in New York,' said Ilya Salkind,

we saw Christopher Reeve, and he was very skinny then. He was an actor but wasn't getting any work. Most guys were coming in for interviews and going out after fifteen minutes. But when Reeve came in we interviewed him for forty minutes. He had the perfect face, he looked fantastic, but Dick Donner said he was too young.

We went back to Los Angeles; we even screen-tested a *dentist* – Ryan O'Neal even said he should play Superman! But he couldn't act and Dick said he was too old. And just then I said, 'Wait a minute. What is this problem about being too old or too young? Who knows how old Superman is? This is a new movie, a new epic of today, it should be someone who is young.' So then I went back down my list of names and I stopped on Reeve. I told Dick and he said, 'He's still too young and skinny.' I said, 'Look, he's skinny but we can build him up, and as for being young – why not?' Well, Dick wasn't all that hot about it, but after we gave Reeve the test, Dick was raving about him.

Salkind hired British actor Dave Prowse, who had played Darth Vader in *Star Wars* and who had himself auditioned for the part of Superman, to put Reeve through a muscle-building regime. But despite what was to prove an exciting new cinema find, media attention was relentlessly focused on Marlon Brando, who, it turned out, would be on screen for no more than ten minutes and receive a reputed $2 million. Not bad for just twelve days work. He would also net 11.3% of the profits. Hackman also received a hefty $2 million.

Meanwhile, some of Hackman's work of the last 18 months was seeing the light of day. The first release, *The Domino Principle*, was, said *Variety*, 'a weak and tedious potboiler starring Gene Hackman as a tool of mysterious international intrigue, and a barely recognizable Candice Bergen in a brief role as his perplexed wife. Stanley Kramer's film contains a lot of physical and logistical nonsense.' Critic John Simon was even more acid: 'Terrible movies tend to start with a preposterous premise and then laboriously work their way to an impossible conclusion. This one however starts with an arrant impossibility and works its way to whatever lies beyond and below that.'

In an attempt to revamp the film for British audiences, it was re-edited and retitled *The Domino Killings*. It finally reached British screens in 1978, and quickly disappeared again.

Then came *March or Die*, which had been hyped to the heavens – but it couldn't overcome the scathing reviews. *Variety* said, 'Biggest disappointment is the"acting" of Gene Hackman who walks listlessly through the major role of a washed-out West Pointer who had given up 16 years of his life to the Legion.' The *Monthly Film Bulletin* said, '*March or Die*, yet another of Lord Grade's wholesome moneyspinners (*sic*) is an overheated mixture of stock characters and antique situations.'

Even before he began *Superman*, Hackman was wondering where his career was heading?

*   *   *

Brando flew into Britain for principal photography on *Superman* at Pinewood Studios in March 1977. He wrapped his scenes within thirteen days and left in early April, just as Hackman arrived to film through to June.

Transformed into Metropolis, the back lot and sound stages of Pinewood were as good as anything that Hollywood could produce, and at a fraction of the cost. The awesome cityscape, built to look like New York's 42nd Street, stretched some 800 feet and incorporated the *Daily Planet* offices, a subway, stores, newsstands, a dozen fire hydrants, and three phone booths.

The film was costing in the region of $40 million – but the Salkinds were actually intending to get the necessary footage for *two* movies. They did the same thing in the case of *The Three Musketeers* with director Richard Lester in 1974, but failed to mention this to the cast, most of whom felt cheated at having been paid only once. This time the cast were aware of the intention to shoot Part II concurrently. Hence, the three villains in the opening sequence to Part I – Zod, Ursa and Non, played by, respectively, Terence Stamp, Sarah Douglas and Jack O'Halloran – were mainly kept in reserve for the sequel. Both Brando and Hackman agreed to a double-film deal provided they could get their scenes done first. While this presented no problems for Brando, having only a couple of scenes in Part I and a few brief holographic visitations in Part Two, Hackman had a lot more work to do. All, however did not go according to plan, as Sarah Douglas explained:

Parts I and II should have been shot together. They concentrated on
Part II to begin with. We hardly did anything on Part I. In fact I did
nine months' work, but obviously it didn't take all that time just to
shoot the three-minute sequence I'm in at the beginning of Part I.
Then Warner Brothers said, 'Hey you guys,' – or whatever Warner
Brothers say – 'you haven't done anything on Part I.' So they
shelved Part II to be completed the next year.

Lex Luthor, a villain with pure evil on his mind, is trying to turn
the Mojave Desert into prime beachfront property by using a
nuclear missile to cause a massive earthquake that sends Southern
California into the Pacific Ocean. As a comic-book character,
Hackman knew he had to play him with humour. 'It was a departure from anything I'd ever done before,' he said. 'Lex is so devious,
he sometimes double-crosses himself . . . just for practice. He lives
under the city of Metropolis because he's too cheap to invest in
above-ground property!'

This was an enterprise that *had* to succeed. If the first film failed,
then the second would prove to be a complete waste of a small fortune. Alexander Salkind, confident of healthy returns, said, 'If you
count the comic buffs, fans of Brando and Hackman and the other
stars, and the science-fiction freaks who loved *Star Wars* – that's our
audience.'

Few of the many stars involved in the film actually got very
close to Brando. Susannah York, as Jor-El's wife, was considered
one of the lucky ones. Trevor Howard, playing one of the Elders
of Krypton, nursed bitter memories of working with Brando in
Mutiny on the Bounty (1962), and felt unfortunate to be back on
a set with him. In a sense, for many of the younger actors working
with Gene Hackman was the next best thing. Said Sarah Douglas,
'He was just so much fun to work with, and yet you knew you
were working with a seriously great actor. He is such a gentleman
too.'

As a newcomer, Christopher Reeve had both the stress and the
satisfaction of knowing that the responsibility for *Superman*'s fate
rested largely on his now much broader shoulders.

You just can't do something like that and be totally cool about it all.
I was really nervous to begin with and I guess everyone must have
thought I was a little uptight. If something went wrong I'd get angry,
because I figured that all these people around me had come from
established careers and if the film failed they'd carry on, but I'd go
back to being a no one. But Gene Hackman said to me, 'I know what
you're going through. I've been through it too.' And to see what he

had attained to was, I guess, a bit of inspiration for me. So he really helped me a lot.

Reeve recalled that on the first film Hackman seemed 'morose'. 'When I asked him, "Gee, Mr Hackman, why did you play Lex Luthor?" he looked at me and said, "You mean besides the $2 million?" ' Despite Hackman's cynicism, he was impressed with Reeve's talent: 'That young feller really comes into his own when he's playing Clark Kent. He's like Cary Grant in his younger days, and you can also see that under the tights and cape there's really a fine character actor waiting to burst out.'

Characteristically Hackman grew bored with the constant technical hold-ups. 'That sort of movie is a terrific holiday for most actors but it has the reverse effect on me,' he said. 'The more technical a film becomes the more inhibited I am. Therefore the harder I have to work.' He cited how just waiting for Superman to fly in on a wire could take up to two hours, making sure the flying looks realistic and that the person holding the wire doesn't get into shot. 'As an actor your energy and attention level become somewhat dissipated by the amount of energy going into that and when it comes time to do your section, it gets a little soft.' In the end he was unhappy with his own performance and admitted, 'I was disappointed when I saw the film.'

As the production ground on, relationships between cast members began to fracture. Sarah Douglas said that by the end of filming it had become

the English versus the Americans. Christopher was, I think, getting a bit wrapped up in Superman. We all started work on the first day together, but by the end of the film Chris couldn't remember any of our names. Having said that, I admit that you do almost get taken over by the character you play and it's very difficult to cut off from that. Certainly Christopher had a lot to live up to, but I was a little disappointed to find he really didn't remember who I was or my name.

Gene Hackman was the one person who was really the same as he was the first time, and we became very good mates. One day we were going to the restaurant for lunch, and on the way we passed a big photograph showing me in a film I did at Pinewood called *The People That Time Forgot*. I looked so different because in *Superman II* I had short hair and all this heavy make-up that made me look very domineering, and I wore a tight black organza outfit with daring little slits everywhere so you think you see me in places you don't; whereas in the photo I was looking all helpless and innocent and had long hair. As we passed the picture, Gene looked at it and said, 'Gee, she's a pretty girl. Not in your class though.' I didn't have the heart to tell him he was looking at a photograph of me.

Hackman's contribution to the first part of *Superman* came to an end in summer 1977. Nor was there much left to do in Part II. Meanwhile, however, he left Pinewood, and England, to return to his family.

Around this time *A Bridge Too Far* was released and immediately did brisk business on both sides of the Atlantic. But for some reason the critics took it upon themselves to act as moralists, accusing the film of trivializing a serious human tragedy in the name of summer entertainment. Whatever the backers' intentions, Richard Attenborough's mission had been honourable. No matter that he had made the best World War II epic since *The Longest Day*, the critical backlash was ferocious. The *Monthly Film Bulletin* said it was 'so wearily, expensively predictable that by the end the viewer will in all likelihood be too enervated to notice Attenborough's prosaic moral epilogue . . . Gene Hackman plays Sosabowski with one-note dolefulness tempered by an extraordinary Polish accent.'

A Bridge Too Far became known as 'a film too far.' The media's drubbing damaged the film, and it struggled to recoup its huge outlay of cash. Though it ultimately went into profit, it was not the huge moneyspinner Levine had hoped for. Hackman felt despondent.

He was being wooed around then by Francis Ford Coppola to come and play Lieutenant-Colonel Kilgore in *Apocalypse Now*. The up-front fee was paltry by the star's standards, but Coppola offered him a percentage of the profits. Hackman turned the offer down. 'Francis has a way of asking you to work on deferments, which I didn't think I should do,' he said. 'But I have all the respect in the world for him. I think maybe he's the best director there is.' Harrison Ford accepted a small role, and Robert Duvall was eventually chosen to play Kilgore, who rides his helicopter into battle playing Wagner from loudspeakers.

Had Hackman accepted, he would have been spending the next month or so in the Philippines. As it was, he felt it was high time to take stock of his life. Meanwhile production on *Superman*, with so many special effects scenes to be shot, rumbled on into the early months of 1978. Both parts had seriously overshot their schedules.

7 A Kind of Death

Hackman returned home to contemplate his future during the summer of 1977. For one thing, he had grown to hate himself on screen because 'I was seeing an old man, an uncle figure of around fifty; I still believed I was a young guy in his twenties.' Then there were the choices he'd made.

> I made four bad pictures in a row – *Lucky Lady*, *The Domino Principle*, *A Bridge Too Far* and *March or Die*. I should have stopped after *Lucky Lady* and gone back to being straight, to taking parts for what they were and not what they paid. Things suddenly seemed very simple. I decided to stop acting before I was forced to stop.

His retirement was purely a matter of survival. His life since winning the Oscar had become 'a long nightmarish blank when I couldn't have told you from one day to the next what I was doing or what I was going to do. I just knew there was a lot of money to be made and I didn't have to think too much about it.'

Perhaps more than anything he recognized that he was going to lose Faye permanently if things didn't change. 'I wasn't easy to live with any more and my home and life were in a turmoil as a result. If I had stayed acting, there would have been a real personal disaster for me. My wife is not an actress, so she could see what was happening to me. She didn't want the effects to rub off on her.'

In an effort to escape the Hollywood lifestyle, he transported the family from their big mansion to their weekend home in Monterey. 'I just want to get out,' he said, 'just have a little Spanish-style house and pick up a truck or something.'

He yearned for the simple life, although this would also be a tall order given the massive wealth he'd accumulated. Art served as a form of therapy, an escape from stress. 'I work in oils and find it enormously soothing. Nothing about it is competitive. It's a very private thing with me. I would never put myself in a situation where my paintings could be judged.' He read a good deal, and learned to sculpt. He played tennis, and derived pleasure from watching his sons racing motorcycles. Whenever he felt the need to escape, he would travel to where the mood took him, buying homes in Europe in the process. 'What's the point of having wealth if you can't enjoy it?' he reasoned.

But before long he found he needed something to energize him. In 1978 he took a five-day course at the Bob Bondurant School of High Performance Driving in northern California, where Clint Eastwood and James Brolin were among his fellow students. He was soon competing in car races at Sebring and Riverside, or taking to the skies in his Pitts biplane either for the sheer pleasure of being in the clouds, or diving and looping in a fashion that would have given studio executives and producers coronaries.

As the scripts mounted up Sue Mengers, his agent, would call him occasionally. 'I'm not interested,' Hackman would tell her each time.

When *Superman – The Movie* was released during Christmas 1978, many critics remarked on the apparently hurried pace of post-production. 'It gives the impression of having been made in a panic – in fear that style or too much imagination might endanger its approach to the literal-minded,' wrote Pauline Kael. The *New Yorker* said that although it was 'one of the two or three most expensive movies made to date, it's cheesy-looking, and the plotting is so hit or miss that the story never seems to get started; the special effects are far from wizardly, and the editing often seems hurried and jerky just at the crucial points.' *Variety* found it 'a wonderful, chuckling, preposterously exciting fantasy . . . Lurking in wacky palatial splendour in the sewers beneath Park Avenue, supercriminal Gene Hackman views this caped arrival as a superthreat befitting his evil genius.'

The sceptical voices of the press were, however, bulldozed by a massive marketing campaign, racking up the highest one-week gross in film history, $18,517,595, in some 500 cinemas. When the picture opened in Britain early in 1979, audiences flocked to it. The same happened throughout the world, and by 1980 it had earned a global gross of more than $300 million.

All of this was a far cry from the shrunken world of Gene Hackman, who was considering starting his own little theatre group in Monterey. Despite still feeling the need to act, when word leaked out that he was planning to come out of retirement, he moved quickly to quash the rumours. 'I lost enthusiasm for the business, not for acting. The business is ugly. There's so much money involved. It's corrupt.' Although he 'tinkered with the idea of starting a theatre group,' he never quite got it together.

He was dong his best to enjoy his retirement. He said, 'I thought that after twenty years of acting I would be glad of a rest. I did everything to distract myself. I thought I was going to enjoy all those things that kept me busy during retirement because I'd never had time to do them before.'

While doing his best to enjoy retirement, he was recalled, along with the rest of the cast, to appear before the cameras in the summer of 1979 – to finish *Superman II*. Sarah Douglas in particular had been waiting a long time for Part II, having appeared only fleetingly in the first film.

> The first year of filming in 1977 I did nearly ten months of work doing *Superman* I and II [she told me] but we didn't complete Part II, so they contracted me to go back the next year. Then they weren't ready; they'd discovered they hadn't done the destruction of Metropolis the first year and hadn't worked out how to do it. So I didn't work but I was paid for the summer. The third year they had me back from August 1979 to March 1980. Picking up *Superman II* where we did [with the trial of the three supervillains] was impossible because we had originally started to shoot the scene three years before and we were trying to remember what we'd been doing.

When Christopher Reeve and Margot Kidder headed back to England to resume filming they whipped up a storm of controversy and outrage on discovering that their director, Richard Donner, had been replaced by Richard Lester. Co-producer Pierre Spengler explained, 'As for Richard Donner, we decided we did not require his talents for *Superman II*. Most of what remains to be done requires technical rather than creative ability.' Despite the producers' denials, Margot Kidder told me she was convinced it was simply a money-saving move.

> I don't know exactly what it was, but whatever it was, it certainly didn't have anything to do with morals. It was an immoral act, in my opinion. Donner was the man who made their first movie successful, who made careers successful, who made them a pile of money, who did half the work on *Superman II* and devoted a huge hunk of his life to it. They turned round and stabbed him in the back, and so there was a lot of resentment about that.

But Richard Lester knew all about it, so he walked into an awkward situation. Luckily, being who he was it was OK. But we definitely did miss Dick Donner on the second one; we were a tight family who'd been together for a year and a half before that and who loved each other, and 'daddy' was no longer there. Poor Richard Lester felt very bad about it himself; he was in an awkward situation.

In fact, half of *Superman II*, or a great deal of it, is Donner's work, and he should be given credit for it. It's his work and characters that we all came to by his direction. The only bitterness on the set was not towards Lester; it was towards the producers.

Originally Lester insisted his name be left off the credits because he recognized that much of Part II was Donner's work. The script and casting had all been shaped by the original director; Lester conceded that he was working from Donner's blueprint – a generous gesture from a much-liked director. The producers, though, knew they couldn't put Donner's name on the credits, and they needed someone's name, so Lester was ultimately credited as sole director.

As well as Donner, other faces were missing from the set. One was Marlon Brando. His scenes in which he appeared holographically to Superman to deliver various messages and fatherly advice had all been recorded three years earlier. However, it soon became evident that he was not going to appear in the sequel at all, and all his lines were being given to Susannah York as Superman's mother. Christopher Reeve became unhappy with the situation, saying, 'I gather that if they'd used those scenes with Marlon they would have had to pay him a huge amount of money as he had a percentage of the gross. So it's a business decision, not an artistic one. And that made me unhappy. The father-son relationship was very important to Part II.'

And where was Gene Hackman? According to the extensive production notes from Warner Brothers, Hackman had returned to Britain to appear in Part II. The truth was rather different; happily retired, he had no intention of working on any more *Superman* films, as Richard Lester explained. 'Gene Hackman had already finished his work on the project although his role features prominently in *Superman II*. So for those scenes of his which he hadn't already shot, I used a double and a voice impersonator.'

Luthor was a character vital to the plot of Part II. With the arrival of Zod, Ursa and Non, the comic-book criminal tries to form an alliance with them, promising to lead them to the son of Jor-El in return for being crowned King of Australia. According to the production notes, Hackman was supposed to have said, 'He was awful enough when he was in control, but now that he has become

Producer/actor Warren Beatty gave Gene Hackman his big break as Buck
Barrow in *Bonnie and Clyde* (1967)

As the skiing coach in *Downhill Racer* (1969) with Robert Redford *left* who
gave him this important role

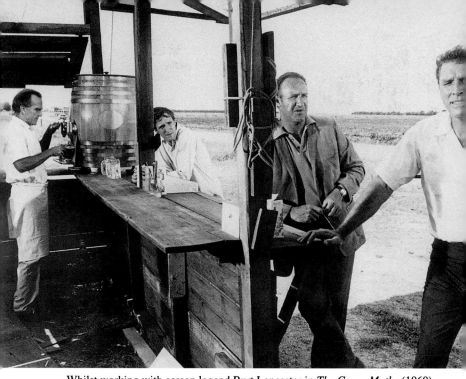

Whilst working with screen legend Burt Lancaster in *The Gypsy Moths* (1969),
Gene Hackman got his first lesson in how a star could control a production

During the filming of *The Gypsy Moths* (1969) Hackman developed a taste for
flying which later became a passion

Stardom and an Oscar came to Hackman when he played 'Popeye' Doyle in
The French Connection (1971)

Hackman proved he could be a
screen hero, carrying Shelley
Winters to safety in *The Poseidon
Adventure* (1972)

Two 'hot' actors of 1973 – Gene
Hackman and Al Pacino – cool off
in the offbeat *Scarecrow*

With one of his favourite directors, Francis Ford Coppola, on the set of *The Conversation* (1974)

Giving a superb performance in one of his most underrated films, *The Conversation* (1974)

Three very unlucky stars, Burt Reynolds, Liza Minnelli and Gene Hackman, in a most unlucky film *Lucky Lady* (1975)

Hackman revealed the depths of his career in *March or Die* (1977), seen here
with Terence Hill

Hackman, Joanna Cassidy and Nick Nolte as journalists covering a civil war,
and having romantic tangles in *Under Fire* (1983)

Director Roger Spottiswoode gave Hackman his best role in years, in the 1983
production *Under Fire*

Left to Right Jane Lapotaire, Gene Hackman, Theresa Russell and Rutger Hauer
in Nic Roeg's *Eureka* (1983)

Gene Hackman finally got a romantic role, with Ann-Margret falling for him in
Twice in a Lifetime (1985)

Hackman displaying his considerable versatility as an actor in *No Way Out*
(1987) by loving and then murdering Sean Young

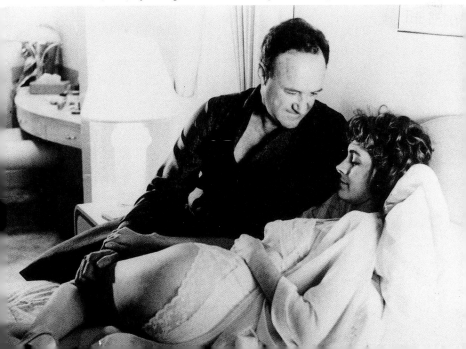

As the ruthless sheriff with a vengeful madame, played by Frances Fisher, in Clint Eastwood's *Unforgiven* (1992) which brought Hackman another Oscar

Out west again, Hackman was the US Cavalry officer out to capture *Geronimo* (1994)

an oily, unctuous underling for a gang of interplanetary hoods, he's even worse. The way he grovels to Zod is a lot like the way Renfield used to fawn on Dracula.' But, of course, he wasn't there.

Hackman's refusal ever to play Luthor again disconcerted the producers, particularly having acquired the rights to *Superman* for twenty-five years. As Ilya Salkind told me, 'We can go on making *Superman* films for years.' No wonder few people realized he had given up acting: the fact that the star had not done a stroke of work under Richard Lester's direction was kept firmly suppressed.

* * *

Late in 1979, Warren Beatty phoned Hackman. 'I'm in England making *The John Reed and Louise Bryant Story* and I want you to come and play a part for me.'

'I've retired,' said Hackman.

'I need you.'

'Oh Warren, please!'

'Look, are you going to make me remind you about *Bonnie and Clyde* and all that stuff about where would you be without me?'

'OK, OK!' he conceded, 'but only a small part.' So Hackman, with no fanfare at all, flew to Britain to work on the film that would eventually be retitled *Reds*. He said, 'Warren always calls me up for these things because I owe him.'

Beatty was both directing and starring as John Reed, the American journalist present in Moscow at the time Lenin returned from exile to assume leadership of the Bolsheviks and begin the Russian Revolution. Reed wrote what he witnessed in *Ten Days That Shook the World*. Diane Keaton played Louise Bryant, the woman in Reed's life, and the part of Irish playwright Eugene O'Neill was taken by Jack Nicholson. The whole production, based at Twickenham Studios, was steeped in secrecy. Between August 1979 and January 1980 Beatty managed to shoot his film both in the studio and on various London locations without a single journalist getting a foot inside the door. I tried – and failed: 'Mr Beatty doesn't want any publicity just yet. He works better that way. Publicity just makes him uncomfortable. He is so involved in the making that he just wants to concentrate on that.'

The film was buried from view until its release in 1981. Hackman's role was so brief – just two scenes as a New York newspaper editor – that he passed virtually unnoticed in the film's 196 minutes. Small part or no, it was surely worth featuring in a film that went on to win Oscars for Maureen Stapleton's supporting performance, Vittorio Storaro's photography, and Beatty's direc-

tion. The latter had been both brave and thoughtful in making
what, in 1981, was a distinctly unfashionable film – a romantic, historical epic – and it proved to be both a personal and a professional
triumph. Moreover, the awards helped to boost a lacklustre showing at the box office.

Finishing his brief stint on the film, Hackman once again slipped
into 'retirement', returning home with some of his taste for acting
reawakened. He tried to forget *Reds* and enjoy his free life. 'I did-
n't really accomplish anything,' he said. 'I just ended up lying
around.' He gave up playing tennis, the solo flying jaunts and the
other hobbies that used to sustain his free time. 'I finally had to
admit that I could not do any of them anywhere near as well as I
can act. That's what I look forward to most when I get up in the
morning.'

Voluntary retirement has proven impossible for all but a rare
handful of stars; Greta Garbo and Marlene Dietrich were excep-
tions, and even Dietrich kept sneaking back. Only an exceptionally
strong-willed actor can turn his back on the adulation, the attention
and, needless to say, the money. But for the most part, it is the emotional reward of the craft that prevents actors from walking away.
The so-called 'acting bug' is a very real addiction. Only those who
genuinely grow tried of acting can retire successfully. And for Gene
Hackman, despite all the fame, the adulation and the riches, the
thing he missed most was the work itself.

'Retirement is a kind of death,' he concluded, 'and no fun at all.
One tends to forget the pain of moviemaking. I guess it's like preg-
nancy – something compels you to go through it all over again.' He
pronounced his retirement over in a final bid to establish himself.
As he told Roderick Mann, 'The only good thing about this break
is that it's got me off the take-the-money-and-run bandwagon.' He
said he would not make three pictures a year – 'there aren't three
good films to make' – and he was going to choose more carefully.

In his directorial debut Robert Redford tried to woo Hackman
for a part in *Ordinary People*. While Hackman liked the project,
there were a number of sticking points, and Redford was not willing to compromise about these areas of disagreement.

Then along came what he considered his 'last chance' – *All Night
Long*, a comedy directed by Jean-Claude Tramont from a screenplay by W.D. Richter. It was totally different from anything
Hackman had done in the past: Jack Lemmon might have fit the
bill perfectly. George Dupler, frustrated at not having been pro-
moted from his executive position with a drugstore chain, punches
a superior in anger and is immediately demoted to night manager
at one of the stores. The local misfits and weirdos cause him all

sorts of havoc. Then one night a girl on a moped pulls up. Enter Cheryl, the kooky girlfriend of George's son, Freddie. Cheryl is married to a fireman who just happens to be George's cousin – he works nights while she keeps Freddie company.

George tries to persuade her that his son is too young for her, and ends up falling for her quirky manner and original views on life. Before long Freddie discovers his girlfriend and father are having an affair; the aggrieved son ignites a marital row that sees George leaving home and taking a room in a hotel. Cheryl encourages him to expand his horizons, so he rents a loft intending to become a renovator. The trouble is, Cheryl cannot choose between George, Freddie and her husband.

Hackman felt that here at last was a chance to 'play a light role for the first time' in a small budget movie, costing just $3 million. Lisa Eichhorn had the role of Cheryl, Diana Ladd was George's wife, Dennis Quaid played Freddie, and Kevin Dobson completed the quadrangle as Cheryl's husband.

Hackman threw himself into film-making with a new sense of purpose. For one thing he still wanted to direct, and this was a superb opportunity to learn. He was, one witness said, 'like a prowling lion on the set, observing every minute detail'. His enthusiasm was sorely tried when he learned of moves afoot to replace the leading lady. With the producer citing 'artistic differences', Lisa Eichhorn suddenly left the production and Barbra Streisand immediately stepped into her shoes.

According to William Goldman, author of *Adventures in the Screen Trade*, the substitution actually came about because Streisand had read the script by W.D. Richter, and had fallen in love with the kooky female character. It just so happened her agent was the wife of the film's director, Jean-Claude Tramont. Exit Eichhorn, enter Streisand. As well as the disruption, more money was at stake. While Eichhorn had been paid $250,000 Streisand cost Universal and the producers Leonard Goldberg and Jerry Weintraub in the region of $4 million. Following the domino principle, the film's budget rose rapidly from a modest $3 million to $15 million: to make a profit the film would now have to be a massive hit.

While Hackman had no gripe against Streisand, he was quick to establish himself as the sole lead of the film. 'She has five or six good scenes and that's it,' he said. 'It would be unfair to audiences to suggest this is Barbra's movie. It's about my character, not hers.'

Striesand's presence bogged the film down, but not through any fault of hers. The quirky role suited a newcomer, like Eichhorn, not a star; a lean, low-budget movie seemed overblown by two stars.

For all that, some of the original concept has remained, with Hackman and Ladd giving perhaps the best performances.

Released in 1981 with little fanfare, the film garnered only modest reviews. Said *Variety*, 'Hackman brings even more to his role than might have been apparent in the script. Playing a clearly subordinate role which she took over from Lisa Eichhorn shortly after lensing began, Streisand is more subdued than usual and effective as such.' But the film itself failed to impress. 'Neither screenplay nor direction seem very clear what they're trying to say, and large chunks of it make no sense at all,' thought the *Daily Mail*.

Hackman's 'last chance' was, unfortunately, a flop, partly because, said Goldman, 'what the studio had done was to take a frail $3 million film and turn it into a $15 million film that was a total disaster and that, when you add in prints and advertising, probably lost them $20 million.'

Hackman had really high hopes for his next role. With his hair and moustache bleached white, he was cast by Nicolas Roeg as Jack McCann, a greedy and rich gold striker who seeks to escape the world. *Eureka*, said Roeg, was 'about ecstasy and what happens after it.' The movie, inspired by the mysterious murder of multi-millionaire Sir Harry Oakes in the Caribbean in 1943, finds Hackman's character also being killed. 'He's a maypole figure around which the other characters dance,' said Roeg. His own real-life wife Teresa Russell was to play Hackman's daughter, who marries a possibly gold-digging gigolo. Joe Pesci, who hit the big time in *Goodfellas* and *JFK*, was cast as a fake entrepreneur who attempts to swindle Hackman and finally sends in his hoods to kill him.

Hackman regarded the script as one of the most unusual he'd ever read. 'It's not your normal adventure story, although it has all those elements. It's not a mystery, although it has mystery involved in it. It's not just a drama about a family, and yet it has that too.' What really enthralled him was the gradual evolution of the character over twenty years. 'And that's what really attracted me to the role – how did he grow, or did he grow, or is he still holding on to the past?'

A director of considerable reputation, Roeg had helmed the modern classic *Don't Look Now*, as well as cult favourites *Bad Timing* and *The Man Who Fell to Earth*. Hackman judged Roeg to have 'a complete knowledge of what the camera can do. Roeg is the sort of director who can exploit an actor for the best advantage of the script.'

The only person who lacked enthusiasm was Faye. The film would bring about a protracted absence, just as she was feeling life after Gene's retirement, was growing more stable. His two-year hiatus had been their last hope of happiness, and she could now see no chance of salvaging what they had.

The film had the backing of MGM, now trying to re-establish itself as a force in Hollywood. In fact, originally Roeg and David Begelman, producer-in-chief at MGM, had intended to make a film about Sir Harry Oakes, but decided they needed to fictionalize it as people like De Marigny and the Duchess of Windsor, caught up in Oakes's story, were still alive. For that reason it became a life of Jack McCann, as scripted by Paul Mayersburg.

Writer and director collaborated closely on the screenplay. Mayersburg told *Sight and Sound*, 'One thing about Nic is that he has never replaced a writer on a screenplay. That comes from loyalty and real conviction about the film he wants to make. In *Eureka* many of the images were suggested by me, and many of the lines of dialogue were suggested by him.' The title for the film came from a suggestion by the girlfriend of producer Jeremy Thomas that there was a link between the script and Edgar Allan Poe's *Eureka*.

Begelman allocated $11 million to make the film, and Roeg made full use of the money, filming in British Columbia, Jamaica, Miami and at Twickenham Studios in Britain. Needing to take advantage of British Columbia's winter and Jamaica's spring, the film required a gruelling schedule of five months. To help relieve the boredom for Hackman, who hated long productions, his son Chris accompanied him, hired by Roeg to work with the crew.

Predictably, the long schedule began to take its toll on Hackman. Although Nic Roeg's working life had started as Richard Lester's cameraman, the style between the two directors could not have been further apart. Hackman's preference was usually for Lester's method of shooting with multiple cameras and rarely doing more than two takes. Roeg by contrast only used one camera at a time because, as a former cinematographer, he enjoyed lighting each set-up individually and took pains to achieve the exceptional photography that is a hallmark of his films. Numerous takes were shot from numerous angles, all requiring different lighting effects. This meant a lot of waiting round for the actors, and Hackman's temper was on an increasingly short fuse.

He and the director began to find themselves at odds, with Hackman demanding greater speed in face of Roeg's highly methodical approach. Hackman's intolerance would rise after each rejected take, and the crew began to remark knowingly about his difficult reputation.

Hackman had perhaps not quite realized the extent to which any Nic Roeg film is the work of an auteur, the product of a grand conception. Roeg and lighting cameraman Alex Thomson captured stunning vistas, punctuated by sudden zooms and edits, hand-held camera shots, and scenes of violence. And whatever the troubles Hackman was going through, or even causing, he emerged with a superb performance.

He also emerged with his private life in shreds.

8 Therapy on the Film Set

Hackman had gone off to make *Eureka* knowing of Faye's unhappiness, but somehow he just seemed powerless to do anything about it. She was happiest when he wasn't working, while he was the exact opposite – even though, by his own admission, his working mode was somewhat morose, even melancholic. But he wasn't miserable, just introspective, and unsettled.

By 1982, with their marriage seemingly beyond repair, he and Faye came to the conclusion that they should part. 'It's been difficult to have a personal life in this business,' he said. 'I've been away so often on location. Pictures aren't shot in Hollywood any more. That affects your wife and it affects your children. I think a celebrity's kids have a hell of a tough life.' At least his children were no longer at a vulnerable age. Leslie was youngest at fifteen, Elizabeth was eighteen and Christopher twenty-two. Frankly this fact eased their separation, for which they cited irreconcilable differences.

The family home was put on the market for $8 million. It was, he said, 'too big for one man and his family.' Leslie and Elizabeth remained with their mother in a smaller house provided by Hackman, while he embarked on a nomadic existence, moving from hotel to hotel. He retained some of his property in Europe, but kept their locations strictly secret.

Despite his problems, he was generous when a friend came to him in desperation, asking for a loan of $3,000 to prevent the bank from foreclosing on his mortgage. He promised to repay the debt in thirty days. Up to three years later, Hackman was still waiting.

The divorced star was plunged into deeper gloom when he learned of the suicide of his lawyer and friend Norman Garey. Now, despite all he had said when coming out of retirement, he threw himself into work. 'It wouldn't be good for me to lie about for the next year or so. For a number of reasons, I'm going to work hard. It's something I know how to do, and it's something I can rely on.' Work took on therapeutic flavour, especially when Hackman found himself playing characters whose personal problems mirrored his own. In fact, while many Hollywood actors would have dived for the analyst's couch to see them through such a crisis, Hackman's best therapy would be gleaned from film sets.

Projects were rattling by at a swift pace. Within weeks of finishing *Eureka* he was back in Mexico for *Under Fire*. Roger Spottiswoode, a Canadian-born director, had read a script by Clayton Frohman which told of the work of true-life Vietnam War photographer Tim Page. While the screenplay itself didn't appeal to Spottiswoode, the core idea of making a film about war correspondents did. Working with Frohman and another writer, Ron Shelton, he crafted a new screenplay.

The story begins in Chad in the late sixties, where two correspondents, Russell Price and Alex Grazier, plus Alex's lover, newslady Claire Stryder, cover the conflict. The action later moves to Nicaragua, where Russell and Claire decide to try to find and photograph the rebel leader. Alex eventually joins them and, while seeking directions from an army unit, is gunned down by a government soldier. Russell having filmed the murder, runs for his life. The president, who has relied on support from the American government, flees the country when Russell's film is shown on television. The rebels emerge victorious.

The film's pivotal scene, where a journalist is shot, was based on a true incident. Here, though, politics does not take a back seat to the 'action', and Spottiswoode expected difficulty in raising the necessary finance. He sent the script out to Gene Hackman, Nick Nolte and Joanna Cassidy, offering them the roles of Alex Grazier, Russell Price and Claire Stryder respectively, and lower-than-usual fees. He had been careful to bypass their agents, knowing they would feel uneasy about their clients getting embroiled in a film about Central American politics. Hackman read and liked it: 'The thing that most appealed to me was the idea of the interplay between the three characters.' In the film Nolte moves in on Joanna Cassidy and steals her from Hackman. 'Within that content we were also covering the war, so it was a fascinating attempt to make a triangle work within the context of a real war.'

He replied in the affirmative within days, as did Nolte and Cassidy. With three major stars under his belt, Spottiswoode was able to raise the necessary finance from Lion's Gate.

In one scene Hackman was scripted to sing 'Spring Can Really

Hang You Up the Most' while accompanying himself on the piano. Spottiswoode had assumed that, having seen Hackman play the saxophone in *The Conversation*, he had musical ability. Not wanting to let the director down, Hackman rented a piano and took lessons. When he launched into the number – singing, playing piano, speaking to Nolte and Cassidy, and finishing in harmony with another singer – he performed it all with utter aplomb. The director could not believe his good fortune. 'He's a writer's and director's delight; an actor who works intensively with the text in preparation. He finds all the options, explores all the possibilities and then comes up with surprises on every take.'

Spottiswoode was no slouch either, filming realistic and riveting action scenes while delivering sensitively handled romantic moments. Both Hackman and Nolte were solid and professional, but Joanna Cassidy excelled in a part that was complex and rich – many miles away from the skin-deep tosh that most leading ladies have to put up with.

Despite his enthusiasm for the role and the film, Hackman still hated the hanging around, and likened being on location in Mexico mid production to being 'in jail'. In his view, the two options for surviving such a mind-numbing eight-week schedule were either to surround yourself with people, 'or you can do it all the way I do – kind of agonize through it.'

He gritted his teeth until the end of summer. After a film he usually retreated somewhere to unwind in time-honoured fashion painting and sculpting. Sometimes he would head off to Monterey, sometimes to Hollywood, and often to Europe. He contemplated directing a script he had bought called *Open and Shut*, about a rape case. While preparing for this task, he told me, 'I've promised myself that I will not allow myself to go on the set on the first morning without having some experience. So what I intend to do is some second-unit work before starting principal photography. I'd prefer not to play in the film as well but it would be very tough for me not to play in it.' Plans to make *Open and Shut* remained indefinitely open.

*   *   *

Hackman had come out of retirement vowing not to make three films a year – but there was little else for him to do. So he accepted an offer from *Scarecrow* director Jerry Schatzberg, who had a script by Barra Grant called *Misunderstood*. This remake of an Italian film called *Incompreso*, made by Luigi Comencini in 1967 was in turn based on a book by Florence Montgomery. Schatzberg said he cried both when he saw the original film and when he read the new script.

The melodramatic, somewhat sentimental story centres on Ned Rawley, a former post-war black-marketeer turned successful shipping magnate, who is living in palatial splendour in Tunisia with his wife Lily. She becomes mysteriously ill and dies, and attempting to bury his grief, he throws all his efforts into his business. In the process he neglects his two sons and is unable to bring himself to break the news of Lily's death to his youngest, Miles, leaving the task to the older boy, Andrew.

Ned promises Andrew he will spend more time with the two boys but his work keeps him from fulfilling his word. He convinces himself that Andrew has come to terms with his own grief, but is berated by his brother-in-law Will for avoiding his duties as a father. The rift between Ned and Andrew grows, and matters come to a head when the boy falls from a tree and is paralysed. On his bed Andrew accuses his father of having only ever loved Miles. When Rawley breaks down and admits his mistakes, father and son are finally reconciled.

Schatzberg managed to raise $8.5 million to make the film, and considered several actors for the part of Ned Rawley. Hackman was on the list, but not at the top. Nevertheless, claims Schatzberg, 'the more I thought about it, the more I realized that he was right.' He sent the script to Hackman who saw in it an opportunity to keep a resolution he had made for himself: to intersperse action movies with more thoughtful, sensitive pictures. 'I have a better view of what I want from acting: personal satisfaction from being proud of the work, and the realization that if I do something not up to my standards, it will come back to haunt me.'

Knowing that this would not always be possible, given the bills he had to pay, Hackman allowed himself to be 'selfish about what I do. I try to hold out for a really good story and script, and if I can't have that, I have to have a lot of money – and good locations.' *Misunderstood* allowed him what he considered to be both a good script and good locations, in Tunisia.

Hackman arrived there for filming in October 1982, and immediately struck up a rapport with two good actors, Rip Torn, who played the boys' uncle, and Susan Anspach, as Rawley's wife. In particular he enjoyed the company of the two young actors, Henry Thomas and Huckleberry Fox, playing Andrew and Miles respectively. 'It was the first time I'd worked with children and it was really fun and interesting,' he said. 'I know W.C. Fields once said the worst things to work with are animals and children because they steal scenes, but I didn't feel like that.'

Working with the boys would have reminded Hackman of his earlier days as a father, as well as reminding him what he had missed in his own childhood. To his horror – and against his will – he had become something of an absentee father. During his marriage he had struggled with the compulsion to work and the need to be with his family, and in the end had been unable to reconcile the two conflicting needs. So he knew how Ned Rawley felt, indeed playing the man served as a form of therapy in how to deal with his own secret and guilty feelings. 'An actor uses his own real memories and emotions as tools of the trade,' he said.

Playing such a dour, distant character required him to get into the right mood before each scene, and when it was over he couldn't automatically snap out of it. But watching the children perform he said, 'It was amazing to see they could be playing a game at one moment, then jump back and do the scene and then resume the games. I wish I could do that as an actor.'

One of the picture's strengths was the tight rein Jerry Schatzberg kept on the sentimentality throughout the picture, only allowing it to become a tear-jerker in the final scene, where Ned tells his injured son, 'I was so blinded by my own sorrow I didn't realize you were suffering too.' Hackman wound up feeling proud of what he'd achieved, and didn't give a damn how well it did at the box office. This project was valuable for the performing experience.

By and large he'd undertaken *Eureka* for the same artistic reasons, and it was just as well he hadn't been counting on a box-office hit. At MGM David Begelman had been replaced, and no one moved in to champion Roeg's film, whose release had been delayed until 1983. In fact the executives at MGM found themselves in a quandary. It was, they felt, an art-house film with a limited appeal and they probably felt the poor expected returns at the box office did not justify the cost of giving the film a full release. After a limited distribution in the United States in 1983, it played briefly in London then plunged without trace.

Some critics liked it enormously, including Tom Milne of the *Monthly Film Bulletin*:

> Between them Roeg and Mayersberg have worked an astonishing alchemy through which an abstraction of the basic patterns of human intercourse is rendered wholly concrete. Embodying Vico's cyclical theory of history, it expounds the despair of humanity's vicious circle from ecstasy to agony, as the impulse to love and possession leads inevitably to loss and destruction.

To *Variety* by contrast, it was 'a Roeg elephant film . . . Even by his own standards, Nicolas Roeg's *Eureka* is an indulgent melodrama about the anticlimactic life of a greedy gold prospector after he has struck it rich. Gene Hackman performs with predictable credit.' For some reviewers the pretentiousness was beyond the pale. 'I've a feeling it will become a cult classic,' said Margaret Hinxman of the *Daily Mail*, 'but no one will convince me that it isn't just the poshest kind of tosh.' She was right; today it is considered a cult classic.

As for *Under Fire*, it was given a full release that same year, and performed moderately well. It was generally considered by critics to be a good thinking-man's action film, 'a complex, genuinely thrilling drama of commitment, the mercenary mentality and the tortuous ironies of history' – *Sight and Sound*. In fact *Under Fire* must be considered one of Hackman's, and Nick Nolte's, best films of the decade.

Misunderstood, much like *Eureka*, was a puzzle to its distributors, who chose to defer the film's release.

*   *   *

In the spring of 1983 a retired Marine colonel, Bo Gritz, returned to Vietnam on a trip, supposedly financed by Clint Eastwood and William Shatner, to search for prisoner-of-war (POW) camps. The subject of Vietnam soldiers listed as 'missing in action' was a sensitive one, especially to the military and government establishments. The news of Bo Gritz's expedition shed light on the suspicion harboured by many that thousands of American soldiers might still be in captivity.

This hypothesis turned into a screenplay called *The Last River to Cross*, written by Joe Gayton, about a Vietnam veteran, Colonel Jason Rhodes, who believes his son, Frank, may be held captive. After failing to get the co-operation of the American government, he decides to return to Vietnam itself. A wealthy industrialist, MacGregor, whose son is also missing in action, finances a raid to be led by Rhodes on a reputed POW labour camp near Laos. Rhodes recruits the rescue party from his old Marine platoon. Arriving in Bangkok, they are disarmed by the authorities but manage to rearm themselves by dealing on the black market. They continue on to Laos and attack the POW camp. Among the rescued Americans is MacGregor's son, who tells Rhodes how Frank had saved his life, fell ill and died.

The script was snapped up by Paramount, which assigned John Milius and Buzz Feitshans as producers and Ted Kotcheff to direct: he had just made *First Blood*, the first Rambo film with

Sylvester Stallone, and was already steeped in background knowledge about the Vietnam War. Immersing himself in further
research, he discovered that the Vietnamese had held French prisoners for nineteen years before being handed over to the French
government. He visited American families whose sons were missing in action. 'It was heartbreaking,' he said, 'to visit a family who
had not seen a son for fourteen years and were hoping he may
one day come back.' A friend who was 'high up in the Democratic
Party' was asked what he thought of the possibility of Americans
still being held captive. 'Of course there are Americans there,' the
friend said.

'What are we going to do about it?' asked Kotcheff.

'What do you want us to do? Go to war?'

Backed by Paramount to the tune of $14.5 million, Kotcheff
began assembling his cast for the film, now called *Uncommon
Valor*. He said, 'I wanted Hackman to play Rhodes because he has
a credible quality, not gung-ho. Any one of us might act his way in
such a situation.' Hackman thought this was as good an action
piece as he was likely to find, and accepted. He was joined by
Robert Stack as MacGregor, with Fred Ward, Reb Brown, Randall
'Tex' Cobb and a young Patrick Swayze.

Kotcheff put his actors through a week of military training to
prepare them, and Hackman emerged looking leaner and trimmer
than he had done for some years. Filming began in California on 6
June 1983, giving Hackman the rare chance to live at home while
he worked – although home was probably a Los Angeles hotel. On
12 July the unit flew to Hawaii to film the jungle scenes for the next
six weeks, working six days a week. A ten-acre Vietcong POW
camp was constructed on Kauai, where the climactic battle was
staged.

Each Sunday Hackman chose to be his usual reclusive self,
relaxing with his paints and easel. It was often this preference for
being alone that gave him the reputation for being melancholic, but
for him solitude was deeply important. Nor did he tend to socialize
with actors.

They talk about their roles and their acting and I don't have anything much to say about that because when I act I don't give it too
much thought or preparation. I like to turn up on the set knowing
my lines but not knowing what I'm going to do. That keeps it just a
little bit scary, gives me an edge. I don't always want to rehearse for
a week or two before we start filming. I do it there, in front of the
camera. It's not something I can talk about or explain. It's just something I do.

The unit moved to Thailand for a final week's shoot, and there the film wrapped in August. Hackman had made good money, working on interesting locations, and for once he thought the film could be a commercial hit. That was also important; he knew he couldn't ignore that aspect of the business all the time. As it happened, the film was also slickly produced, better than the average action film and lacking the likes of Stallone and Schwarzenegger not one bit.

Paramount, realizing they were on to a winner, rushed the film through post-production and had it ready for release at Christmas. In just the holiday season alone it took around $30 million. Some critics thought that Hackman was largely wasted in it. 'All the top talent involved – especially Gene Hackman – is hardly needed to make *Uncommon Valor* what it is, a very common action picture,' commented *Variety*, adding, 'True to a long tradition of war films, by the time the tough really get going it's only a question of who won't come back from the dangerous mission. But at least each of the main characters does his best to make you care whether it's him.'

The *Monthly Film Bulletin* said it was like a big-screen version of *The A-Team*, while others dismissed it as a right-wing fantasy. Much of which goes to show a lack of understanding of the film business by the so-called experts, for the truth is, if you don't make films for the masses, you don't get to make films at all. That's why Hollywood is still thriving. An actor like Hackman, who wants to make films of which he can be personally proud even though they may be of minority interest, must stay in the running by making some films that people will pay to go and see.

* * *

In 1984 he and Faye began divorce proceedings. He took some solace, according to some newspaper reports, in the company of Betsy Arakawa, a Hawaiian pianist who was only a little older than his first born, Christopher. But while he was saddened by the total breakdown of his marriage, he was feeling more at ease with life as he turned fifty-four.

He attended the Oscars in April, presenting Linda Hunt with the Best Supporting Actress award for *The Year of Living Dangerously*. *Under Fire* had received one nomination, for Jerry Goldsmith's music, but in the event it lost out to Bill Conti's score for *The Right Stuff*.

After a delay of almost two years *Misunderstood* finally emerged in spring 1984. *Variety* found it to be 'sombre and largely

unsentimental'. Said the *Hollywood Reporter*, 'Hackman's character forces him into something of a straitjacket, and the suspicion
persists that the father doesn't feel nearly as deeply for his sons as
he evidently did for his wife. A few glimpses of genuine care or
warmth might have helped.' But Janet Maslin wrote in the *New
York Times*, 'Without Gene Hackman and two appealing young
actors to hold the audience's attention, there wouldn't be a movie
here at all.' Deemed as a film with little commercial appeal, which
took very few bookings in America, it wasn't screened at all in
Britain but released straight on to video.

Hackman had been floating the idea of a return to the stage for
some time; also that he would like to work with Dustin Hoffman.
Hoffman seemed to have the solution when he decided to return to
the stage himself in *Death of a Salesman*, and asked Hackman to
join him. But by then the latter had signed to do *Twice in a
Lifetime*. It was a film Hackman thought too valuable to give up
even for the chance to work with Hoffman – and on stage.

British actor/writer Colin Welland had written a play for British
television called *Kisses at Fifty*, the story of a Manchester steel-
worker who undergoes a mid-life crisis, and leaves his wife to take
up with a local barmaid. Bud Yorkin, who had previously directed
a handful of films that ranged from the appalling *Inspector
Clouseau* to the moderately enjoyable *The Thief Who Came to
Dinner*, decided he'd like to turn the teleplay into an American
motion picture, believing that it could be transposed from
Manchester to Pittsburgh, Pennsylvania. Raising a budget of $8
million himself, he commissioned Welland to rewrite the script to
become *Twice in a Lifetime*.

Welland spent six months living in Pittsburgh to research the
new version. While visiting one of the pub-like bars there, he witnessed a young woman storm in with her mother and confront her
father, who had shacked up with another woman. Welland inserted
the scene into his screenplay.

For all the screenwriter's location research Yorkin decided to
shift the action from Pittsburgh to Seattle, because he felt its archi-
tecture and weather were more 'cinematic'. The cumulus clouds, he
felt, had 'that wonderful look you get from enough dampness and
rain which gives you a texture difficult to get elsewhere'.

Welland's story emerged to Yorkin's satisfaction. At the outset
his main character, Harry Mackenzie, seems content with his life at
the steelmill, around which his working life and all his friendships
revolve. His wife Kate and daughters Sunny and Helen throw him
a fiftieth birthday party, but he manages to cut the party short and
leave for the Shamrock Bar for a drink with his friends. There he is

bowled over by an attractive new barmaid, Audrey.

Working the nightshift, Harry seldom comes into contact with Kate, who works by day at a beauty parlour. Down at the Shamrock, Harry becomes more acquainted with the widow Audrey, and sharing each other's problems, they begin to arrange clandestine meetings. Once they are seen together by Kate's boss, their affair quickly becomes public knowledge, and Harry's family is devastated. Kate blames herself for his dissatisfaction. Audrey tells him he must choose between her or his wife, and Harry opts for his mistress. Sunny bursts in on Harry at the Shamrock Bar where she gives full vent to her bitter feelings.

Time passes and Kate begins a new life for herself, going to bingo, accompanying her daughters to a disco – even a male strip show. Ten months after the separation, Helen gets engaged and her older brother Jerry returns from California for the wedding. Time has healed some of the family's pain even though Sunny cannot forgive or forget. Jerry sympathizes with his father, and Kate feels that what happened may ultimately have been for the best. Helen appreciates her father's concern that she may be marrying too young, but assures him her life will be different to his. On the wedding day he attends the church to give her away, but decides it best for everyone not to attend the reception afterwards. He goes home to Audrey.

Yorkin's first choice to play Harry was Hackman. On reading the screenplay he felt compelled to do it because, as he told me,

it offered a different kind of challenge. The character isn't particularly sympathetic in his action, but you had to keep an audience interested and caring about him. I guess this story moved me more than a lot of other things I'd done more or less immediately before. I'm at an age where I get offered these fatherly parts now – the father and son relationship – but this one interested me because the father changes. He's got a hard edge to him but he's also got a soft side, and the son seems to have inherited these qualities.

The longer you're an actor, the more you become attracted to doing things you've never done. I've become more attracted to relationships in films like *Twice in a Lifetime*. Films that come out of relationships rather than the story of a man against the system become more interesting. I knew it wasn't going to be a commercial choice but it was such an interesting part to play.

Yorkin lined up the rest of his cast – Ellen Burstyn as Kate, Ann-Margret as Audrey, Amy Madigan and Ally Sheedy as the daughters, and Darrel Larson as the son – and gathered them together in

Los Angeles for a week of rehearsals. Hackman, who never liked much preparatory work, felt that on this occasion the time was well spent. 'It was a difficult acting piece and I think without the rehearsing we did the film wouldn't have worked on any level.'

The story resonated with much of Hackman's recent experience. Ditto director Yorkin. 'We were both going through a divorce,' said Yorkin, 'and I guess the film was something of a therapy for both of us.'

After the week's rehearsal, the unit moved to Seattle on 16 July 1984, for a week's location work. Then they returned to Los Angeles for a further five weeks to shoot the interior scenes. It didn't take Gene long to realize that this film was going to drag him through the emotional wringer. 'It was a little painful for me to play that role, and although I thought I could use some of what I was going through at the time, it didn't really work out that way.'

One scene was particularly difficult to cope with; it was the one based on fact, where the daughter confronted the father, and it seemed to affect everyone. Said Hackman, 'It was such an uncomfortable scene to do, and being uncomfortable and self-conscious is something we all dread. It makes us vulnerable, so when we came to shoot it, just about all the actors wanted their lines reduced; some just didn't want to do it.'

Even so, thanks to Welland's thoughtful script and Yorkin's sensitive direction, what emerged was more than just a schmaltzy family drama tugging at the heart strings. Touching without being sentimental, Welland had also injected some sharp humour to keep it from sinking under a tidal wave of gloom and depression. The bleak Seattle location also prevented this from becoming a glossy melodrama.

After fifty-five days, Hackman's work on the film was complete, and he decided to enhance what was his favourite way to unwind and relax after a film by taking lessons from a Russian painter. He may not have been tempted back to the set quite so soon had not the next offer come from one of his favourite directors, Arthur Penn.

The film, *Target* (originally *On Target*), was a departure for Penn – a spy melodrama – but he accepted it.

I was working on another film that fell through when Richard Zanuck and David Brown offered me this script called *On Target*. There'd been a lot of films which took a rather snide attitude, which thought they were 'so cool', and I thought it would be fun to make what was really just a good yarn, and go for the kind of excitement that Hitchcock did in films like *North by Northwest* and *The Man*

Who Knew Too Much. I knew I wanted Gene Hackman because this kind of film was like a formula, and you hope to find other aspects through the acting, and with Hackman you find yourself as a director open to subtle things he can offer.

Hackman said the script he saw was poor, but that Penn convinced him it would be improved upon. This one explored another father–son relationship, and under Penn's instructions, as well as to satisfy Hackman, this aspect of the script was enhanced. Otherwise, said Hackman, it was a routine action film. 'With this kind of film the audience accept it as a genre movie, so they already believe you are attractive and sympathetic; you don't have to lay it on the line but they have to believe it or it doesn't work on any level. Just so long as they go out of the theatre saying, "That was entertaining," that's all that matters, and I've done my job.'

Hackman played Walter Lloyd, a highly conventional middle-class businessman whose wife, Donna (played by Gayle Hunnicutt), goes to Europe on vacation while he remains to spend time with their drop-out son, Chris (Matt Dillon). Walter convinces his son to go fishing with him, but during their trip they receive news that Donna has gone missing.

Chris presumes that his mother has simply abandoned a mundane marriage, but Walter, concerned that she has been kidnapped, flies to Europe to search for her, taking his son with him. En route he is forced to tell Chris that he once worked for the CIA and has been living incognito for years. His background, he fears, may have something to do with Donna's disappearance, and, indeed, it transpires that Donna has been kidnapped by an East German spy in revenge for the death of his family. The chase leads through Hamburg and Berlin before she is finally rescued.

Another incentive to do the film was the fact that Penn was shooting in France and Germany, and Hackman didn't want to pass up the opportunity to see more of Europe. Filming got underway in Paris on 8 October 1984, on a budget of $11 million, with a schedule of sixteen weeks. Away from Hollywood, Penn was able to flout union rules and to hire a small and more mobile crew of about thirty people. Hackman observed that 'each one of them truly loved film, and they really cared about what we were doing. It was one of the best crews I've ever worked with anywhere'.

The unit moved to Germany for three weeks' location shooting in Hamburg where the script called for the leading man to dive into icy water. Producers Brown and Zanuck wanted a stunt man to do the scene, but Hackman, at the age of fifty-four and with one gammy knee, insisted on doing it himself. 'It's part of the actor's job to do as much as he can,' he maintained. 'It's important. I have to signal my son from the water to run. It had to be me. So why not get it done and get it over with?' Not to mention the fact that he was always exhilarated by danger. Under the supervision of the stunt director, Hackman donned thermal underwear, then a frog-man's suit, and his ordinary clothes on top. At the signal he plunged in, Penn got the shots he needed, and Hackman emerged, shivering and soaked, but exultant.

Not surprisingly Hackman remained as restless as ever between scenes, keeping himself occupied by observing the technical aspects. David Brown remembers, 'I've never known an actor who spends so little time relaxing in his trailer between takes. Gene wants to know everything that goes on.' That was because he was fighting off boredom by preparing himself to become a director.

Nighttime shooting in Hamburg began to take its toll on all the crew. The late autumn was bitterly cold, especially at night. Despite the piping hot goulash fed to the unit to keep them going, Hackman admitted that by 'three or four o'clock in the morning you really want to quit. One night shoot didn't finish until gone five in the morning.'

After Hamburg Penn took his small unit to Berlin to film a scene at Checkpoint Charlie, then returned to France and the Studios de Boulogne. Certainly the script made no great demands upon the cast, but Penn was more concerned with making this a strictly action-only film. No doubt if he'd had time he would have polished the script more, but he was under orders from his employ-ers, Zanuck and Brown, to get the film finished on time and on budget. It was early 1985 when the film wrapped.

Still intent on directing, Hackman kept an eye on the post-pro-duction phase of *Target*, following its progress through to release in 1985. It was expected to become a big commercial success, but it took only $10 million in the United States although its European release ensured it broke even. Many critics seemed to take it all too seriously and highlighted the film's cliché-ridden plot – or perhaps Penn failed to get across his point that the clichés were meant to be enjoyed. *Variety* found it to be 'a spy thriller that's not only com-pletely understandable and involving throughout, but also continu-ally surprising on the way'. It also noticed some gaping flaws. 'It also strangely contains a few scenes of dreadful writing, acting and direction.'

Twice in a Lifetime was also released that year and received fair but not overwhelming notices. David Denby, in *New York*, found that Hackman is 'such a powerful yet unempathic performer, with so intimate, easy and unforced a relation to the reality of whatever situation he's in, that you simply accept what he does as an expression of his entire being'.

Variety noted a weak spot: 'Hackman is stalwart and determined in his resolve to make a new life with Ann-Margret, but she is far too sexy and he is far too underdeveloped for anybody to understand what she sees in him.' It did add, however, 'Audiences will love Burstyn's warm wrinkles and visit with her daughters to a male strip joint, as well as Hackman's workmanlike heroism.'

Pauline Kael took exception to the film, saying, 'It is like a sermon on the therapeutic value of adultery, divorce and remarriage, given by a minister who learned all he knows from watching TV.' Nobody expected this film to set box-office records, and Yorkin was pleased when the film broke even with a return of $9 million.

*   *   *

Having headlined several films in a row, Hackman chose to take a bit of a back seat for the next one, mainly so he could have the experience of working for Sidney Lumet. He regretted having once turned down one of America's finest directors, with films like *Twelve Angry Men*, *Fail Safe*, *The Hill*, *Serpico*, *Dog Day Afternoon*, and the one Hackman let get away, *Network*. Another incentive was that, as his friend Al Pacino had testified, Lumet was one of the *fastest* directors in Hollywood, meaning that Hackman would not be spending quite so much time hanging around between scenes. As Paul Newman said of Lumet, 'He's the only guy who could double park in front of a whorehouse. He's that fast.'

Furthermore it was comforting to know that *Power*, the movie in question, rested squarely on the shoulders of Richard Gere and Julie Christie. Gere played Pete St John, a ruthless and amoral public relations consultant who contrasts starkly with his highly ethical mentor and partner, Wilfred Buckley, played by Hackman. Julie Christie played Gere's ex-wife, Ellen, a journalist and friend of Wilfred's.

Pete and Wilfred come to loggerheads when they each decide to back opposing candidates in the Ohio Senate election after Senator Hastings (E.G. Marshall) resigns. Ellen decides to investigate the reason for his resignation and uncovers all sorts of shady dealings that lead Pete to redeem himself by joining forces with Wilfred. David Himmelstein, a former journalist, speechwriter and press aide, sought to illustrate through his script the power of the media to manipulate and package politicians. The point of the picture was, said Lumet, 'that it doesn't matter if you believe in your client or not. The whole political process has become dehumanized'.

Lumet rehearsed his actors before filming in summer 1985. He told me,

> I do this because it makes shooting so much quicker. The first thing I do is get the actors to spend a week pinning down their performances: they have the chance to improvise and shape things the way they want, and I'm able to start working out my camera angles while watching them. The next week they polish their performances, getting everything right, because that's the way they'll do it in front of the cameras. Then we move to the set and film it according to plan, and it all moves so much faster that way. It saves the actors a lot of time waiting around, and makes the whole process more economical.

Hackman was stimulated by Lumet's method, saying 'The whole thing felt like a play. It's like, by the second Friday you're ready to open on Broadway if you could. It's a very involved and complicated process. And we got a lot of theatrical performances, which is refreshing, as opposed to a lot of naturalness that you see in a lot of films with people throwing stuff away.' He felt that everybody gave fine performances but made a special mention of a young black actor making a start in films. 'I thought Denzel Washington was wonderful,' he said. 'A very strong actor.' A decade later, when Hackman worked with him on *Crimson Tide*, Washington recalled, 'Gene and I were in *Power* ten years ago. We rehearsed together but our characters didn't meet in the film.'

Another great pleasure for Hackman in making *Power* was getting the chance to work again with E.G. Marshall with whom he'd appeared in the early sixties television series *The Defenders*. Marshall, one of the *Twelve Angry Men*, was one of Lumet's favourite actors.

On location in New York, Hackman was mesmerized by the speed and efficiency maintained by Lumet scene after scene. 'We were moving locations in New York City sometimes two, three times a day,' said Gene. 'They would move the entire crew to another location. Some films that I've worked on, you couldn't move once in a *day* – you'd just lose the rest of that day.'

Despite all the rehearsing, the planning, the enthusiasm, the outcome was poor. *Variety* called it 'a facile treatment of big-time politics and media'. David Denby, writing in *New York*, thought the film should have been called *American Gigolo Goes to Washington*, but he conceded, 'Hackman, whose mastery of film acting is one of the few remaining glories of American movies, has never been more adept at suggesting the social routines – the little greetings, jokes, delusions – that get a man through the working day.' It earned just $3 million, and was not released in Britain.

9   It's Only a Movie!

After *Power* wrapped, Hackman had little time to unwind in front of his easel: he was back before the cameras in October 1985, in New Richmond, Indiana, for *Hoosiers*. The title is a nickname for the inhabitants of Indiana, which is considered to be the basketball capital of the world. Not surprisingly the film would be retitled for Britain, where it was known as *Best Shot*.

Angelo Pizzo, one such 'hoosier', wrote the screenplay, which was inspired by a victory scored by the humble Milan High School over the mighty Muncie Central in the State High School Basketball Tournament Championship of 1954. Pizzo set his story in 1951 because, he said, it was 'a time before the intrusion of television, the last era of true regionalism in America'.

Pizzo received three offers to buy his script, but each time he resisted because they refused to meet his own demands. He was insistent on producing the film himself, that the film be shot entirely in Indiana, and that his friend David Anspaugh direct. Anspaugh had not directed a feature film before but had won an Emmy and a Director's Guild Award for his work on an episode from *Hill Street Blues*; he'd also directed episodes from *Miami Vice* and *St Elsewhere*. Pizzo also stipulated that Gene Hackman play the tough coach, who, in his efforts to push a small-town high school on to victory, uses the experience to purge himself of his own shortcomings. Pizzo said that he had written the part specifically with Gene Hackman in mind.

Perhaps because they didn't like the idea of using a first-time film director, or simply because they didn't like the idea of a writer being producer, the studios withdrew their offers. Then producer Carter De Haven – whose father and grandfather, both also called Carter De Haven, were film-makers in the silent days – read and liked the script. He said he was 'struck by the way it rang true about a certain time, place and event in America'. He invited Pizzo to co-produce the film with him, was willing to give Anspaugh the chance to direct and eager to shoot in Indiana. Pizzo was surprised and delighted by the producer's invitation. The only outstanding question was whether or not Hackman would agree to play the coach.

Fortunately the script contained a key element for Hackman: a man who changes after some kind of spiritual journey. The fact it was a sports-oriented film limited its general appeal, but he liked it enough to say yes, to De Haven's complete delight.

The producers began scouting for locations, hoping to find a single town in Illinois they could use for the whole film. While New Richmond could function as the wider setting, De Haven and Pizzo were unable to find everything they needed, such as a gymnasium of that period, or a high school. The fictional Hickory therefore had to become a composite of other Indiana towns such as Knightstown, Lebanon and Ninevah. Vintage cars were begged, borrowed or stolen, and the only extant 1939 Chevrolet bus outside of the Smithsonian Institution was acquired to become the Hickory team bus. Costume designer Jane Anderson re-created clothing of the period, and unearthed a hidden cache of authentic fifties cheer-leaders' sweaters and skirts.

It must have been a curious experience for Hackman to find himself filming on a set so remarkably similar to his home town of Danville, Illinois, as it was in the fifties. Extras, recruited among the locals and wearing contemporary fashions, poured on to the New Richmond streets that had also been dressed to reflect the period. Hackman had the feeling he had seen it all before. He said, 'They seem the same to me. Everybody is wearing the same clothes they were in when I left Danville. It's really kind of peculiar. It doesn't feel like a period film at all to me.' His feeling of *déjà vu* was heightened by the fact that Danville was a mere sixty miles away.

Another nostalgic moment came when he met 85-year-old Mrs Fanny Stephens, his mother's best childhood friend. She showed him photographs of herself and his mother when they were teenagers, and related how they used to watch the silent movies, then go home and act them out. He said, 'Maybe it was from my mom I caught the acting bug.' He was considerably touched by the episode, and it made the film a more personal experience.

The film's story reflected the attitudes of a bygone rural America. The townspeople are unsettled by the arrival of Norman Dale, a former college coach who, ten years earlier, had been suspended from major-league coaching for striking a player. Having frittered away many bitter years, Dale is invited by an old friend, the Hickory High School principal (played by Sheb Wooley) to coach the local basketball team. While his ways seem harsh to the farm boys and their parents, he wins over a few friends, including the town drunk (Dennis Hopper), whom he helps to rehabilitate, and an attractive schoolteacher (Barbara Hershey).

His coaching is slow to produce results, but just as the town is about to give up on him, a former star player turns up and inspires the rest of the team to follow Dale's coaching. Before long the team is winning games and they find themselves qualifying for the state championships. Dale leads the team to victory despite all odds.

With its theme of underdog-makes-good, the film's concept was hardly a novel one, but even for those with no interest in basketball, there was much to enjoy, not least Hackman's own performance, which flourished under Anspaugh's brisk direction. It was a feel-good-about-America film, and Hackman felt pretty good about it too. On its release in 1986 *Variety* said, '*Hoosiers* is an involving tale . . . that paradoxically proves both rousing and too conventional, centred around a fine performance by Gene Hackman as the coach . . . [The] first half offers Hackman many special moments.' It noted that the film 'belongs to Hackman, but Dennis Hopper gets another opportunity to put in a showy turn as a local misfit.'

There were two Oscar nominations, for Jerry Goldsmith's music, and for Dennis Hopper's supporting role. Neither won, but the film was thrust under the media spotlight, an unintended effect that paid off commercially: it became Hackman's most successful film in years – apart from *Superman* – earning $25 million in the US market alone.

* * *

In 1986 the divorce between Gene and Faye was finally settled. He never revealed how much alimony he had to pay – he has somehow always managed to keep his private life under wraps, even in the goldfish bowl of Hollywood – but suddenly his workrate shot up in the ensuing years. Observers thought he needed the money for the divorce settlement. It's probably just as true that he worked even harder because, without family ties, he was a free agent. Not that he was lonely, for he had friends, mostly from other walks of life, notably doctors and painters. Betsy Arakawa was still a close friend. His only actor friends remained Dustin Hoffman and Robert Duvall, and though they were always on the lookout for work they could do together, that goal somehow kept eluding them. Hackman still harboured ambitions to perform on stage again, and expressed interest in *The Iceman Cometh* and *Long Day's Journey Into Night*.

Instead he decided to make a film, *Deceit*, which studios regarded as a poisoned chalice; and then a role he had sworn he would never play again: Lex Luthor, in *Superman IV: The Quest for Peace*. He had avoided having anything to do with the third *Superman*, and since then the film rights to the comic strip hero had been taken up by the Cannon Group, based at the former Elstree Studios, just outside London.

Deceit was a stab at superstardom by its leading as yet little-known actor, Kevin Costner, to be directed by Roger Donaldson, a New Zealander whose only notable efforts had been the Anthony Hopkins/Mel Gibson flop *The Bounty*, and *Marie* with Sissy Spacek. Studios remained unconvinced that Donaldson was a hot property, and Costner also failed to inspire confidence. Producers Laura Ziskin and Robert Garland managed to get financing from Orion – one major factor in clinching the deal was that Hackman had agreed to do the film, now retitled *No Way Out*.

It was actually an unofficial remake of *The Big Clock*, made in 1948 and featuring Charles Laughton as a powerful publisher who murders his mistress and then, aware that the act had been over-looked, assigns his crime editor, Ray Milland, to find the witness. The twist is: Milland is the witness and spends the film trying to cover his own tracks while trying to prove that Laughton actually did it.

This new version takes the same premise but sets it in the Pentagon. Costner plays a naval Lieutenant-Commander, Tom Farrell, who meets a gorgeous good-time girl, played by Sean Young, at an official function. It turns out she is the mistress of the Secretary of Defence, David Brice, played by Hackman. Farrell takes her home and during the taxi ride back, they strip off on the back seat and make love.

When Brice realizes she is two-timing him, he murders her in a jealous rage, only to realize that someone has witnessed the crime. Unaware that the witness is Farrell, he orders him to find the intruder whom, Brice maintains, is the real killer. Farrell knows that by doing his job properly he will lead the trail to his own back door, and he therefore searches for a way to prove that Brice is the real killer. But as events unfold and the evidence begins pointing to Farrell, he finds himself trapped.

Filming began on 7 April 1986 in Los Angeles, with additional location work planned in Washington DC and New Zealand. Even if this picture was made by Hackman for the money and its sheer commercial value, it was nevertheless a good choice. Classic thriller moments abounded – sex, murder, secrets, pursuit and a seemingly no-win situation. It was a shame that Sean Young's character had to be killed off quite so soon; but from the murder scene onwards the story races along without a chance to move back from the edge of your seat, all the way to its stinging final scene.

Costner dominated the film with his charisma – proving all the sceptics wrong – but nor was Hackman left behind, pulling off one of his classic 'heavy' roles, full of charm and danger. Released in 1987, the film was a huge success, establishing Costner as a new star in Hollywood and re-establishing the tremendous power of one of America's finest character actors, Hackman. Costner never forgot how no one would touch this movie, and he was determined that in time he would have power to produce his own films. Come this time, he resolved to get Hackman to work with him again.

Having finished work on *No Way Out*, Gene flew to Britain to begin work on *Superman IV; The Quest for Peace*. The film had been a long time in the planning – three years had passed since *Superman III* – and the green light had depended largely on Christopher Reeve's availability and enthusiasm, which had severely waned. He recalled that the Salkinds and Pierre Spengler had originally wanted him to sign to do four movies but he had declined right at the start. 'Since there wasn't even a script I said no.' After *Superman III* he vowed never to rehash the role again.

> I had tired of playing him the way he was. I wanted more control over the character to bring him up-to-date in line with how today's audiences see him as a hero for the eighties. To do this I had to have a hand in developing the storyline with two screenwriters, Mark Rosenthal and Lawrence Konner. I enjoyed the creative input, and this was one of the conditions on which I agreed to play Superman again.

The direction of the script could not be settled until Hackman could be persuaded to play Luthor. Either that or get another actor to play the part. Hackman, however, must have thought twice about letting a role he had created pass to somebody else. At least on *Superman III* the character had been completely excluded from the story. He agreed, saying later, 'It's the kind of role that lends itself to a lot of action and scope, and when you get to an age when you're cast in older-man-type roles there's a lot of energy inside you that you feel you want to get out. I like playing Lex Luthor because I can use up some of this energy.'

Sprung from a chain-gang, Luthor is back in circulation as an arms entrepreneur dedicated to 'keeping the world safe for war profiteers'. Superman, meanwhile, becomes alarmed that the Earth is in danger of destroying itself with nuclear weapons, and announces his plans to hurl the world's nuclear arsenal into the sun. With the world free of nuclear weapons, Luthor plans to make a fortune on the black market as the more sceptical power-hungry states begin stockpiling weapons – just in case.

Luthor also has another agenda: to destroy Superman and take over the world. He sets out to achieve this by stealing a strand of Superman's hair from a museum, adding a 'genetic reactor' and attaching the package to a missile that, on contact with the sun, will create the invincible Nuclear Man. Superman, in his efforts to destroy the threat of atomic war unwittingly aids Luthor in creating Nuclear Man, who can melt iron with a touch, and corkscrew through buildings from a vertical take-off. Superman must discover his one Achilles' heel in time, before the Earth is devastated and finally ruled by Lex Luthor, still proclaiming himself as 'the greatest criminal mind on Earth'.

Margot Kidder, also back as Lois Lane, was delighted that the film was in new hands, having been demoted to a small supporting performance in *Superman III* after making clear her views about Richard Donner's dismissal. Jackie Cooper also returned as Perry White, editor of the *Daily Planet*.

The end result seemed to cast some doubt over the accuracy of the $30-$40 million Cannon Films were said to be budgeting. Cost-cutting measures seriously affected the look of the film. London Underground was a poor substitute for the New York Subway, while Milton Keynes looked unconvincing as Metropolis. The special effects seemed less-than-special too, and there was a terrible accident at Elstree Studios when stunt man John Lees fell twenty feet while being hoisted up on wires. His legs were badly broken and he successfully sued Cannon Films, who were found to be negligent.

Reeve was disappointed with the final print, and vowed that this would be his last outing as Superman. Tragically he would never be able to retract that promise after a fall from a horse while show-jumping in Virginia, in May 1995, that left the actor paralysed.

Released in 1987, the film ran a modest eighty-nine minutes compared to the two-hour-plus earlier blockbusters. *Variety* commented,

> The earlier films in the series were far from perfect, but at their best they had some flair and agreeable humour, qualities this one sorely lacks. Hackman gets a few laughs, but has less to work with than

before, and everyone else seems to be just going through the motions and having less fun doing so.

Maurice Speed, writing in his 1988/89 *Film Review* annual, thought this film, 'a good deal more endurable than *Superman III,*' but summed up his opinion of the special effects with, 'You'll believe a man has wires!'

Despite the production weaknesses on *Superman IV*, Hackman on the set was a different man to the one Reeve had first encountered. 'On the first film he was morose,' said Reeve, 'but this time he really enjoyed himself.' Despite his ordeals, Hackman, it seems, had emerged more relaxed, less melancholic and easier to work with. He said, 'I'd hate to be around doing *Superman IX*, but I enjoyed myself on this one and stopped worrying about what people think about my doing it a long time ago.'

* * *

Hackman had seen the 1981 French thriller *Garde Vue* (*The Inquisitor*) and decided he wanted to direct a remake of it. Structured around an insightful police interrogation, the film concerns a wealthy lawyer, arrested on suspicion of raping and murdering two children. Hackman felt he could make his directorial debut with a small budget, concentrating on the performances. Hollywood studios, doubtful about its profitability or perhaps nervous about another actor trying to direct, failed to take the bait in 1987.

That year he looked forward to working again with John Frankenheimer, this time on Ernest Hemingway's *Across the River and Into the Trees*. Reputed to be an 'unfilmable novel' all previous attempts to get it on celluloid had failed. John Huston had planned to film it, and among the stars who had at times hoped to play the lead character were William Holden and Burt Lancaster. Hackman was delighted finally to land the central role of a veteran of the two world wars who winds up living in Venice. There he makes one last attempt at sport and love with a nineteen-year-old girl. But the project ultimately lived up to its cursed reputation, and the film was cancelled.

Perhaps out of frustration at having a pet project pulled from under his feet, Hackman chose to do *Bat 21*. There could have been little to attract him to this movie apart from the fee – he claimed, rather unconvincingly, a dearth of money. His role was that of a US airforce colonel, known as Bat 21, who has spent most of the Vietnam War sitting behind a desk rather than seeing the front line.

But when he finds himself stranded in Vietcong-occupied territory, he must draw on his own hidden reserves to get him home. His only other help comes in the form of Danny Glover in a reconnaissance plane.

Directed by Peter Markle for Tri-Star, the film unevenly blended buddy-movie back-slapping and pacifist philosophizing, with too many pauses in-between the action to be popular. The film's American release in 1988 was met with indifference and went straight on to video in Britain.

Empire described Hackman as 'the undisputed master of the art of rotten career moves,' and he proved them right by following up *Bat 21* with the weak and stagey *Full Moon in Blue Water*, which seemed like an indulgent antidote to an action film – though it couldn't make up its mind if it wanted to be a character drama or a comedy. Hackman played a beleaguered Texan bar owner whose wife drowns and whose business is threatened by insolvency. Teri Garr played an amorous bus driver, Elias Koteas was Hackman's simple-minded employee and Burgess Meredith played Hackman's father-in-law. The *Monthly Film Bulletin* described it as 'a comedy as soft-centred as they come ... just about insufferable.' It quickly sank without trace after its 1988 release.

Possibly disenchanted that his career was getting bogged down in a morass of dire films, he became all the more determined to direct.

> I'd like to be able to understand the actor's problems, and also to be able to put the story on film. It's very hard for actors sometimes to be objective. They tend to want to do moments. Directors want to do scenes. So the problem, as I see it, is trying to make the transition from what the actor wants to what the film needs.

He also recognized that the chances of getting studio backing would be considerably greater if the project could demonstrate some commercial viability. He shelved the idea of remaking *Garde Vue*, and at the beginning of 1988 he was on the lookout for an indisputably commercial project – no straightforward matter. Occasionally, however, a film-maker can stumble across that rare commodity: a film everyone is waiting for. In the top ten of the *New York Times* list of best-selling books, *The Silence of the Lambs* by Thomas Harris successfully sequelled the FBI thriller *Red Dragon*, by the same author, which director Michael Mann had made into the small-scale cult picture *Manhunter*.

The bizarre tale of *The Silence of the Lambs* focuses on a young FBI trainee, Clarice Starling, who is forced by her superiors to forge a relationship with insane psychiatrist Dr Hannibal 'the Cannibal' Lecter, who is in prison for killing and eating numerous victims. The FBI believe Lecter can give Clarice information that will help her to find a serial killer who has murdered and skinned fourteen women.

The book was an enormous bestseller, and Hackman knew it could be a movie sensation too, so he bought the screen rights with the intention of making it his directorial showcase. 'It's one of the most cinematic books I've ever read. As I read it the movie was clicking in my mind.' Studios began kicking themselves at not having had the foresight to snap up the rights to the book themselves.

Hackman wanted Michelle Pfeiffer to play Clarice Starling and John Hurt as Dr Lecter. Hackman intended to take the role of Sterling's superior, Jack Crawford. But before he could begin work on it, he had to do a film with British director Alan Parker – *Mississippi Burning* – which had already been agreed.

The script, said Parker, 'was a mixture of fact and fiction,' based on actual events surrounding the killings by the Ku Klux Klan of three young Civil Rights workers, two white – Mickey Schwerner and Andy Goodman – and one black – James Chaney – on the night of 21 June 1964 in rural Mississippi. Chaney's killer complained to the others, 'You didn't leave me nothing but a nigger, but at least I killed me a nigger.'

This fragment of genuine dialogue and the horrific events themselves were the springboard for Chris Gerolmo's screenplay. In 1964, when the murders hit the national headlines Attorney General Robert Kennedy persuaded FBI chief J. Edgar Hoover to hunt down the killers. Senior Inspector Joseph Sullivan masterminded an operation that involved hundreds of FBI agents. The screenplay concentrated on two fictional agents, one a Northerner, the other a Southerner. Parker wanted Hackman to play the Southerner, a man who favours a worldly-wise approach in contrast to the Northerner's righteous zeal.

The screenplay retained many key factual elements: a witness is driven around with a paper bag over his head to prevent him from being recognized by the local Klansmen; a CBS news cameraman is attacked by a suspect; the defendants are originally cleared on a technicality, just as it happened in reality. The real FBI investigation was hampered by a wall of silence shielding the killers, and it took forty-four days for the agents to discover the whereabouts of the three bodies, even after offering a $30,000 reward. The screenplay, by contrast, had the FBI recruiting a freelance black enforcer, who terrifies the mayor into spilling the beans.

The story departs mostly from real events in implying that the two Feds leave the town a better place than it was when they had arrived. The deputy sheriff's wife, who helps put the Klan behind bars, utters, 'There are lots of good folks in this town who will know what I did was right.' Hollywood wanted only an upbeat ending.

It was these 'embellishments' of real events that would later whip up controversy. But Parker knew how Hollywood operated, and so did Hackman. Parker openly admitted the film was 'very obviously fictional' and that the two invented white Feds who find themselves in the middle of real events were simply a reflection of the way Hollywood works, which means providing the audience with less of a history lesson and more of a story of two fascinating though fictional characters.

Parker would later say that he didn't make films 'for fourteen intellectuals at the Cinematheque in Paris,' but for the widest possible audience. 'I've got a responsibility to take the producer's $15 million and do this right.' And that's partly why he wanted Gene Hackman. As the other agent he cast Willem Dafoe. Curiously, although neither actor could then have been described as major box-office names, Hackman's growing reputation as a latter-day Spencer Tracy, and Dafoe's looking like star material in 1988, Parker needed only his own name as a hotshot director to give the package that crucial commercial gloss.

Like most Hollywood projects, when this one was first conceived in 1985, Hackman and Dafoe were the last actors Orion, who had bought the story from Gerolmo, had in mind. They saw the film as a contemporary police epic with Clint Eastwood and William Hurt, minus much of the political debate. Milos Forman and John Schlesinger were mooted as possible directors, with Alan Parker being approached late in the day. Parker liked the story but wanted to make changes, and Gerolmo quickly became alarmed at what he saw as the decimation of his original work. He told *Empire* 'After Alan was hired it quickly became apparent that he was intent on redoing the script.' For a while Parker and Gerolmo worked together, but the plain fact is that when a director of Parker's status wants a script to go his way, that's the way it goes. 'He really browbeat me into making all his changes,' said Gerolmo, alleging that on their first day of working together, Parker became 'very bombastic and ugly, calling me an amateur, a dilettante and saying my script was stupid and lazy'. The writer said that by the end of that first day Parker was brandishing his script in the air and shouting 'This isn't worth making.'

Not surprisingly, Parker recalled events differently. He says he tried patiently to work with Gerolmo 'to fix the script, which didn't work very well,' but as so often happens in movies, the director finally rewrote the screenplay himself. Parker insists that he is not difficult 'for ego reasons – but for the work'. He was, in essense, a powerful film director who would make the film his way, and when Gerolmo complained to Orion, they backed Parker. They needed the picture ready for release by Christmas 1988.

Parker's way was to write on his own, getting input on some aspects from his actors. For example, in the scene in which Hackman receives the final crucial information from the deputy sheriff's wife, the director had suggested that his character ought then to make love to her on the floor. Hackman objected, and later said, 'I felt that was excessive and would distract from her as a human being, and from her courage in terms of what she has just revealed. She didn't do it because she wanted to make love to me, but because she thought it was right.'

Parker played down the disagreement: 'Gene must be referring to something we discussed before we started filming. Perhaps when I was rewriting the script and was debating how far the relationship should go between the agent and the deputy's wife, Gene got worried I might be trying to do an *Angel Heart* on him.'

Filming began during the summer of 1988, in Mississippi. As Hackman would recall, 'It was hot. Even in the middle of the night.' The scene in which he and Dafoe discover a black youth, played by Simeon Teagus, lying curled up and beaten in backwoods brambles, was shot after midnight in a swamp near Vicksburg. Swarms of insects plagued the cast and crew.

Parker called 'Action!' as Hackman and Dafoe, soaked with perspiration (the real thing – not make-up), came across the youth writhing in agony. Dafoe reached down to cradle the boy's head while Hackman stood, emoting anger and frustration. Dafoe said his line, and Parker called, 'Cut!' and suggested that Dafoe try to pull up the youth's pants, which are around his knees, indicating that Dafoe would try to preserve the boy's dignity. They did the scene again. 'That's very good. Let's do it once more,' said Parker. So they did. And then again. Journalist Patrick Goldstein noted how Hackman raised his eyes to the sky and said, 'Jeez, it's hot out here. It just seems to get hotter as the night goes on.'

If Hackman was becoming irritable, he tried to keep it under control. There was, by Parker's own admission, one argument he and Hackman had – just the one 'and it only lasted two and a half minutes'. He maintained that both of them were 'just two professionals and we saw each other's point of view and we were very comfortable together. That's why his performance is as good as it is.'

Parker was full of praise for Hackman's skill:

He has an instinctive way of working that makes scenes work and quick and easy. There was the scene in the barber shop where Gene takes over from the old barber who's shaving the deputy sheriff, and the way he took that razor was like a magic trick – the hands transfer it in a flash. That's a difficult thing to do and you might not be able to do it a second time, but with Gene you don't have to do many takes. Now if Mickey Rourke had been playing the part, he would have needed fifty takes because he simply cannot repeat anything because he'd have to change it each time. But with Gene he can do it again, and you only have to shoot a couple of takes.

That scene was staged inside an authentic old-style barber shop in Jackson called the Paramount Barber Shop. It had hardly changed since 78-year-old Daniel Salony opened it in 1939. During filming, Hackman's performance was so vigorous that as he carried out his interrogation of the deputy sheriff brandishing a razor blade, he managed to break two of the barber's chairs. When Orion compensated Salony with a cheque for $50, he complained that it actually cost him $75 to get the chairs repaired, so the barber was reimbursed in full.

Hackman proved imaginative throughout production, and Parker allowed him the freedom to suggest changes to the script. On one occasion Parker, Hackman and Dafoe sat reading through a scene in which Gene had to persuade a local Klansman to co-operate with the police inquiry, when Parker said, 'I have a problem here. I don't know what this man would do that gives him the superiority he needs to establish here.' He suggested that maybe Hackman could smash a glass over the Klansman's head, but to Gene that seemed unnecessarily violent. He had his own idea. 'Let me grab his balls,' he said, and even tried it out on Willem Dafoe to make his point. It was the perfect solution to the scene.

For the locals, the production provided an opportunity to work as extras. Six hundred of them stood in a muddy field ten miles outside Jackson one night, pretending to be the White Citizens' Council, hollering on cue as they listened to actor Stephen Tobolowsky deliver a rousing speech as a Klu Klux Klan leader. Shivers ran down a lot of the local spines. Many of the onlookers could recall the days when this was all very real, and one woman remarked, 'I just keep saying to myself what they said about *Jaws* – it's only a movie, it's only a movie.'

Attitudes might have changed since 1964, but racism was still thriving in the deep South. Hackman was startled when he popped into the local cleaners and the man behind the counter said, 'You're the actor that's in that nigger movie they're making down here.'

That was one reason Parker chose to film in Mississippi itself. 'If you're going to make a movie about that attitude,' he said, 'you should be where you see it every day.'

Shooting in the actual state where the events themselves happened gave the picture a true-to-life, gritty feel, but much else was changed, such as the names of the Klansmen and those of the Civil Rights workers who were murdered. There had to be a disclaimer in the credits that 'the characters are fictitious and do not depict real people either living or dead'.

That combination of fact and fiction, in which the real murder of three young men paved the way for movie actors Gene Hackman and Willem Dafoe to demonstrate their acting skills, landed the film in trouble when it came out at the end of 1988. Respected American historian David Halberstam, who was in Mississippi in 1964 writing for the *New York Times*, wrote in *Premiere*,

> There is a Mississippi out there that Parker is welcome to create. But he did not invent his own incident. He chose to base his story on a true event which, of course, piques our curiosity even more. It is no longer his Mississippi; it is instead the Mississippi of those three young men who were so remarkably brave that summer.

Vernon Jarett of the *Chicago Sun-Times* argued that the film 'treats some of the most heroic people in black history as mere props in a morality play', while *Time*'s Jack E. White described the film as 'a version of history so distorted that it amounts to a cinematic lynching of the truth'. Author Seth Cagin, who reported the event in 1964, said in *Vogue*, 'The film's suggestion that the FBI resorted to dirty, un-American tactics to defeat the Klan not only distorts the truth, but feeds directly into a Klansman's favorite fantasy – glorifying his martyrdom and endorsing the Klan's preferred self-image as victims of federal tyranny.'

Actor and director Spike Lee saw it differently. 'For Alan Parker to say that the FBI was a great friend of the Civil Rights movement, that's a bare-faced lie. J. Edgar Hoover did many things to sabotage the Civil Rights movement. J. Edgar Hoover hated black people. He was fucked up, wasn't he? That's not what Alan Parker tries to tell us, though.'

The controversy raged on. Parker told Richard Lowe of *Empire* in 1991, 'That film was a very realistic story, though whether it was the definitive film about the black civil rights struggle is a different matter, because it was never *meant* to be.' He believed it was the most realistic film ever made about the Civil Rights struggle and had hoped other movies, directed by black directors, would follow.

'Unfortunately the controversy was such that it killed any other film being made.'

But the film had its defenders among the critics. Barry McIlheney wrote in *Empire* that it

> hurtles along at a gripping pace . . . Hackman is marvellous as Anderson, charming the deputy sheriff's wife (Frances McDormand) one minute, grabbing a local thug by the balls the next . . . It sets a standard of convincing dialogue, high-impact performance and aggressive direction that could prove hard enough to match.

What mattered most to the film's backers was that it drew huge audiences: Hackman had scored his biggest success for ages, beating even *Hoosiers*.

10   The Art of Rotten Career Moves

Even before *Mississippi Burning* was released, word had spread that Hackman had given one of his best-ever performances. Producers and directors began to regard him as a talisman, conferring class upon everything he did. The offers came his way in spades, but the quality of the scripts he chose was questionable. Some thought Woody Allen's *Another Woman* worthwhile, but his appearance in the film was fleeting. Gena Rowlands was the star, winning plaudits from critics as a married, fifty-year-old philosopher who moves into a New York apartment to write a book, and finds herself overhearing analysis sessions from the psychiatrist's office next door. She becomes particularly intrigued by one patient, played by Mia Farrow, who relates how her marriage is gradually disintegrating. The eavesdropping sparks of painful memories in Rowlands's life; she relives past events through dreams, flashbacks and chance encounters – and throughout she is haunted by the memory of a former lover, played by Gene Hackman.

It was a measure of Hackman's stature in 1988 that a respected director like Allen should want him for such a small but important role – even if *Empire* thought 'Hackman strains credulity and everyone else mopes without much conviction' in what it described as a 'drab psychological drama'. But *Variety* liked it, saying the 'film that emerges is brave, in many ways fascinating, and in all respects of a calibre rarely seen'. Tim Pulleine in the *Monthly Film Bulletin* was even more enthusiastic: 'Not only Allen's most wholly personal movie since *Stardust Memories* but arguably the most substantial achievement of his career.' Unless you were a card-carrying Woody Allen admirer, the chances are you'd probably find it all rather gloomy. But it highlighted Hackman as a highly important actor, a status confirmed by being one of the most Oscar-nominated actors alive – and for *Mississippi Burning* he was shortlisted once more.

Insiders knew that there were only two real contenders for the 1988 Best Actor Oscar: Gene Hackman for *Mississippi Burning* and his lifelong friend Dustin Hoffman for *Rain Man*. Privately they congratulated each other. As for the other nominees – Tom Hanks for *Big*, Edward James Olsen for *Stand and Deliver* and Max Von Sydow for *Pelle the Conqueror* – bookies and punters were giving them little chance of winning against the powerful and popular performances of Hackman and Hoffman.

On the night it was Hoffman who was summoned to the podium. When he collected his Oscar he said, 'I'm very honoured, and I thank the Academy for your support. And I also thank Tom Hanks and Max Von Sydow and James Olsen, and my good friend Gene Hackman for their wonderful work, even if they didn't vote for me ... I didn't vote for you guys either!'

Hackman was not distraught at losing to his friend, or at 'losing' full stop. 'The value of an award like an Oscar is how much it will add to the gross of the picture and to your fee for your next picture,' he once told me. 'It's great to win awards but you have to put them in perspective. Besides, I'm just not competitive; I don't want to beat other actors. I just want to do good work.'

While the evening's result did not dash his spirits, he did pause for thought while watching scene after scene from *Mississippi Burning* every time it was nominated for editing, sound, photography (the only award it finally won), supporting actress (Frances McDormand), Hackman, Alan Parker and best picture. The clips of Parker's dark, violent and essentially true account of man's inhumanity forced him to reconsider his commitment to *Silence of the Lambs*. He could stomach violence in a factually based film like *Mississippi Burning*, but if the cocktail also included psychopathology and cannibalism – all in the name of fiction – he didn't think he could face what could be a wallow in the dark side of humanity. 'It's a wonderful work,' he said of Harris's book, 'but it's one thing to read it and another to show it.'

Just days following the Oscars, he surprised industry-watchers by announcing he would not go ahead with *Silence of the Lambs*. If ever a film was eagerly awaited by the American public – this was it. Orion Pictures, hearing of its sudden availability, snapped it up and assigned Jonathan Demme to direct. Meanwhile Michelle Pfeiffer took another look at the outline being shaped into screenplay form by Ted Tally and decided, like Hackman, that she was 'unable to come to terms with the overpowering darkness of the piece'. She dropped out, and Jodie Foster stepped into her shoes.

When John Hurt proved unavailable, Orion offered the role of Lecter to Anthony Hopkins.

In the end *Silence of the Lambs* cost $19 million to make and earned $124 million in eighteen weeks when it was released in 1991. To many in the business, Hackman's decision to sell on the film rights was incomprehensible, especially given his run of flops, punctuated by the occasional *No Way Out* and *Mississippi Burning*. But he stayed on an even keel, even after *Silence of the Lambs* had won a huge profit and an Oscar for Hopkins. Hackman had never been guided by any great career plan, and had even attempted to retire after the first *Superman*. But the fact that he seemed to squander his recognized talent in so many unworthy films suggested that his judgement, more than anything else, was seriously in question.

Hackman reiterated the misgivings that forced him to give up the film rights to *Silence of the Lambs*. 'There's too much violence in the world. A violent film must have some redeeming qualities,' he said. Not that he thought *Silence of the Lambs* was a bad film. He just believed there was no good reason for giving the public a feast of violence and horror, apart from making money – and he could still do that as an actor.

* * *

Throughout 1989 Hackman was working to excess, making films virtually back to back; inevitably, as in the seventies, issues of quality took a backseat. He continued to live up to *Empire*'s description as 'the undisputed master of the art of rotten career moves,' as proved by his next choice, *Loose Cannons*. Perhaps it looked funny on paper. Perhaps he liked being top-billed with a major co-star, Dan Aykroyd, in a police-buddy story heavily reminiscent of *Lethal Weapon 2*, *Midnight Run* and *Beverly Hills Cop*. Perhaps he needed the money.

Hackman breezed through his role of the gruff cop with a whole career's worth of experience under his belt. Aykroyd, his partner, has a nervous breakdown behind him and is given to lapsing into multiple personalities. He is brought back into service only because his uncle, a police captain, pulls strings. Consequently Hackman finds himself saddled with a manic policeman by his side as they attempt to solve some gruesome murders and fight off a small army of neo-Nazis with Uzis. To sum up, this sorry excuse for a comedy has to be one of the worst Hackman's ever made. 'Dan Aykroyd's dexterous multipersonality schtick is the only redeeming feature of this chase-heavy comedy,' thought *Variety*, 'while Gene Hackman continues his over-flowing resume with shameful losers.'

In search of a winner, Hackman opted to make an action piece that seemed to have something worthwhile to say. In *The Package*, a cold war political thriller that, in 1989, seemed a touch out of date, he played a military security officer who is sent home in disgrace when he fails to stop an American general being killed at a Berlin summit. He takes with him a 'package' – a court-marshalled GI – played by Tommy Lee Jones. *En route* Hackman is attacked and Jones escapes to carry out his secret assignment – an assassination that will put a stop to a nuclear pact about to be signed by the American president and the Soviet leader (who is clearly based upon Gorbachev). Hackman finds his every move hindered by his superiors, but with help from his wife (Joanna Cassidy), he fights on to prevent the assassination.

Hackman knew that this was not going to be a 'life-changing experience for audiences', but simply offered what he and director Andrew Davis hoped would be a rollercoaster ride of thrills. The backdrop of *glasnost* served to create a more rounded and sympathetic portrait of the Soviets, even though villains of every nationality abounded.

Historic events made the film an easy target for critics; after all, by 1990, when the film was released, the Berlin Wall had come down, the Soviet Union was breaking up and the world was feeling safer than it had since the late fifties. These events diffused the impact of the film, as Angie Errigo noted in *Empire*, although it 'still emerges as a reasonably gripping yarn ... One needs to keep on one's toes to keep up with the sinister doings, but the 'lone man against the odds' stuff clings to some semblance of credibility with good performances from all the principals and some tough action.' Many dismissed it as just another melodramatic thriller.

In a sense, the film lost out to *The Hunt for Red October*. Having also just missed the Cold War boat it nevertheless managed to draw a considerable audience by offering something new in the way of special effects action: instead of being set in the air or in space, the action took place under the sea in a new kind of nuclear submarine. By the time *The Package* hit the screens, the public had no desire to look back, or under their beds for Reds: a more optimistic view was required. Interestingly, the same *glasnost*-inspired plot would emerge a year or so later in *Star Trek VI: The Undiscovered Country* with the Federation of Planets and the Klingon Empire.

Whether these films were disappointing or downright bad, offers of work from producers and directors continued to flood in, secure in the knowledge that, whatever happened, Hackman would always do his job superlatively. As James Cameron-Wilson wrote in

Film Review, 'Even in stinkers like *Misunderstood*, *Full Moon in Blue Water* and *The Package*, the actor rises above the material, giving a performance that seems effortless and totally real.'

* * *

There was no let-up in 1989; Hackman starred in *Narrow Margin*, a remake of a 1952 crime melodrama that some consider a minor classic. Director Peter Hyams obviously thought enough of it to give it a new lease of life. This man's approach to film-making was almost unique in that he nearly always photographed the films that he also wrote and directed (and often produced); *Capricorn One* and *2010* are cases in point. On a Peter Hyams film nobody works harder than him. And that may be the reason why his films always fall just short of being excellent: he simply takes on too much himself. Nevertheless, he has made highly competent, successful films, and Hackman must have recognized this in signing up for *Narrow Margin*.

In the original version Charles McGraw had been one of two Los Angeles detectives escorting the widow of a racketeer from Chicago to testify before the grand jury. When his partner is killed by pursuing gangsters, McGraw and the widow spend the film outwitting the killers on the train from Chicago to Los Angeles. For the remake Hyams turned the detective into a deputy district attorney and cast 59-year-old Hackman opposite Anne Archer as the widow.

Archer, perhaps best remembered as Michael Douglas's wife in *Fatal Attraction*, said she accepted this film because, number one, 'working with Gene Hackman' and, number two, 'I recognized it was a page-turner; I felt it would be a commercially successful film.' She also conceded that being one of many actresses chasing very few scripts, the choices are often limited. 'I just picked the thing that I thought was the best at the time.' About her distinguished leading man, Anne Archer told *Empire*'s Phillipa Bloom, 'He's such a sweetheart, and he's very supportive; one of the most supportive actors one ever has an opportunity to work with.'

Unlike the 1952 train journey, this one took the two protagonists through Canada, and whereas in the original, McGraw and his leading lady Marie Windsor became romantically involved, Hyams kept things platonic between Hackman and Archer; at the age of fifty-nine Hackman decided he was too old to start playing romantic leads.

In his trailer in-between scenes, he revealed his rather ambiguous attitude towards filming to journalist Nancy Mills. She asked him why he continued to work so hard. 'I don't know – I guess I've been doing this for so long, I don't know what else to do.' He had numerous houses in the United States and across Europe, but he admitted he found it difficult staying in one place for any length of time. Constantly moving from new set to new location, his was the life of a nomad. He admitted that he did get tired of filming, but he found that life away from the camera was just as unbearable after a couple of months. 'It's a very strange life. It's like being in the circus, I suppose.'

The film was heightened by some spectacular stunt work and excellent production values, with a price tag of $21 million (Richard Fleischer's 1952 version had cost $230,000). With careful guidance from experts, Hackman was able to do many of his own stunts, such as hanging on to the train and climbing over the top of it while it was in motion. Anne Archer went into the project thinking that she would not be required for any of the stunt work. 'It's not something I'm accustomed to doing as an actor,' she said. 'Nor did I consider it part of my craft. I thought that was for stunt people.' Peter Hyams, however, told her he needed her to do some shots where the audience could see it really was her clinging to the side of the speeding train or clambering over it.

Learning that Hackman was doing his own stunts, she reluctantly decided to agree. So Peter Hyams was able to get the valuable footage he needed. Later she found out that the gentlemanly Hackman had told others, 'Well, when I saw Anne was willing to do her own stunts I thought, well, if she's gonna, who am I not to do them too?' Said Archer, 'Neither one of us told each other, but we both thought if the other was willing, maybe we should!'

Thin cables protected both actors from falling to an almost certain death. Archer said, 'Even with the cables, it was still terrifying. It wasn't much comfort, because you'd still fall. You might not plunge to your death, but you might hang there, and who wants to do *that*?'

She and Hackman at least had the satisfaction of knowing that Hyams had planned every shot meticulously, so there was no wasted footage; everything they did was used in the film. According to Hyams, Hackman brought special qualities to the role. 'Gene isn't going to make the hearts of the women watching flutter, and he isn't going to do super spectacular stunts, but what you get is a man who makes acting look so easy that he makes it all believable. And that's all a director can ask of any actor, to make the part believable.' And that he did, while Hyams did his usual customary job of making a fast-paced, glossy thriller with plenty of well-staged action scenes that always kept it watchable.

Variety picked up on some of the film's basic weaknesses: 'Peter Hyams fails to make his story involving . . . Hackman adds panache to a one-dimensional role. Archer is stuck with a nothing part, given barely one monologue to express her character's feelings.' Tom Tunney, reviewing the film for *Empire*, seemed to like it enough to give it a 'good' rating, but, remembering the original version, said,

> This is a bit of an also-ran by comparison, though the many significant revisions to the original's plot mean that knowing the twist ending of the earlier film won't totally spoil the very different way things pan out here . . . What this sometimes witty time-filler never quite manages is a genuine sense of confined menace.

Released in 1990, it was only a moderate success. Like *The Package*, it really found its market on video. In fact, the video market had by that year become such an important outlet for any film that producers were working out their budgets and potential income to take into account video rentals and sales; Hollywood had discovered there was gold in those VCR's. Only the most expensive films such as *Waterworld* needed to make massive profits on cinema release before giving over to video release. A moderately budgeted film could get away with moderate box office providing it had video appeal as well.

But Hackman had more on his plate than mere money. His health became a much more serious issue when he suffered a suspected heart attack. Fortunately while he was not incapacitated by the seizure, it was enough to lead to tests in hospital that confirmed his heart was not holding up under the strain. Too much work, a generally restless nature, and his fluctuating weight were all factors. He was going to have to watch his diet, cut down on drink and work less. That last sacrifice would be the hardest to make.

If Hackman had to slow down, he could at least play supporting roles, usually in films that tended to be better than the ones in which he was the actual star. Such was *Postcards from the Edge* in 1990, a screen treatment of actress Carrie Fisher's best-selling book. Fisher had shot to stardom as the princess in distress in *Star Wars*, but after a battle with alcohol and drug addiction, she retired to write a book that was loosely based on her own experiences as the famous daughter of the even more famous Debbie Reynolds and Eddie Fisher. When Mike Nichols wanted to turn it into a film, he got Fisher to write the screenplay.

Hackman was fourth down the cast list in *Postcards from the Edge*, but he enjoyed himself. 'I get to do a good part with a good

cast, and I don't have the burden of the film on me.' Carrying the
weight of responsibility were Meryl Streep and Shirley MacLaine.
Despite the known links between the story and Carrie Fisher's own
life, Nichols insisted that MacLaine was not portraying Debbie
Reynolds, nor Meryl Streep Carrie Fisher. Yet the story of a young
actress who, in attempting to escape her Hollywood mother's
shadow, resorts to drugs and alcohol certainly could not have been
closer to Fisher's own hellish experiences. 'The movie and the book
certainly have their roots in reality,' she said. 'The construction,
though, is just entertainment. For example, my mother doesn't
really drink.'

It was ironic, then, that the studio's first choice to play the
mother's role was Debbie Reynolds. And she agreed to do it too.
But Mike Nichols ruled out that prospect as too bizarre, and
Shirley MacLaine was offered the role instead. She came to the
film with her own doubts. 'I told Mike Nichols that I couldn't play
Debbie Reynolds. And frankly, I also questioned how Meryl could
play Carrie Fisher.' Nichols told her that Reynolds and Fisher
should be viewed as 'basic models' for the characters.

For the part of a sternly paternalistic director, Hackman was
ideal; he'd worked with enough directors to be able to pick and
choose little foibles to create an authentic portrayal. There was a
particularly ironic twist in Nichols's choice of Hackman: he had
fired him from *The Graduate*. But that had been twenty-three years
earlier, and since then no film director doubted Hackman's abilities, least of all Nichols himself. In their book *The Movies of the
Eighties* co-authors Ron Base and David Haslam describe
Hackman as 'perhaps the most respected American movie actor
since Spencer Tracy.' He could be difficult and irritable, they noted,
'but on screen his performances were seamlessly natural.'

Hackman could be compared to the great Fredric March,
arguably one of America's two greatest actors – the other being
Tracy. March never quite reached Tracy's legendary heights, but
then, in his younger days, the latter needed the companionship of a
Gable or a Hepburn to magnify his star. By contrast March never
went in for screen partnerships (although his frequent stage partner was Florence Eldridge). After notable starring roles in several
Cecil B. De Mille epics, he grew to become respected, admired and
held in awe. Ultimately he made an indelible mark on acting, with
some great stage performances and a handful of excellent pictures
such as *The Best Years of Our Lives*, *Seven Days in May* and *Inherit
the Wind* (in which he starred with Tracy). Nor was he too high and
mighty to miss making good money appearing in more lightweight
moneyspinners like *Christopher Columbus* and *Hombre*.

Hackman's career resembles that of March, but minus the stage reputation.

For years Hackman had perpetuated an image of himself as an 'ugly' man, and had long given up the hope of playing a romantic lead. But if he didn't know it, Shirley MacLaine wrote in her memoir *My Lucky Star* that she thought Hackman was 'romantically attractive' and related the time she had met him at a party some years earlier. She revealed how when he came into the room, he walked with 'a captivating sexuality', and, more generally, observed that a man's walk could speak volumes more than his words, and a woman's words more than her actions. 'I would have changed all that if he'd made the slightest suggestion,' she wrote.

Postcards from the Edge offered Hackman a solid supporting role. So too did Dennis Quaid, playing a Hollywood brat, and Rob Reiner as a supercilious film producer. But the film belonged to Streep and MacLaine, although it was only the former who was Oscar-nominated for her performance (she didn't win). Nevertheless, Hackman clearly seemed to belong, just down the cast list, in this sharp-witted tragi-comedy that offered a fascinating snapshot of the sometimes murky world of Hollywood.

Although playing a minor role, Hackman still managed to get some good personal notices. 'Hackman [is] in typically brilliant form,' was the view of *Empire*'s Barry McIlheney who found the film 'hugely entertaining, highly recommended'. *Variety* praised Hackman for his 'sternly paternalistic director,' found Meryl Streep 'refreshingly guileless in a role requiring casual clothing and no accent,' and thought that Shirley MacLaine as the impossible stage mother 'makes it her own until, stripped of her glamour in the climactic scene, she abandons the rampant egotism of the character to reveal the frightened creature underneath.'

With what he called a 'dicky heart' to consider, Hackman had to give up some of his more invigorating hobbies, like stunt-flying. But he still continued to fly, and in October 1990, while test-flying a single-engined plane 2,500 feet over California, the engine just suddenly cut out. He battled to restart the engine for ten seconds before it came back to life. His friend and PR man Richard Guttman said, 'It was pretty scary, but Gene's had a pilot's licence for about twenty years, and he stayed calm. He decided not to buy that particular plane.'

After his heart scare Hackman might have been wary of taking on the pressure of a starring role, but he was confident that the screenplay for *Class Action* would not require too much physical action. Michael Apted was directing a film that would allow Gene to indulge in a worthy cause – civil rights – but without violence. He played a lawyer who has devoted his life to defending the weak and the oppressed – a sort of courtroom Robin Hood. But this do-gooder has flaws, which is what attracted Hackman to the part: he tends to revel in the glory his victories bring him, and he is always prepared to take whatever steps are necessary to win his cases.

He also has a daughter – a lawyer, of course – who can't forgive him for the way he once treated her mother, calling him 'a superior, self-righteous bastard.' The screenplay sets the stage for a court-room battle, when she defends an automobile company sued for allegedly knowingly selling faulty vehicles; she must square up to her father, who represents the maimed survivors from crashes in which the cars exploded on impact. This part of the film is actually based on a true-life class action case in which it transpired that a certain automobile company had tried to bury their discovery that a model had a fault which was a potential deathtrap.

Mary Elizabeth Mastrantonio played the daughter, having found fame as Maid Marion opposite Kevin Costner in *Robin Hood: Prince of Thieves*, and in the cult classic *The Abyss*. Two cracking performances, from her and Hackman, plus some good courtroom scenes prevented the film from deteriorating into a soppy, sentimental soap opera.

On its release in 1991, the film was generally greeted with mixed reviews. Said *Variety*, 'Winning performances by Gene Hackman and Mary Elizabeth Mastrantonio, and potent direction by Michael Apted pump life into the sturdy courtroom drama formula once again.' Kim Newman in *Empire*, however, thought a lot less of it, finding that it 'becomes unbearable whenever the lead characters talk about their relationship'. But she conceded that what it had going for it was Gene Hackman who 'can redeem the shoddiest characterization through sheer presence and his obvious enjoy-ment of a nicely turned line of dialogue.'

James Cameron-Wilson, writing in *Film Review*, was impressed with Mastrantonio, 'once again proving to be one of America's best young actresses. Of course, Gene Hackman is always good, regard-less of the quality of the film.' As for this film, Cameron-Wilson liked it, describing it as 'an intelligent courtroom drama that makes few concessions to the commercial market'. Ultimately that was its problem, for it didn't really find its niche in a film market domi-nated by often mindless action pictures. And excellent as both Hackman and Mastrantonio are, neither is a name to draw in the punters. Had Michael Apted been able to cast opposite Hackman one of the very few top female stars of the time, such as Julia Roberts or Michelle Pfeiffer, *Class Action* would undoubtedly have had a lot more pulling power. But Twentieth Century Fox were unwilling to allot to the film the kind of money that could pay for both Hackman plus a Roberts or a Pfeiffer.

Hackman had another unsuccessful stab at comedy in 1991, in *Company Business*, a rather tedious blend of humour and espionage. He played a former CIA agent, sent to collect and bring back a Russian spy, played by former ballet star Mikhail Baryshnikov. When things get fouled up, they go on the lam together. Nicholas Meyer, who stole the plot of *The Package* to turn into *Star Trek IV*, directed this one, and one can't help feeling he's used the same basic premise once again.

Perhaps a less secure actor might have been worrying about his future. In the three years since *Mississippi Burning* Hackman had made seven films, none of which really enlarged his reputation, even if they swelled his bank balance. Given his heart condition, the frenzied pace of work had to stop. It was time for a break. 'I've been painting, and working on a full-size plane – and I'm enjoying it,' he said in 1991. He felt that time off would give him a truer perspective on his career. 'After you get away for a while, the need for excitement wanes and you can be more objective about what's attractive about film-making.'

He decided that, for the sake of his health, he would also give up the idea of directing for now, even if he was only putting his dreams on hold. The screenplay of *Open and Shut* was one he still wanted to do as an actor, but now he hoped another director would take it on. There was also a screen treatment he liked which he hoped he could do with Dustin Hoffman and Robert Duvall. And he had the idea of remaking *La Cage aux Folles*, the 1979 French comedy hit that starred Michel Serrault as Albin, a temperamental drag queen, and Ugo Tognazzi as Renato, his 'husband'. Hackman regarded the part of Renato as one that would offer him a whole new challenge. 'I'm not going to get leading men roles,' he said, 'but there's still work for me. I don't think I've reached my best or highest point yet.'

He was, perhaps, about to, but not until Clint Eastwood could soften his resistance.

11   The Way West

Hackman wanted nothing to do with the script Clint Eastwood sent him. With the working title of *The William Munny Killings*, it was the kind of movie he detested – a Clint Eastwood western – and to anyone who has ever known anything about movies, that meant violence. From the first major Eastwood western *A Fistful of Dollars* through the seven that followed (excluding *Paint Your Wagon*), Eastwood had become notorious for depicting extreme violence, and although he and Hackman had been on friendly terms for years, they had never worked together, partly because Hackman could not face the carnage. The difference in this case was that the film did not set out to use violence to titillate the audience.

The story sees William Munny, a one-time drunk and killer, now settled down with two children, a wife in her grave and a small pig farm. A young would-be gunslinger, the so-called Schofield Kid, comes by with news of a reward on offer for killing two cowboys, put out by the whores of Big Whiskey after one of them is cut up. Munny finally decides he cannot duck the prospect of earning money by putting a wrong to rights and he picks up his old friend Ned Logan and joins the Kid on route to Big Whiskey.

Meanwhile in the town of Big Whiskey, English Bob, a notorious gunslinger, arrives with his own biographer in tow. His real reason for being there is to collect the reward. The town's sheriff, Little Bill Daggett, has him brutally beaten and driven out of town as an example to any other gunslinger who tries to take up the whores' offer.

Next comes Munny, Logan and the Kid. Daggett gives Munny a beating, but he is cared for away from town by the local whores. Once recovered, he and his two partners track down the cowboys and manage to kill one. Sickened by this act, Ned decides to go home, but en route he is captured and taken to Daggett, who tortures him to death.

Finally Munny and the Kid finish off the job when the Kid shoots the second cowboy dead. He admits he's never killed anyone before and is traumatized by the experience. Hearing that Ned has been murdered by Daggett, Munny sends the Kid home while he rides into town and kills Daggett and his deputies. Returning then to his small home, he once more hangs up his guns and becomes father and farmer again.

The fact that every Eastwood western had been a box-office success meant nothing to Hackman. Not even the fact that Hackman was Eastwood's first and only choice for the role of the ruthless sheriff moved Hackman to reconsider the offer. 'He's one of the best actors in America,' said Eastwood, 'and I needed someone who had great charm – and the sinister aspect.'

Hackman's resistance began to soften the more Eastwood prevailed upon him to reconsider. 'I swore I would never be involved in a picture with this much violence in it,' said Hackman, 'but the more I read it and the more I came to understand the purpose of the film, the more fascinated I became.' According to Eastwood, Hackman 'liked the tearing down of the adulation of killers, showing how someone who participates in violence has to carry that within his soul for all his life. The sheriff was not an absolute villain; he faces death with a tremendous amount of bravado.' Hackman agreed to do the film that was finally called *Unforgiven*.

Eastwood said his own reason for making *Unforgiven* in 1991 was 'Current events. That's why I chose to make this movie after the script had been around for 15 years. It's more timely now with the world's desensitization to violence, and the misinterpretation of justice.' He admitted he had been partly responsible for the rise in violent films but liked this one 'because even the perpetrators of the violence are touched by it, and a lot of good people are victims'.

Although the film was set in Wyoming, the fictional town of Big Whiskey was constructed in Alberta, Canada. Over a period of thirty-two days veteran set designer Henry Bumstead supervised construction of the town – a living, breathing environment in which exteriors and interiors could be shot, far away from Hollywood.

Filming began in October 1991 and lasted for fifty-two days. Along with the rest of the cast and crew, Hackman would arrive on set and leave each day on horseback; Eastwood had decreed that to keep the historic atmosphere no motor vehicles were allowed on the set.

Hackman soon discovered that Eastwood's style of directing

was to his taste. 'I've taken a lot of time,' he said, 'to learn the ability to tell people, "Don't just do something, stand there!" '

'He says very little to you,' said Hackman, 'which I appreciate
because much of what's said to you by a lot of directors is all ego,
and they say it for the people who are around the camera.' In the
little he spoke, Eastwood usually blocked his actors' movements,
and then gave them a free hand in rehearsal. Said Hackman,

> With Clint, you didn't rehearse prior to the film. We blocked the
> scene in terms of knowing where you're going, what props you're
> going to handle, and most of that is for the camera operator so that
> he's not surprised. And then pretty much you're left to your own
> devices, which is real fun film-making because you're not really sure
> what's going to happen, nor are the other actors. And in many cases
> out of that comes a sense of it happening right in front of your eyes.

As Eastwood put it, 'Sometimes I let the actors play it a little bit,
tell them "Why don't you guys just walk around and talk about it
and you'll see it," and they'll instinctively do something interesting. The scene sort of unravels itself.' Often if things were going
well during the on-set rehearsal, Eastwood would say, 'Let's just
shoot this,' and unlike many directors, he settled for one or two
takes, often using the filmed rehearsal. This suited Hackman, ever
the intuitive actor, as did the fact that Eastwood shot fast – a good
deal faster than most directors, according to producer David
Valdes:

> Clint likes to shoot fast; I think a lot of that is because he is an action
> director and most of his pictures are action, and he feels by moving
> quickly on the set, by moving the set-up so he's not taking seven,
> eight, nine takes on the same thing, moving the action just a little bit,
> helps everybody keep moving just a little faster and that again trans-
> lates on to celluloid.

Hackman as actor and Eastwood as director was an effective combination. 'Gene is great, very fast,' said Eastwood. 'You always
have to be ready to roll with him.'

Possibly one of the most relaxed directors of all time, Eastwood
created a laid-back atmosphere on set, which for Hackman became
one of the most pleasurable experiences of his career. Despite the
violent nature of his character, he felt sufficiently lighthearted to
join in with the occasional gentle horseplay between takes. During
a break in filming he entertained Eastwood's leading lady (and
girlfriend) Frances Fisher and her camcorder by performing a piece

from *Henry V* in the style of Marlon Brando. 'A horse, a horse, my kindgdom for, er . . . erm . . . er . . . uh . . . a horse!'

The scene in which Eastwood and Hackman meet for the first time called for a very exacting rehearsal. Hackman had to knock Eastwood down by pistol-whipping him and then brutally kick him; the movements were carefully choreographed, even if it was routine stuff for these veterans. Even so, a sudden loss of concentration or a missed mark could have resulted in injury. In scenes like this, there is no room for clowning. They ran through the movements, Eastwood landed on the floor and lay curled up, pretending to be in agony, as Hackman moved to the bar and reached for a bottle of liquor. From the floor Eastwood groaned, 'Pour me one of those too.' Hackman laughed, the crew laughed, then they got on with it and did it in a single take.

But when things went wrong, Eastwood could get in a temper, such as during the filming of the climactic scene when Eastwood shoots it out with Hackman and his deputies. The blank cartridges in Eastwood's gun wouldn't fire and he scowled and grumbled creating tension on the set. New, stronger blanks were loaded, and as the cameras rolled it all went smoothly as Eastwood wounded Hackman and shot dead the rest of them. He quickly eased the tension by firing off his last blank, looking into the camera with his famous cold-blooded squint and snarling: 'Print that!'

For Hackman the picture was over. He said, 'I only worked on it for three weeks. When you get to my age your attention span tends to go.' Whether he realized it at the time, Hackman departed from that big film set in Canada having given one of the finest performances of his career. It also proved to be one of Eastwood's, and the critics lavished praise on it when it reached cinemas in 1992. Many were calling it Eastwood's best western. Some said it was his best film full stop. Some predicted it would be his last western and *Empire*'s Angie Errigo figured that if it was,

> it's a grand one to ride out on – dark, gripping and embracing complex themes . . . Altogether, this is as fine a piece of craftsmanship as one could expect of Eastwood, with Hackman and [Morgan] Freeman's performances standing out, and given the sombre tone there are entertaining surprises and even some good laughs to be had . . . This is a must-see if one cares whither the western goes, and an *extremely* satisfying one for all Eastwood fans.

Hollywood being Hollywood, the film heralded a brief revival of the western genre, and in 1993 *Unforgiven* won awards at home and abroad. The Los Angeles Film Critics' Association awarded

Hackman Best Supporting Actor, Eastwood Best Director and Best Actor, and the film itself Best Picture. The National Society of Film Critics also named Hackman as Best Actor, Eastwood as Best Director and the film Best Picture. Hackman was Best Supporting Actor again in the opinion of the New York Film Critics' Circle.

Just a week before the American Academy Awards show, the British Academy of Film and Television Arts doled out their awards. The BAFTA had never been an award to lure many American nominees over to Britain, so in 1993 the ceremony in London had a satellite link-up with Universal Studios, where the Hollywood Brits and a few Hollywood actors had gathered to be a part of the show. Among them sat Gene Hackman, nominated as Best Supporting Actor. Clint Eastwood, who had been nominated for his direction of *Unforgiven*, couldn't attend, and didn't win anyway: the accolade went to Robert Altman for *The Player*. But Gene Hackman was voted Best Supporting Actor and accepted his award with typical humility, and perhaps just a hint of embarrassment.

The Oscars, of course, were the big ones, and *Unforgiven* found itself nominated for several; Hackman, naturally, was a serious contender for Best Supporting Actor. But prior to that came the prestigious Golden Globes Awards, which are considered to give an indication of what may follow at the Oscars. *Unforgiven* didn't win Best Motion Picture – that went to *Scent of a Woman* – and Eastwood didn't win Best Actor – that went to Al Pacino for ditto. But Eastwood did win Best Director, and Hackman was voted Best Supporting Actor.

A few weeks later, on 29 March, the Academy Awards Show got underway at the Dorothy Chandler Pavilion. When Hackman arrived he was asked by one of the waiting reporters about his expectations for a Best Supporting Actor award. He said, 'It's the kiss of death.' In the event, the evening was a triumph for him and Eastwood, who picked up the Best Director award. In fact Eastwood came away clutching two Oscars, the second for Best Picture. Even the film's editor, Joel Cox, was recognized by the Academy.

After the show, the victors were ushered to the press room to give their first public utterances as Oscar winners. Hackman had earlier vowed to call it a day if he won, but now he told the assembled reporters he'd withdrawn his resignation. When asked why *Unforgiven* had captured the imagination of the cinema-going public, he replied, 'I think it's because we grew up with those romantic westerns. But this one is a little different in its approach. I thought it was too violent when I first read it, but I feel very fortunate that someone did convince me.' Looking at his Oscar, he said, 'Where will I put it? On my desk, I suppose.'

In 1995 he told Edward Murphy in *Film Review*, 'Of course, I like the awards. But I don't believe the concept of acting awards has any real weight. I think it's difficult to compare my performance in *Unforgiven* with Denzel Washington's in *Philadelphia*. They are so different, how can you compare?' Having come to rest on a higher plateau, Hackman had become arguably the most respected living actor in America. More than just an actor's actor, he had metamorphosed in the eyes of the public into a true star, and the acting profession could not boast anyone more distinguished. He was conceivably the most sought-after actor in town, not as a megastar to headline big-budget films, but as someone whose name immediately conferred upon a production a true touch of class.

This is exactly what Sydney Pollack had in mind when he acquired Hackman's services to lend heavyweight support to Tom Cruise in *The Firm* (1993). Based on John Grisham's novel, the film stars Cruise as Mitch, a newly qualified and highly gifted lawyer out of Harvard, who finds himself courted by a Memphis law firm Bendini, Lambert & Locke. Big-hearted company boss Avery Tolar offers him a luxury house and a more-than-generous salary. Mitch takes the bait and moves himself and his wife Abby down to Tennessee. At first deliriously happy, the couple begin to suspect that something is seriously awry in this small firm supposedly dealing in tax affairs. For one thing, the company seems to have a higher than normal mortality rate and no one ever actually leaves the company before retirement.

An FBI agent reveals to Mitch that the company is in fact a front for the Mafia's money-laundering operations, and the agent tries to enlist Mitch's co-operation as an insider. Mitch finds he has only two choices: dish the dirt on the dangerous company, or face twenty years in prison when the Feds finally break Bendini & Co. Mitch plans and finally executes a master plan that has him breathlessly trying to keep one step ahead of Avery Tolar's henchmen.

On paper, the film bore all the hallmarks of a really good movie – possibly a great movie. Sydney Pollack was a director who knew how to make high-quality films without losing sight of the commercial target. Other good omens were that John Grisham's book was a huge bestseller, while Tom Cruise was a young star with massive box-office appeal. Gene Hackman, coming in as a recent Oscar winner, was the frosting on the studio's cake.

Actually, Hackman was not Pollack's first choice to play the part of the charming but ultimately dangerous Avery Tolar. He had originally wanted to rewrite the part for a woman and hoped Meryl Streep or Glenn Close might be wooed. But John Grisham was adamant that the firm in question was conceived as male-dominated and insisted it remain so. While Pollack capitulated on that point, he went his own way on many of the others. Indeed, even before it reached the screen, the movie had accrued its fair share of controversy.

When Pollack heard of Grisham's irritation at many of the changes Pollack was making in transferring the book to the screen, the director riposted, 'He knew that it was going to be different, otherwise he wouldn't sell his books to Hollywood.' However, Grisham's agent, Jay Garon, said that the author tended to write in a style that was ideally suited to the cinema. 'He never does it intentionally. It just happens that Grisham's structure is very scenic, and each chapter is like an episode for a movie connecting with each other. That's the way he happens to write.'

Pollack, however, refused to simply shoot the book. 'Everybody kept saying,"Oh, it's a perfect film, just do the book." It's just not informed thinking. You can't read a movie, you watch it. If I filmed the book exactly as it is written, it would be terrible.' Grisham signed his deal with Paramount for the film rights – for $600,000 – in 1991, even before Jay Garon had completed a publishing deal for the book. He quickly went on to sign subsequent deals for *The Pelican Brief* and *The Client*.

Of course, Hackman knew from the start that this was a 'Tom Cruise movie'. No problem on that front. In fact, he had had it on good authority from Dustin Hoffman, with whom Cruise co-starred in *Rain Man*, that here was a young star bursting with talent and eager to prove to the critics he was not just a pretty face. Yet a mystery arose when the film's posters began advertising the film: Gene Hackman's name was missing from it.

Certainly no public argument had led to this strange state of affairs. In fact, Hackman announced with dignity that he had asked to have his name removed from both posters and credits because, he said, he didn't want the public to have the impression that this was a 'buddy-buddy' movie. That was the official reason, anyway. However, according to *Film Review*'s columnist Tony Crawley, Hackman's contract called for his name to be above the title, while Cruise insisted his name alone went up there. Certainly the final poster featured little more than a blown-up photograph of Cruise's face, with his name emblazoned across the top of the title. If this had been the original intention of the Paramount advertising department, Hackman may well have been miffed and insisted his own name be removed altogether. Paramount managed to get round the dilemma in the end by splashing a line from the *Daily Mirror*'s review: 'A SMASHING NIGHT OUT . . . memorable performances by CRUISE and GENE HACKMAN.'

The film met with uniformly good reviews, and while Cruise failed to overwhelm most of the critics, Hackman garnered most of the accolades. As *Empire* said, 'Hackman, brilliant, as always.' And John Marriott in the *Daily Mail* wrote, 'Gene Hackman suggests the unspoken darkness with barely a raised eyebrow. As gritty and physical a presence as ever, [he] excels as the unnerving consigliere.' As for Cruise, Marriott thought that 'in the hands of Sydney Pollack, Cruise powers a well-honed nailbiter which is too eventful to let him express much thought'. Sheridan Morley, in the *Sunday Express*, thought Pollack had spoiled the film with its excessive length of almost three hours. 'There's nothing wrong with *The Firm* which couldn't be solved by chopping about 50 minutes off its running time.'

Screen Mirror was much more enthusiastic: 'What takes *The Firm* above other suspense dramas are memorable performances by Cruise and Gene Hackman as a corrupt legal partner with menacing joviality.' But while most critics refused to take Cruise seriously, that didn't stop his legions of fans from flocking to see *The Firm*; it was a mammoth success. Toppling *Jurassic Park* off the number-one spot, it managed to rake in $100 million in just twenty-three days. Apparently Paramount were so grateful to Cruise for helping to wipe away the losses incurred by *Sliver* that they bought him a Mercedes. Hackman, meanwhile, quietly got on with conferring his own golden touch on every film he made.

* * *

Because of *Unforgiven* and the few other westerns he'd been in, Hackman by 1990s standards had come to be recognized as a specialist of the genre, mainly because so few others had been riding horses and packing six shooters since the demise of the cowboy film. In fact, there were very few true surviving western stars other than Clint Eastwood and Jack Palance, and possibly Charlton Heston who were still making films and occasionally playing cowboys. So while the western enjoyed its brief Indian summer in the wake of *Unforgiven*, Hackman was sought for most such movies being made throughout 1993.

Almost as soon as *Unforgiven* became a winner, Kevin Costner started making plans to return to the genre he had helped to revitalize with *Dances with Wolves*; a remake of *Gunfight at the OK Corral* was mooted to be in the air at Warner Brothers. In fact,

Costner's ambitions far exceeded this concept. He was planning to tell the saga of Wyatt Earp's life, from youth to middle age and death at the end of the nineteenth century. Like *Dances with Wolves*, the real inspiration for Costner's latest foray derived from old-time epic westerns such as *Cheyenne Autumn* and *How the West Was Won*.

Another retelling of the OK Corral legend was being discussed simultaneously with Brad Pitt pencilled in to portray Wyatt Earp. Almost as soon as Costner announced his plans, news emerged that the Brad Pitt version had been shelved. One Warner Brothers executive commented, 'Kevin is so much the top gun right now that it would be a very brave young gunslinger to challenge him.'

And in the best tradition of the western, a young gunslinger did strap on his holster. Almost as soon as Brad Pitt had dropped out of the rival film, Kurt Russell stepped into the boots of Marshal Earp. Two films were now seemingly being floated on the same subject: *Wyatt Earp* with Costner and *Tombstone* with Russell. Was Hollywood so short of imagination that the same old ground had to be covered – especially now that the saddle had been mounted with a fresh sense of vigour. But in fact Costner had something different in mind.

His vision clearly sprung from good old American values:

> You must make offerings in the work you do, and in my heart I know mine are honourable offerings. I am intrigued by the past – I have been since I was a little boy. It's a longing for a more innocent time. We live in a cynical age. We're all jaded. A lot of our heroes have turned out to have clay feet. It's a primal emotion to want to make the bad good, to hope things will work out in the end. You have to try and conduct your life in some way, and movie heroes are great patterns. A film idol is anybody who's done the right thing in a situation where I wasn't sure what to do. One of my favourites was Henry Fonda.

Fonda, of course, played Earp in John Ford's classic version, *My Darling Clementine*.

He took the project to Lawrence Kasdan, who had begun his directing career with *Body Heat* in 1981, and had written *The Empire Strikes Back*, *The Return of the Jedi* and *The Raiders of the Lost Ark*. He had also made one of the few westerns of the eighties, *Silverado*, which had featured a young Kevin Costner. That film had flopped, although Costner maintained the film's poor showing had more to do with the distributor's indifference than Kasdan's work. Now that the western was making a come-back, Costner and

Kasdan set to work on what they hoped would be the definitive film, not just of the famous gunfight, but of the man himself. This meant exploring Earp as an outlaw, a disappointment to his father, then a lawman. The two men's instincts married commerce with quality. They agreed that Gene Hackman would be perfect as Earp's father – not only because of his manifest abilities, but also because he was currently regarded as an identifiable western 'star'.

Hackman considered their sales pitch having reached a new stage in his life. Perhaps because he had won his second Oscar, because he had turned sixty, and because of his heart condition, he was feeling less and less inclined to work, claiming, 'Usually when I get up in the morning to go to work, I say,"This is the last one I'm doing. I don't want to do anymore." But knowing myself and what a whore I am, I'd probably miss it.'

When he read the script for *Wyatt Earp* he saw an opportunity to be involved with a big-budget film – costing $65 million – that everyone considered would be a guaranteed box-office success; and yet because it was in essence a cameo, it required his services for little more than a couple of weeks. He also approved of Costner from their time together on *No Way Out*, and little in the way of violence was required for this character. He accepted, and Costner was delighted to be reunited with him on screen.

The experience proved happy for Hackman who, now so much more relaxed than ten years earlier, was revelling in his status as a respected elder statesman of the American film industry. He executed his part with his usual professionalism and delivered another seemingly effortless performance.

All the really hard work was invested by Dennis Quaid as Doc Holliday. Going for complete authenticity, Costner and Kasdan wanted this Doc Holliday to look like he was truly sick with consumption. So, accepting the challenge, Quaid lost three and a half stone and came up with the frailest-looking Doc Holliday in screen history; it was also easily the best performance of the film.

Filming on the epic seemed to drag on as Kasdan meticulously shot everything to fill the three hours he and Costner felt were needed to tell their story. Usually films that ran three hours or more were considered box-office poison, mainly because it meant that cinemas could pack in fewer performances in a day. But Costner had acquired a reputation for successful three-hour-plus films such as *JFK* and his own *Dances with Wolves* (which every major studio had predicted would be a disaster). He had a philosophy about films of the nineties:'I'm sick of movies that are just two hours long. They're just designed to get you in and get you out.'

Tempers rose and disagreements reported between Kasdan and

Costner seriously tested their long friendship. Then, disaster struck. *Tombsone* was finished first. Moving along at a brisk pace, the latter's running time had been limited to a more repeatable 129 minutes. It also made use of old timers such as Robert Mitchum as a narrator, and Charlton Heston in a largely wasted cameo role. Val Kilmer played a remarkably healthy-looking Doc Holliday, and the whole thing led up to the climactic gunfight at the OK Corral. The film was rushed into release to beat Costner's epic, and critics liked it enough to encourage the public to go and see it.

The competitive rivalry between the two films became intense. Talking to David Aldridge in *Film Review*, Val Kilmer said, 'Ours came out first and is doing well, so I'm sure they're worried. I'm curious about the Costner film because they've been filming it only about fifty miles from where I live, in New Mexico. But our script is so good – why are they bothering?'

Many had high expectations of *Wyatt Earp*. The common thread linking the film to Costner's earlier successes, *Robin Hood: Prince of Thieves* and *Dances With Wolves*, was, according to Costner

> poignance. The cards of narrative have to keep flopping too. There must be tremendously careful construction and attention to detail. My movies can't be salvaged by car chases. The fashion in action movies is to stress the action and cut out the character's development, yet all the camera work in the world can't disguise there's not a story.

Tombstone fitted neatly with the trend Costner was decrying. Reaching cinema screens at the beginning of 1994, it made a quick killing at the box office, earning $6 million in its first weekend in America. By the time *Wyatt Earp* was ready for release in the summer of 1994, it was generally considered to be too long and leisurely, though the film attracted some ardent admirers among the critics. CRN's Susan Granger found it to be 'a spectacular epic', in which 'Kevin Costner is riveting' and 'Dennis Quaid is dynamite.' Emma Norman, reviewing it for *Screen Mirror*, thought it 'the best in the recent crop' of westerns. She liked all the performances but said that the 'revelation is Quaid who acts everyone off the screen . . . It's his presence that brings the film to life. It is a larger-than-life movie, over-long and over-elaborate, but it is fascinating.' Despite the fact that it was a far superior film to *Tombstone* – and may even become a cult classic in time – it did not meet with success in America, and was given a limited release in Britain. The same fate faced the four-hour *Gettysburg*, released around the same time.

Wyatt Earp's failure damaged Costner, who tried to revive his reputation with an all-action adventure, *Waterworld*, which became an even bigger disaster. But for Gene Hackman, playing a rather forgettable cameo in this marathon western, it hurt not at all.

*   *   *

While Costner was still wrapping up production work on *Wyatt Earp*, Hackman had already climbed back in the saddle again, in *Geronimo* for Walter Hill. John Milius's script followed the Apache chief's exploits, which led to the American government ordering his arrest, and the ensuing pursuit, during which a young cavalry officer finds himself torn between loyalty to his uniform and his growing conviction that the government is out to annihilate the Apaches. His conscience ultimately forces him to aid Geronimo.

While the 1962 film of the same title had starred white American, Chuck Connors, as the legendary Apache warrior, in the nineties version, the title role was given to an authentic Indian actor, Wes Studi, who had previously appeared in *Last of the Mohicans*. Robert Duvall was cast as a tracker and Jason Patric as the conscientious young cavalry officer. When Hackman learned that his friend Duvall had signed up for the film, he couldn't resist accepting the role of the older cavalry officer in pursuit of Geronimo.

True to an America chastened by the treatment meted out to its native tribes, the film eschewed the traditional cowboys 'n' injuns clichés: rather it attempted to portray the historic events with honesty while still giving the audience plenty of excitement along the way. Studi remarked, 'We're not putting Geronimo on a pedestal and saying he did nothing wrong. He was simply reacting to the way his people were being treated by the US Government.'

For a man with heart trouble, Hackman bore up well under the rigours of this epic outdoor western, allowing his horse to take much of the strain as he led his cavalry of extras into the spectacular location of Moab in Utah during summer 1993. In between scenes he retreated to his trailer to escape the intense heat, and enjoyed the companionship of Duvall. In the thirty or so years since their careers had got off the ground, this was only the second film they had appeared in together. And it had proved impossible for Gene to work with Dustin Hoffman at all, such was the often intricate way in which stars are packaged into films. Despite, or perhaps because of, this they remained the closest of friends. 'Even though I know Dusty and Bobby are stars,' said Hackman, 'I still can't picture either of them except as living in this cold-water flat in New York, much like the one I had.'

Geronimo was the realization of a dream for Walter Hill, the one-time screenwriter and western buff who began his directing career with the excellent and much under-rated Charles Bronson drama *The Streetfighter*. That, like many of his ensuing films, was shot like a western. His chance to do the real thing came in 1980 with *The Long Riders*, when he believed he'd found his ideal métier. As it was, he had to wait until 1993.

His dream amounted to little in the end. As luck – or bizarre Hollywood strategy – would have it, another film of the same title covering the same page of history hit the screens at the same time. Neither film was widely shown, emerging briefly in 1994, although Hill's version was the only one to make it to British screens, and then only on a limited release. For some reason Hollywood, having decided to churn out westerns, quickly got cold feet, resulting in a rapid decrease in production, and a lack of effort in their distribution. In hindsight the genre would be regarded as a passing fad that produced mostly expendable films.

Among these was *The Quick and the Dead*. The screenplay by Britain's Simon Moore told of a woman who sets out to avenge the death of her father. Moore, who had directed *Under Suspicion*, wanted to produce and direct his own western, but when Sharon Stone read the script, she coveted the idea of producing it herself, and bought it outright for a million dollars. Moore still hoped to direct it, but Stone gave the job to Sam Raimi, whose *Darkman* and *Army of Darkness* had proved modest successes.

Stone, desperate to break away from the sexy siren mould that had made her a star, decked herself out in a wide-brimmed hat and long coat reminiscent of Clint Eastwood's Man with No Name. Stone rides into the town of Redemption to take part in a shooting contest in which the targets are the other competitors. The first prize is a lot of money; the second prize is a coffin. However, she has a secret reason for being there; she wants to kill the ruler of the lawless town: his name, appropriately, is Herod.

Why Hackman involved himself in this bizarre attempt at a star's makeover is a mystery. Perhaps the money on offer brought out the 'whore' in the great character actor. Unlike Daggett in *Unforgiven* who was several shades of grey, Herod was simply black; to add a little colour and verve to an otherwise cardboard character, Hackman, in bowler hat and whiskers, turned him into something of a dandy.

Stone and Raimi had managed to get TriStar interested in financing the film but the company hesitated in 1993 because Stone's previous film, *Sliver*, had earnd only around $36 million in the domestic market, although it went on to reel in around $100 million outside America. Nevertheless, because it succeeded only by a slender margin, TriStar were reticent about greenlighting the $30 million Stone needed to make her western. And it didn't help that Gene Hackman was resisting all efforts to corall him into the picture. He disliked the script for its violence, and felt the need to relax after the rigours of *Geronimo*. But TriStar were keen to have him, as were Stone and Raimi, and they collectively pulled a seduction job on him that eventually had him signing along the dotted line. TriStar then gave the film the official thumbs-up, and shooting began in November 1993.

Because the story was basically a series of gunfights, Sam Raimi carefully choreographed each showdown as though they were ballets. Sergio Leone worked in just the same way, developing his style from *A Fistful of Dollars* through to *Once Upon a Time in the West*. Even the costumes were supposedly originals used by Leone in *The Good, the Bad and the Ugly*, *Once Upon a Time in the West* and *My Name is Nobody* – Sharon Stone discovered them in a vault in Milan. Not surprisingly *The Quick and the Dead* wound up looking like a pastiche of, or possibly a homage to, the Leone westerns. But whether intentional or not, the problem was that Leone's style was itself a pastiche, and this reworking just seemed too heavy-handed. On the other hand, this western at least had an original storyline, which couldn't be said for many of the others made in 1993. And it had a unique look to it, with the town of Redemption looking more like something from a Stephen King story, complete with Herod's satanic-looking house at the end of the street.

Redemption had been constructed at Mescal in the Arizona desert, around fifty miles from Tucson. The days were baking, while at night the temperatures were sub-zero. Gene had the luxury of a house in Tucson to live in throughout production. At the age of sixty-three he had every right to ensure he was accorded four-star treatment. On the set Stone was the boss, but Hackman had reached iconic status. He had turned sixty-four when the film wrapped in February 1994.

The distributors held back the film until September 1995, hoping to miss the rush of westerns on and off the screens. As most were falling by the wayside, *The Quick and the Dead* came at the tail-end of a genre that had been rediscovered and killed off by the end of 1994.

It delighted some critics and irritated others. Simon Rose in *Screen Mirror* felt 'Sam Raimi has unintentionally produced a comedy . . . While it might have made for an amusing ten minutes, it makes for an incredibly turgid feaure-length movie.' Marianne

Gray, writing in *Film Review*, had mixed feelings about what she described as 'a daft film but huge fun . . . this is an uneven, uneasy fantasy,' but she considered it 'a one-off and I enjoyed its oddness'. As for the acting she said, rather predictably, 'Stone is OK (looks better than she acts) but Hackman as the elegant, evil Herod of this particular hell-hole is just great.'

Hackman probably never even saw the finished product; he rarely watched any of his films by this time. 'I think of myself as being much younger than I am, and I see this old guy up there with the bald head and the paunch. It's depressing.'

12 Just a Hanger-on

Hackman was often threatening to retire, and it seemed that the failure of his three Westerns had the Hollywood accountants discounting him yet again. The threats were usually lame, but by 1994 Hollywood's reaction towards Hackman was genuinely somewhat mixed. On the one hand he was considered one of America's greatest actors of all time; yet on the other he was not considered a bankable star – at least, not on his own. Like Spencer Tracy, his financial value was realized only when he had a star partner. That is pure Hollywood mentality, of course. In Hollywood Arnie and Sly are bankable stars, even though each have had their own box-office disasters. Hackman's disasters have, fortunately, usually been someone else's.

It was this Hollywood mentality that, despite *Unforgiven* and *Mississippi Burning*, despite two Oscars and all the nominations, saw powerful studio accountants looking down their noses at Hackman. The feeling was pretty much mutual.

> The power-brokers who put the deals together are just financiers, and that doesn't feel right to me. There are a lot of people who can live in a corporate world and have a good life. I hope people question authority, protest against inequities. But I have my doubts. We live in a country where everyone likes to be very comfortable.

Fortunately Hackman had his champions among the elite of Hollywood producers, and he continued to be in demand by creative personnel, who kept putting his name at the top of their preferred cast lists. The trouble was that the studios' financiers only ever wanted Warren Beatty, Robert de Niro or Al Pacino, and this is exactly what happened while production partners Don Simpson

159

and Jerry Bruckheimer were trying to put together a package for *Crimson Tide*.

The film came from an idea mooted by Mike Stenson, a vice-president of Disney's Hollywood Pictures, which, like Touchstone, had been set up to produce the kind of films that Uncle Walt would never have approved of. Stenson asked Simpson and Bruckheimer, 'What would happen if you crossed *The Caine Mutiny* and *Fail Safe*?' To find out, the producers hired screenwriter Michael Schiffer and novelist Richard P. Henrick to come up with a story.

When news comes that a rebel Russian unit has captured a former Soviet nuclear missile base, nuclear submarine USS *Alabama* is put on alert. It receives an initial message to prepare for launching its missiles. But then a second message is cut off. Captain Ramsey is intent on carrying out the nuclear attack but his second officer, Lieutenant-Commander Hunter, insists that they must make every attempt to get the complete second message, which might well be cancelling the first order. Ramsey maintains that not to launch will result in defeat and annihilation for the United States, while Hunter argues that to fire the missiles without getting confirmation of the second message might precipitate a nuclear holocaust. When Ramsey tries to carry out the attack, Hunter takes over the ship. Officers loyal to Ramsey lead a counter-mutiny, and the story unravels through to the end. Finally, the second message is conveyed in full, announcing the end of the crisis and calling off the attack.

Simpson and Bruckheimer spent eight months developing the script, and by early 1994 they were seeking their two lead actors. They wanted Gene Hackman to play Captain Ramsey, whereas the studio favoured Warren Beatty. The Los Angeles earthquake had just devastated Beatty's home, and he was staying at the Bel-Air Hotel, right next door to Simpson's house. It proved very convenient for Beatty to frequent Simpson's house over the next month to discuss *Crimson Tide*. Simpson said, 'Warren deserves some credit for how good this movie is, if it's good, because he challenged us on a lot of points.'

But Beatty just would not agree to proceed any further and, as Simpson put it, they were not prepared to 'dance forever'. The studio still wouldn't consider Hackman, so Simpson and Bruckheimer moved on to Al Pacino, who was also staying at the Bel-Air. Pacino usually avoided action films, but on this occasion he told Simpson, 'I want to say, "Yes, take me to bed." '

Next, in search of a director, they approached Tony Scott, with whom they'd made *Top Gun, Beverly Hills Cop II* and *Days of Thunder*. Scott said he'd be interested in directing if Quentin

Tarantino could do a rewrite on the characters. 'I thought he could really bring something fresh to them,' said Scott. 'I mean, he's flavour of the year, but for a very good reason, because he's clever and really does bring a whole new light to how people communicate.'

Tarantino breezed through the rewrite, giving the characters some telling dialogue, including a discussion between Ramsey and Hunter about Lippizaner stallions, and incorporating jokey references to the Silver Surfer and *Star Trek*. Another Tarantino touch was the scene in which a crewman quizzes another on submarine movies such as *The Enemy Below* and *Run Silent, Run Deep*. The *wunderkind* also decided that rather than letting the audience feel that Hunter is the good guy with all the right answers, the audience should be kept on the edge of their seats in a state of suspense and ambivalence.

With Pacino interested, Brad Pitt was approached to play Hunter. After a month Pacino was waiting for Tarantino's finished rewrites; all the producers wanted from Pacino was a firm confirmation that he'd do the part. He wouldn't give it, and with a start date of August looming they had to move on without him. Once Pacino dropped out of the picture, so did Pitt. Meanwhile Hackman's agent rang to say that having read the original script he thought Gene would want to do it.

Denzel Washington's agent called the producers and suggested they consider him. Simpson and Bruckheimer found the proposition interesting, but told the agent, 'We can't cast that part until we know who the other part is going to be played by.' They were back on the Hackman trail, but the studio remained unconvinced, especially when his agent announced he would cost them $4 million. But Simpson and Bruckheimer, knowing Hackman would be ideal, persevered and finally persuaded the studio to let them have their way. Then they cast Washington, for a fee of $6.5 million.

Further rewrites were executed by Robert Towne, who had helped put *Bonnie and Clyde* into shape at the beginning of Hackman's career. Towne recalled, 'They didn't have a beginning or an ending, and they didn't have a scene where the philosophies of the two lead characters were distinguished.' So as a 'favour' he wrote two scenes to articulate the conflicting ideas on warfare between Ramsey and Hunter. 'They paid me a few dollars,' he said, 'but the big payment I expect from this is the pleasure of seeing Gene Hackman act in a scene I wrote.'

Then Steven Zaillian, who won an Oscar for *Schindler's List*, rewrote Tarantino's version, although in the end it was Michael Schiffer who received sole screenwriting credit. This mixing and matching on a screenplay is, of course, common practice in Hollywood, going all the way back to the days of *Gone with the Wind* when various people worked on the script but only Sydney Howard received credit. Screenwriters are often likened to paper tissues – use 'em and dispose of 'em – and producers and directors feel that rough approach is perfectly justified. Bruckheimer put it, 'This validates the old studio system.' Schiffer remained on set throughout filming to rewrite when necessary.

Over a two-week period Scott and the producers sat down with Hackman and Washington to rehearse. During this time Scott came up with the idea of giving Ramsey a snap-happy Jack Russell terrier that he keeps on board the submarine; he based the dog on one owned by his brother Ridley. Washington suggested that the speech about the Lippizaner horses, which originally came at the beginning of the script, was put towards the end. Hackman himself added a line for the very end of the film: 'You were right about the horses.' 'These are all great movie moments which came from team work,' said Bruckheimer.

All seemed ready to go towards the end of summer 1994. Then the US Navy, without whose co-operation the film would be nigh-on impossible, demanded that the mutiny be taken out of the story and supplied a detailed alternative plot treatment. To the producers, it was akin to them telling the US Navy how to run a nuclear submarine. They refused to change their story, and the navy refused to co-operate. Consequently, they had to beg, steal and borrow the shots they needed of the submarine at sea, and they managed to get the French Navy to lend them an aircraft carrier.

The interiors were shot at Culver Studios in Los Angeles, where a claustrophobic set was built on top of a gimbal – a moving platform. This was tilted as steeply as 30 degrees for scenes when the submarine is either diving or rising. Coca-Cola was sprayed over the set floor to form a sticky film and keep the very expensive actors from slipping and hurting themselves. Hackman found it particularly hard going on his knees, and said it was 'a little rough' having to work with multiple cameras, as Scott tended to do. 'He uses long lenses also, so every time he does a close-up you're talking to someone ten or twelve feet away at the side of the camera, and that's a little disconcerting.'

Denzel Washington noticed nothing disconcerting about Hackman during the close-up scenes. He told Tony Crawley, 'When I was off-camera giving him lines for his close-ups, I watched him. And, man, this guy is good! Very relaxed. To Washington, Hackman is 'one of the great actors'. He also said, 'In his position, it'd be easy to get lazy or slow down. Instead, he's very, very professional.

Always knew his lines, always ready, always on time. I like to think he knew he was with someone who could act also. Maybe that helped to give him new energy.' In fact Hackman had already praised Washington's abilities ten years earlier on the set of *Power*.

Hackman was modest, but not falsely so, about his own acting ability. He told *Premiere*, 'What happens to you as an actor is that you gain a certain amount of poise and people discern that as acting. The audience also gives you points on a scale of one to 100. Since I've been here thirty-five years, I'm already thirty-five points ahead.'

He said that he found playing Captain Ramsey easy, mainly because of the type of movie this was in which 'you always have a goal; there's a place you have to go, a high and a low. There's a second act break and there's a flat part.' It was a formula he understood and said, 'in terms of finding a line to play, it's much easier'.

He was not even concerned about the W.C. Fields adage about never acting with animals – he'd already broken the rule about children on *Misunderstood*. Woody was the Jack Russell terrier he had to work with, and Woody, like most of his breed, snarled and snapped a great deal, which was perfect for his role in the film as the captain's pet. Hackman had to feed the terrier pieces of hot dog, and said, 'You have to get your hand out in a hurry. They're kind of nippy, these Jack Russells. They'll nail ya.'

One of Scott's techniques was the use of diffusion smoke, invisible to the film's audience but creating a photographic quality for interior scenes that Scott favoured. Breathing in that smoke, said Washington, 'has cut a few years off our lives'. Nevertheless, Hackman only had praise for Scott. 'I'd seen Tony's other movies and I liked his style. This is a very stylish action movie. I think it would be foolish to pretend it's anything else.' He thought, however, that the film explored the dilemma of making decisions on matters that affect humanity.

By mid October, with the filming half completed, tension on the set appeared to be getting the better of some cast members. While shooting the scene in which James Gandolfini, one of the officers loyal to Hackman, comes to remove Washington from the conning room, Gandolfini surprised Washington during the first take by grabbing him a lot more fiercely than he had done in rehearsal. Washington pushed him back, and suddenly they were involved in a shoving match.

Tony Scott, in his usual salmon-pink shorts, purple Gore-Tex sneakers and baseball cap, perched on his director's chair in front of the monitors several feet away, decided to call a lunch break, hoping the actors would cool off. But when they came back it hap-

pened again. Scott sat rigidly, believing his film was about to fall
apart. Then the two scuffling actors broke into laughter. Not a single person, not even Hackman who'd stood silently wondering
what breed of actor he was working with, had known that
Washington and Gandolfini had been plotting this prank.

Washington was less easy-going when Tarantino turned up on
the set to see how his contribution to the script was going. He may
have wished he'd stayed away, because Washington, no longer kid-
ding around, began to berate him for his treatment of race in his
films and particularly for his frequent use of the word 'nigger'.
Tarantino, embarrassed by this argument in front of the crew, suggested they went elsewhere to pursue the matter. Washington
refused, saying, 'Let's discuss this now if we're going to discuss this.'
Later neither of them would elucidate what had happened. 'I'm not
into discussing it in the press or anything like that,' said
Washington. 'He's a fine artist and I told him my feelings. So he
knows what I had to talk about.'

Outside in the parking lot, Tarantino had a happier experience
meeting up with Hackman who had just finished for the day. To
Tarantino, Hackman was one of the cinema greats. He began
telling Gene about his psycho-sexual theories about *Top Gun*,
saying that the film was really about 'man's struggle with his own
sexuality,' and that all the fighter pilots represented the gay world
and Kelly McGillis represented heterosexuality.' 'Yeah,' chuckled
Hackman, 'and the airplanes are the penises – yeah, yeah!' He
asked if he had shared his theory with Scott (*Top Gun*'s director),
and Tarantino replied he'd been telling him for years; Scott had
never found it particularly amusing.

Hackman enjoyed meeting Tarantino. 'Quentin is a terrific
movie fan, and chatting to him was like talking to a movie encyclo-
paedia.'

By the end of November, the last scenes were being shot at
Chapman University in Orange County. Hackman happily signed
autographs for the watching students. He seemed in particularly
fine spirits now that his work on the film was almost over, and he
keenly anticipated a break at one of his European hideaways. He
hummed 'Anchors Aweigh' as he walked back to the set, ready to
do a scene that involved Woody.

When he had to take an open cut-throat razor with a flash of
hands in *Mississippi Burning* he managed the potentially dangerous feat without missing a beat. But with the snapping dog he was
a lot less confident. The cameras rolled, and he reached to take the
leash. He fumbled, and Scott yelled, 'Cut! Once more, please!' They
tried again, and again he fumbled. On the third take he managed to

take the leash without mishap to his ankles.

With his work on the film over, he flew back to one of his European retreats. He had always been reclusive by most Hollywood standards. In the early days, before *The French Connection*, no one had been interested in his personal life. When he hit the big time, he briefly came under the scrutiny of the gossip columnists – but only briefly, for they received little ammunition. He didn't get into fights; he wasn't a handsome Warren Beatty-type with a new girlfriend every month; he hadn't been in jail: in fact, there was little to pique the public imagination, and the columnists quickly diverted their attention away to more public property.

So when his marriage began falling apart, no one noticed. There were not even headlines when he retired in 1977: he just quietly announced to his agent he wouldn't be working any more. Similarly his come-back inspired no fanfare in the press; nobody, it seemed, had noticed he'd been gone, thanks perhaps to his role in *Superman II*, which few knew had been filmed as long ago as 1977.

His private life had always remained just that. 'I really am not that fascinating a personality,' he told me,

> so there's little about me for people to know about. And I guess it's because I'm so normal that has made my life of disinterest and has also made me successful as an actor. I've felt that audiences respond to the proletarian man they see in me. On the other hand, that doesn't make for headlines. So I've got it great both ways.

But he has always been enormously possessive of his privacy, too. Rarely has he given interviews, and has generally refused to help promote the films he was in, often because he could leave that to the likes of Clint Eastwood, Tom Cruise, Kevin Costner or any of the other high profile stars with whom he co-starred.

After his divorce his existence became semi-nomadic, living out of suitcases in different hotels, and to a certain extent, minus a family, could remain that way. Free from responsibilities, and in an effort to escape the trappings of Hollywood life, he spent more and more time in-between films at the numerous properties he owned in Europe. When not painting pictures, he was painting his homes. 'I love doing DIY,' he said. 'It empties my head in-between movies.'

Crimson Tide was released in the autumn of 1995 and was generally cheered by the critics. *Sight and Sound* took it for what it was, a film with a structure that 'owes a debt to *Speed* which proved that the fail-safe way to keep a 90s audience gripped is to cram a preposterous succession of races against the clock into a real-time frame.' Simon Rose wrote in *Screen Mirror*, '*Crimson Tide* had me jumping out of my seat in fright. It's a superbly crafted, worryingly-plausible and hugely enjoyable thriller.' Although he found the two main characters somewhat clichéd, he said, 'These two great actors could keep us spellbound performing the British Rail timetable.'

Anwar Brett of *Film Review* recognized the film's various qualities but felt 'it is the powerful, layered performances from Hackman and Washington that shoot it into a higher orbit'. The film was, he said, a showcase for 'two excellent actors at the top of their form, sparring like two fighters ... Hackman just seems to get better and better with age; he can convey physical toughness without lifting a finger and is able to turn the most innocuous line into a veiled threat or barbed insult.'

The fact that any actor could emerge from an action-suspense thriller with so much praise said a great deal about Hackman's acting skills and, more than anything, the high esteem in which he was now held by everyone throughout the industry, from producers and directors, to actors, critics and journalists – by all but the accountants. But *Crimson Tide*'s success was to change that.

*   *   *

Danny DeVito, the diminutive actor who, like his friend and occasional co-star Michael Douglas, had established himself as a producer, was persuaded by director Barry Sonnenfeld to buy the rights to Elmore Leonard's prime crime novel *Get Shorty* in 1992. DeVito must have been hesitant since other films based on Leonard's books such as *Glitz*, *52 Pick-up* and *Cat Chaser* had all failed to do well. However, Quentin Tarantino, who was heavily influenced by the works of Leonard, had begun buying up the rights to some of his novels, and Sonnenfeld, who desperately wanted to make *Get Shorty*, needed someone with clout in Hollywood to prevent this one from falling into Tarantino's hands.

So DeVito bought the rights and assigned Frank Scott to write the screenplay. Knowing he needed a couple of star names to convince a studio to back it, he succeeded in raising interest from, first, John Travolta and then Gene Hackman, whose agent told DeVito that Hackman's price was equal billing with Travolta and $7 million. With the two stars on board, DeVito went to MGM who gave their blessing and, more importantly, their finance.

Hackman said that these days his choice of film was very much dictated by 'the chance to work with good people. I don't have much ambition left now, but it's great to work beside the people who are"hot" in the industry right now.' Few came hotter than John Travolta, a star who rose and quickly fell in the late seventies and early eighties, only to rise again, triumphantly, in Quentin Tarantino's *Pulp Fiction.*

Hackman returned to Los Angeles, where the film was to be shot. A much calmer air surrounded Hackman at age sixty-five, and he had fun playing his role of B-film producer Harry Zimm. For once, Hackman could alter his facial appearance by wearing false teeth, and he warmed, too, to the film's broad comedy. On set he casually played down his own talents and contribution: 'I don't think I do anything great. I get to do the easy stuff. It's the writers and directors who have the hard part of bringing the story alive. I'm just a hanger-on, really.'

John Travolta played Chili Palmer, a Miami loan shark and obsessive movie fan, on the trail of Leo Devoe, a dry cleaner who, having faked his own death, still owes money to the Mob. When Chili gets an assignment to go after Harry Zimm, a producer of B films who's looking to move into the major league, he takes the opportunity to pitch an idea to Harry for a film about a loan shark who comes to Los Angeles on the trail of a man who's faked his own death. Harry tells him the story has no ending, and besides which, he already has a hot script – *Mr Lovejoy* – which he is developing as a property for film star Martin Weir (Danny DeVito), the ex-husband of his girlfriend, former scream queen Karen Flores (Rene Russo). Chili feels inspired to turn his hand to film producing.

Gangster Bo Catlett (Delroy Lindo) collects a stash of Columbian drugs at Los Angeles airport and leaves the payment of $500,000 in a luggage locker. The courier is scared away from the airport by a DEA stakeout, and turns up at Catlett's house wanting his $500,000. Catlett kills him, and then tries to pressurize Harry and Chili into collecting the drug money. Chili's boss, Ray 'Bones' Barboni (Dennis Farian), arrives in Los Angeles, finds Harry, beats him up and frames him for the killing of one of Catlett's men. While Harry is in hospital, Chili sets up his own film production.

When the Columbians turn up wanting their money from Catlett, he kidnaps Karen and demands that Chili bring the money he needs to his house. Chili arrives and Catlett tries to kill him but is himself fatally shot. Chili returns to his hotel, where 'Bones' turns up, finds the key to the airport locker, assumes that's where he'll find the money Chili has collected from Leo Devoe, and goes off to pick it up. Chili gets on with filming his own life story.

The film's satire is closer to the truth about Hollywood than its producers would ever admit. Certainly the premise of a charming crook who arrives in Hollywood and blends in with the local fraternity is in no way far-fetched, and in some ways this is an updated version of Benjamin 'Bugsey' Siegel's story, who did pretty much the same in the late thirties. The film certainly has the stamp of authenticity and the in-jokes fly thick and fast, keeping the audience laughing along with its makers.

It wasn't to everyone's taste. *Sight & Sound*'s John Wrathal thought that 'John Travolta is perfectly cast' and that the film was 'certainly entertaining' but felt 'the end result is disappointingly trite'. He objected to the

> farcical style which robs the story of any sense of danger, and reduces the deaths to throwaway jokes. Worse, with the commendable exception of Russo as Karen and Lindo as Catlett, Sonnenfeld allows the cast to camp it up. De Vito has always been a ham, but Hackman here gives his most trivial performance since Lex Luthor.

But Simon Rose of *Mirror Screen* called it 'a brilliant comedy-thriller. Travolta takes coolness as far as it can go without becoming a parody ... When a movie's as sly, witty and clever as this, you find yourself sitting back with a big, stupid grin on your face. Anyone who loves movies will be besotted.'

Hackman really had little to do in the film, but it did no harm for him to be associated with this hip success, and it reawakened his taste for comedy.

* * *

By 1996 he had achieved very few of his stated ambitions. Despite his weak heart he still harboured a sneaking desire to direct, though he was doubtful if it would ever happen. 'There are just too many hassles,' he said. Neither was he likely to return to the stage. But one ambition he did have finally came to fruition – to remake *La Cage aux Folles*. Originally he'd wanted to direct it, but that was, by 1996, out of the question because of his heart problem. He had talked to a number of directors in the hope of interesting them in the project, including Mike Nichols. Given that Nichols was responsible for almost bringing Hackman's film career to a shuddering halt thirty years earlier, it said something about both men that they had such a good working relationship. Nichols had enjoyed directing Hackman in *Postcards from the Edge*, and had been looking for a more substantial part to offer the actor.

Hollywood looked to the success of the Australian hit comedy, *The Adventures of Priscilla, Queen of the Desert*, which proved that a mainstream American audience would flock to a film about drag artists. Being what it is, Hollywood simply copied the formula and came up with its own successful drag queen comedy drama, *To Wong Foo, Thanks for Everything! Julie Newmar*. Its success meant that Mike Nichols could get the backing he needed from United Artists, Blackwell and Bruce Ericksen to produce and direct the American version of *La Cage aux Folles – The Birdcage*.

For the Americanized version, drag artist Albin became Albert, and 'husband' Renato became Armand. Otherwise, the screenplay by Elaine May essentially followed the storyline of the original French version. At the Birdcage nightclub Albert, otherwise known as star drag queen 'Starina', throws a tantrum in his dressing-room, convinced his 'husband', Armand, is having an affair. Albert refuses to go on stage until Armand reassures him he is not being unfaithful, and when 'Starina' finally goes on to perform, Armand goes off to meet the mystery man, who turns out to be his son, Val.

Val reveals he is going to marry the daughter of Senator Keeley, an ultra right-wing co-founder of the Coalition for Moral Order. The press are out to dig any dirt on the senator, especially since his closest political ally was discovered dead in bed with a prostitute. Val wants his father to help him impress his future in-laws, a prospect that fills Armand with dread, knowing what kind of man the senator is. But he goes along with the ploy as Val invites the Keeleys over to meet his parents. Val's mother agrees to join Armand at his house for the sake of their son. Albert, refusing to be left out of the evening, decides he will pose as Val's uncle, but despite all attempts to make him more butch, he is unable to put a lid on his effeminate mannerisms. On the fateful night he turns up in drag posing as Val's mother.

Senator Keeley is charmed by Val's 'mom', even though 'her' wig keeps slipping. The evening deteriorates when Val's real mother turns up, followed by reporters intent on ridiculing the senator. The only recourse left to the beleaguered dinner-party guests is to disguise Keeley and sneak him past the hungry photographers. He leaves, in drag, with his wife, as 'We Are Family' plays on the soundtrack.

Nichols approached the multi-talented Robin Williams to play Armand, and he agreed to do it. Hackman had originally wanted to play Renato, but at the age of sixty-five, he was clearly too old. So Nichols suggested he play the role of the ultra-right Senator Keeley.

'With any new script I'm sent, I usually think first and foremost what kind of experience I'll have with the director or the other actors,' said Hackman. With Nichols as director, Robin Williams as Armand, and the chance to fulfil a long-standing ambition, Gene was unable to resist. 'It was a wonderful part,' he said. 'Senator Keeley is central to the story but I'm able to leave it to the younger actors to do all the energetic stuff.' With both Williams and Hackman giving the film star weight, Nichols was able to cast a lesser name for the part of Albert and chose Nathan Lane. Dianne Wiest played Louise Keeley, Dan Futterman was Val and Christine Baranski played Katharine.

Since the play and original film had been set in the seventies, Nichols and Elaine May updated the political material to include references to the gays-in-the-military debate, and the subject of a gay father's rights. Senator Keeley alludes scathingly to Robert Mapplethorpe, and dismisses Bob Dole as being 'just too liberal'. But in a nod back to the seventies, Nichols decided to use the music of the decade, particularly the disco classics.

Hackman had always preferred the improvisational approach to film acting, and with this one he got to see the art being performed by one of the masters, Robin Williams. Just getting through scenes without cracking up into gales of laughter was often a challenge at times for the entire cast. Much of the fun transposes itself to the screen. But somehow the final result seemed diluted, and it may be simply because it was done earlier, and better, by Edouard Molinaro.

Not surprisingly, most critics compared it to the original. Paul Burston, in *Sight & Sound*, wrote,

The first question to ask is, why remake it? Much as in the art of female impersonation itself, there is a fine line between paying homage and becoming a drag. It's a shame that Mike Nichols doesn't seem to realize this. *La Cage aux Folles* may have had its faults, but at least it worked as farce. *The Birdcage* is simply a travesty.

But there was praise for Hackman who, wrote Burston,

with his dragmatic exit in a blonde wig as Senator Keeley, gives the scariest drag performance by a confirmed heterosexual male since Terence Stamp's in *Priscilla*. Hackman may well have been lumbered with playing a two-dimensional stereotype, but he is the only person to emerge from this sorry affair with any dignity.

In 1996 Hackman signed to work with Britain's most glamorous movie couple Hugh Grant and Liz Hurley in their own £14 million production, *Extreme Measures*. It was filmed during the summer under the direction of Britain's Michael Apted. Exterior scenes were filmed in New York where the action takes place, but interiors were shot in Toronto where the cost of filming proved less costly.

While Hurley remained behind the scenes, Hugh Grant took the starring role of a doctor who uncovers a plot being perpetrated by colleague Gene Hackman. The attraction for Gene was the fact that while his character was the film's heavy, he was not a particularly evil man but a good doctor deep down and one of the world's great medical minds. Grant discovers that the plot centres around Hackman's work in finding a cure for one of the world's most common ailments. Close to a breakthrough but frustrated at only being able to experiment on animals rather than human guinea pigs, Hackman rounds up the unwitting homeless of New York.

Hugh Grant said that the film 'feeds the paranoia of everyone about hospitals and what really happens to you when you go into hospital: are they necessarily treating you for the best?'

Throughout filming Hackman, as usual, kept a low profile as the world's media focused its interest, not surprisingly, on Grant and Hurley whose relationship had managed to survive the scandal created by Grant a year earlier when he was caught in Los Angeles with a prostitute.

After filming, Hackman took the rest of the year off. Finally he seemed to have slowed down. 'I'm tightening my work schedule and I'll make just one film a year,' he announced. Of course, he has said words to that effect in the past, but turning sixty-six in 1996, he seemed to have at last accepted that he had nothing more to prove. The path of his career has been strewn with achievements. He virtually began his film career as an Oscar nominee, became a top star in the seventies earning a fortune, took early 'retirement', and came back to become arguably the most respected American actor since Spencer Tracy and Fredric March. He was never a mere supporting actor, nor just a character actor, nor was he a Hollywood megastar. And that has been his unique success. 'It's true that I've had a greater versatility in the roles I've played because I've fallen somewhere between star and character actor,' he said.

But after all he has accomplished, he is not prepared to rest on his laurels. 'I don't look back too much and mourn or cheer over the best roles,' he has said. 'I just look towards the future.'

The future, he said, held no mysteries. 'I don't think I'll ever do anything else but act. I don't think I could be successful in anything else.' If he did ever retire for a second time he would, he said, 'paint pictures on a small farm in Connecticut'.

Bibliography

Books

Base, Ron, and Haslam, David, *The Movies of the Eighties*. Macdonald, 1990.

Bergan, Ronald, *Dustin Hoffman*. Virgin Books, 1992.

Eames, John Douglas, *The MGM Story*. Octopus Books, 1986.

Finler, Joel W., *The Movie Directors Story*. Octopus Books, 1985.

Hirschhorn, Clive, *The Universal Story*. Octopus Books, 1983.

Holden, Anthony, *The Oscars: The Secret History of Hollywood's Academy Awards*. Little, Brown, 1993.

MacLaine, Shirley, *My Lucky Stars*. Bantam Press, 1995.

Parker, John, *Warren Beatty: The Last Great Lover of Hollywood*. Headline, 1993.

Reed, Dr. Donald A., *Robert Redford*. Popular Library, 1975.

Thompson, Douglas, *Sharon Stone: Basic Ambition*. Little, Brown, 1994.

Zec, Donald, *Lee Marvin*. New English Library, 1979.

Magazine and newspaper articles

Aldridge, David, 'Going West', in *Film Review*, March 1994.

Austin, John, 'Lucky Lady', in *Photoplay*, November 1975.

Bassom, David, Murphy, Edward, and Crawley, Tony, 'The Tide is High' in *Film Review*, December 1995.

Bloom, Phillipa, 'Anne Archer', in *Empire*, February 1991.

Bygrave, Mike, 'Hackman at 51', in *Mail on Sunday*, 31 October 1982.

Castell, David, 'Will the Real Gene Hackman Stand Up Please?' in *Films Illustrated*, September 1978.

Cates, Gilbert, 'Life with Father', in *Action*, August–September 1970.

Davis, Victor, 'Popeye Doyle is Back on Spinach', in *Daily Express*, 11 January 1985.

Friedkin, William, 'Anatomy of a Car Chase', in *Action*, March–April 1972.

Goldstein, Patrick, 'It's Only a Movie', in *Empire*, June 1989.

Hibbert, Tom, 'Spike Lee', in *Empire*, April 1993.

Lewin, David, 'Hard Man Gene, back as Mr Nice Guy', in *Sunday Mirror*, 1 March 1981.

Lurie, Rod, 'Having a Lousy Time', in *Empire*, February 1991.

Mann, Roderick, 'What Gene Discovered When He Quit', in *Sunday Express*, 14 January 1979.

Milne, Tom, 'Eureka', in *Sight and Sound*, autumn 1982.

Mueller, Matt, 'The Book Club', in *Empire*, October 1993.

Ritchie, Michael, 'Snow Job', in *Action*, August–September 1970.

Walker, Beverly, 'Gene Hackman', in *Empire*, July 1991.

Filmography

Mad Dog Coll. 1961. Thalia Films. Directed by Burt Balaban. Produced by Edward Schreiber. Screenplay by Edward Schreiber. Photographed by Gayne Reschner. Music by Stu Phillips. Cast: John Davis Chandler, Neil Nephew, Brooke Hayward, Jerry Orbach, Telly Savalas, Vincent Gardenia, Kay Doubleday, Glenn Cannon, Tom Castronova, Joy Harmon, Gene Hackman. 87 minutes.

Lilith. 1964. Columbia/Centaur Productions. Produced and Directed by Robert Rossen. Screenplay by Robert Rossen and Robert Alan Arthur, from the novel by J.R. Salamanca. Photographed by Eugene Shufttan. Music by Kenyon Hopkins. Cast: Warren Beatty, Jean Seberg, Peter Fonda, Kim Hunter, Anne Meacham, James Patterson, Jessica Walter, Gene Hackman. 114 minutes.

Hawaii. 1966. United Artists/Mirisch. Directed by George Roy Hill. Produced by Walter Mirisch. Screenplay by Dalton Trumbo, from the novel by James A. Michener. Photographed by Russell Harlan. Music by Elmer Bernstein. Cast: Julie Andrews, Max Von Sydow, Richard Harris, Carroll O'Connor, Elizabeth Cole, Diane Sherry, Heather Menzies, Torin Thatcher, Gene Hackman. 186 minutes.

First to Fight. 1966. Warner Brothers. Directed by Christian Nyby. Produced by William Conrad. Screenplay by Gene L. Coon. Photographed by Harold Wellman. Music by Fred Steiner. Cast: Chad Everett, Marilyn Devlin, Dean Jagger, Bobby Troup, Claude Akins, Gene Hackman, James Best. 97 minutes.

A Covenant with Death. 1966. Warner Brothers. Directed by Lamont Johnson. Produced by William Conrad. Screenplay by Larry Marcus and Saul Levitt, from the novel by Stephen Becker. Photographed by Robert Burks. Music by Leonard Rosenman. Cast: George Maharis, Laura Devon, Katy Jurado, Earl Holliman, Sidney Blackmer, Gene Hackman, John Anderson, Wende Wagner. 96 minutes.

Banning. 1967. Universal. Directed by Ron Winston. Produced by Dick Berg. Screenplay by James Lee, from a story by Hamilton Maule. Photographed by Loyal Griggs. Music by Quincy Jones. Cast: Robert Wagner, Anjanette Comer, Jill St John, Guy Stockwell, James Farentino, Susan Clark, Howard St John, Mike Kellin, Gene Hackman. 102 minutes.

Bonnie and Clyde. 1967. Tatira-Hiller-Warner Brothers. Directed by Arthur Penn. Produced by Warren Beatty. Screenplay by David Newman and Robert Benton. Photographed by Burnett Guffey. Music by Charles Strouse. Cast: Warren Beatty, Faye Dunaway, Michael J. Pollard, Gene Hackman, Estelle Parsons, Denver Pyle, Dub Taylor, Evan Evans, Gene Wilder. 111 minutes.

The Split. 1968. Spectrum/MGM. Directed by Gordon Flemyng. Produced by Robert Chartoff and Irwin Winkler. Screenplay by Robert Sabaroff, from the novel *The Seventh* by Richard Stark. Photographed by Burnett Guffey. Music by Quincy Jones. Cast: Jim Brown, Diahann Carroll, Ernest Borgnine, Julie Harris, Gene Hackman, Jack Klugman, Warren Oates, James Whitmore, Donald Sutherland. 89 minutes.

Riot. 1968. Paramount/William Castle. Directed by Buzz Kulik. Produced by William Castle. Screenplay by James Poe, from the novel by Frank Elli. Photographed by Robert B. Hauser. Music by Christopher Komeda. Cast: Jim Brown, Gene Hackman, Ben Carruthers, Mike Kellin, Gerald O'Loughlin, Clifford David, Bill Walker, Ricky Summers, Warden Frank A. Eyman. 96 minutes.

Marooned. 1969. Frankovich/Sturges/Columbia. Directed by John Sturges. Produced by Mike J. Frankovich. Screenplay by Mayo Simon, from the novel by Martin Caidin. Photographed by Daniel Fapp. Cast: Gregory Peck, Richard Crenna, David Janssen, James Franciscus, Gene Hackman, Lee Grant, Nancy Kovack, Mariette Hartley, Scott Brady. 133 minutes.

Downhill Racer. 1969. Wildwood International/Paramount. Directed by Michael Ritchie. Produced by Richard Gregson. Screenplay by James Salter, from the novel *The Downhill Racers* by Oakley Hall. Photographed by Brian Probyn. Music by Kenyon Hopkins. Cast: Robert Redford, Gene Hackman, Camilla Sparv, Joe Jay Jalbert, Timothy Kirk, Dabney Coleman, Jim McMullan, Oren Stevens. 101 minutes.

I Never Sang for My Father. 1970. Jamel/Columbia. Produced and Directed by Gilbert Cates. Screenplay by Robert Anderson, from his own play. Photographed by Morris Hartzband and George Stoetzel. Music by Al Gorgoni and Barry Mann. Cast: Melvyn Douglas, Gene Hackman, Dorothy Stickney, Estelle Parsons, Elizabeth Hubbard, Lovelady Powell, Daniel Keyes. 92 minutes.

Doctors' Wives. 1970. Frankovich/Columbia. Directed by George Schaefer. Produced by Mike J. Frankovich. Screenplay by Daniel Taradash, from the novel by Frank G. Slaughter. Photographed by Charles B. Lang. Music by Elmer Bernstein. Cast: Richard Crenna, Janice Rule, John Colicos, Diana Sands, Gene Hackman, Rachel Roberts, Dyan Cannon, Carroll O'Connor, Cara Williams. 102 minutes.

The Hunting Party. 1971. Brighton Pictures/Levy-Gardner-Laven. Directed by Don Medford. Produced by Lou Morheim. Screenplay by William Norton, Gilbert Alexander and Lou Morheim. Photographed by Cecilio Pania Gua. Music by Riz Ortolani. Cast: Oliver Reed, Candice Bergen, Gene Hackman, Simon Oakland, Mitchel Ryan, L.Q. Jones, G.D. Spradlin, William Watson. 108 minutes.

Cisco Pike. 1971. Columbia/Acrobat. Directed by Bill L. Norton. Produced by Gerald Ayres. Screenplay by Bill L. Norton. Photographed by Vilis Lapenieks. Music supervision by Bob Johnston. Cast: Kris Kristofferson, Gene Hackman, Karen Black, Harry Dean Stanton, Viva, Joy Bang, Roscoe Lee Brown. 94 minutes.

The French Connection. 1971. D'Antoni/Schine-Moore/Twentieth Century Fox. Directed by William Friedkin. Produced by Philip D'Antoni. Screenplay by Ernest Tidyman from the book by Robin Moore. Photographed by Owen Roizman. Music by Don Ellis. Cast: Gene Hackman, Fernando Rey, Roy Scheider, Tony LoBianco, Marcel Bozzuffi, Frederic de Pasquale, Bill Hickman,

Ann Rebbot, Harold Gary, Arlene Farber. 104 minutes.

Prime Cut. 1972. Cinema Center. Directed by Michael Ritchie. Produced by Joe Wizan. Screenplay by Robert Dillon. Photographed by Gene Polito. Music by Lalo Schifrin. Cast: Lee Marvin, Gene Hackman, Angel Tompkins, Gregory Walcott, Sissy Spacek, Janit Baldwin, William Morey, Clint Ellison. 86 minutes.

The Poseidon Adventure. 1972. Kent/Twentieth Century Fox. Directed by Ronald Neame. Produced by Irwin Allen. Screenplay by Stirling Silliphant and Wendell Mayes, from the novel by Paul Gallico. Photographed by Harold Stine. Music by John Williams. Cast: Gene Hackman, Ernest Borgnine, Red Buttons, Carol Lynley, Roddy McDowall, Stella Stevens, Shelly Winters, Jack Albertson, Pamela Sue Martin, Arthur O'Connell, Eric Shea, Leslie Nielsen. 117 minutes.

Scarecrow. 1973. Warner Brothers. Directed by Jerry Schatzberg. Produced by Robert M. Sherman. Screenplay by Garey Michael White. Photographed by Vilmos Zsigmond. Music by Fred Myrow. Cast: Gene Hackman, Al Pacino, Dorothy Tristan, Ann Wedgeworth, Richard Lynch, Eileen Brennan, Penny Allen, Richard Mackman. 112 minutes.

The Conversation. 1974. Coppola Company/Director Company/Paramount. Directed by Francis Ford Coppola. Produced by Francis Ford Coppola and Fred Roos. Screenplay by Francis Ford Coppola. Photographed by Bill Butler. Music by David Shire. Cast: Gene Hackman, John Cazale, Allen Garfield, Frederic Forrest, Cindy Williams, Michael Higgins, Elizabeth MacRae, Teri Garr, Harrison Ford, Mark Wheeler, Robert Duvall (uncredited). 113 minutes.

Zandy's Bride. 1974. Harvey Matofsky/Warner Brothers. Directed by Jan Troell. Produced by Harvey Matofsky. Screenplay by Marc Norman, from the novel *The Stranger* by Lillian Bos Ross. Photographed by Jordan Cronenweth. Music by Fred Karlin. Cast: Gene Hackman, Liv Ullmann, Eileen Heckart, Harry Dean Stanton, Joe Santos, Frank Cady, Sam Bottoms. 116 minutes.

Young Frankenstein. 1974. Gruskoff/Venture/Crossbow/Jouer/Twentieth Century Fox. Directed by Mel Brooks. Produced by Michael Gruskoff. Screenplay by Gene Wilder and Mel Brooks. Photographed by Gerald Hirschfeld. Music by John Morris. Cast:

Gene Wilder, Peter Boyle, Marty Feldman, Madeline Kahn, Cloris Leachman, Teri Garr, Kenneth Mars, Gene Hackman. 108 minutes.

Night Moves. 1975. Hiller/Layton/Warner Brothers. Directed by Arthur Penn. Produced by Robert M. Sherman. Screenplay by Alan Sharp. Photographed by Bruce Surtees. Music by Michael Small. Cast: Gene Hackman, Jennifer Warren, Edward Binns, Harris Yulin, Kenneth Mars, Janet Ward, James Woods, Anthony Costello, John Crawford, Melanie Griffith, Susan Clarke. 99 minutes.

Bite the Bullet. 1975. Persky/Bright/Vista/Columbia. Produced and directed and written by Richard Brooks. Photographed by Harry Stradling Jnr. Music by Alex North. Cast: Gene Hackman, Candice Bergen, James Coburn, Ben Johnson, Ian Bannen, Jan Michael Vincent, Mario Arteaga, Robert Donner, Robert Hoy. 131 minutes.

French Connection II. 1975. Twentieth Century Fox. Directed by John Frankenheimer. Produced by Robert L. Rosen. Screenplay by Robert Dillon, Laurie Dillon and Alexander Jacobs. Photographed by Claude Renoir. Music by Don Ellis. Cast: Gene Hackman, Fernando Rey, Bernard Fresson, Jean-Pierre Castaldi, Charles Millot, Cathleen Nesbitt, Pierre Collet, Alexandre Fabre, Ed Lauter. 119 minutes.

Lucky Lady. 1975. Gruskoff/Venture/Twentieth Century Fox. Directed by Stanley Donen. Produced by Michael Gruskoff. Screenplay by Willard Huyck and Gloria Katz. Photographed by Geoffrey Unsworth. Music by Ralph Burns. Cast: Gene Hackman, Liza Minnelli, Burt Reynolds, Geoffrey Lewis, John Hillerman, Robby Benson, Michael Hordern, Anthony Holland, John McLiam, Val Avery. 118 minutes.

The Domino Principle. 1976. Associated General. Produced and directed by Stanley Kramer. Screenplay by Adam Kennedy, from his own novel. Photographed by Fred Koenekamp and Ernest Laszlo. Music by Billy Goldenberg. Cast: Gene Hackman, Candice Bergen, Richard Widmark, Mickey Rooney, Edward Albert, Eli Wallach, Ken Swofford, Neva Patterson, Jay Novello. 100 minutes.

March or Die. 1977. Dick Richards/Associated General/ITC. Directed by Dick Richards. Produced by Dick Richards and Jerry Bruckheimer. Screenplay by David Zelag Goodman. Photographed by John Alcott. Music by Maurice Jarre. Cast: Gene

Hackman, Terence Hill, Catherine Deneuve, Max Von Sydow, Ian Holm, Jack O'Halloran, Marcel Bozzuffi. 107 minutes.

A Bridge Too Far. 1977. Joseph E. Levine/United Artists. Directed by Richard Attenborough. Produced by Joseph E. Levine and Richard P. Levine. Screenplay by William Goldman from the book by Cornelius Ryan. Photographed by Geoffrey Unsworth. Music by John Addison. Cast: Dirk Bogarde, James Caan, Michael Caine, Sean Connery, Edward Fox, Elliott Gould, Gene Hackman, Anthony Hopkins, Hardy Kruger, Laurence Olivier, Ryan O'Neal, Robert Redford, Maximilian Schell, Liv Ullmann. 175 minutes.

Superman – The Movie. 1978. Dovement-International/Warner Brothers. Directed by Richard Donner. Produced by Pierre Spengler. Executive Producer, Ilya Salkind. Screenplay by Mario Puzo, David Newman, Leslie Newman and Robert Benton. Photographed by Geoffrey Unsworth. Music by John Williams. Cast: Marlon Brando, Gene Hackman, Christopher Reeve, Margot Kidder, Valerie Perrine, Ned Beatty, Jackie Cooper, Marc McClure, Susannah York, Trevor Howard, Harry Andrews, Terence Stamp, Sarah Douglas, Jack O'Halloran, Glenn Ford. 143 minutes.

Superman II. 1980. Dovemead-International/Warner Brothers. Directed by Richard Lester. Produced by Pierre Spengler. Executive Producer, Ilya Salkind. Screenplay by Mario Puzo, David Newman and Leslie Newman. Photographed by Geoffrey Unsworth and Bob Paynter. Music by Ken Thorne. Cast: Gene Hackman, Christopher Reeve, Ned Beatty, Jackie Cooper, Terence Stamp, Sarah Douglas, Jack O'Halloran, Margot Kidder, Valerie Perrine, Susannah York, E.G. Marshall, Marc McClure. 127 minutes.

All Night Long. 1981. Universal. Directed by Jean-Claude Tramont. Produced by Leonard Goldberg and Jerry Weintraub. Screenplay by W.D. Richter. Photographed by Philip Lathrop. Music by Ira Newborn. Cast: Gene Hackman, Barbra Streisand, Diane Ladd, Dennis Quaid, Kevin Dobson, William Daniels, Ann Doran, Jim Nolan. 87 minutes.

Reds. 1981. Paramount. Produced and directed by Warren Beatty. Screenplay by Warren Beatty and Trevor Griffiths. Photographed by Vittorio Storaro. Music by Stephen Sondheim and Dave Grusin. Cast: Warren Beatty, Diane Keaton, Edward Herrmann, Jerzy Kosinski, Jack Nicholson, Paul Sorvino, Maureen Stapleton,

Nicolas Coster, M. Emmet Walsh, Gene Hackman. 196 minutes.

Eureka. 1982. Recorded Picture Company/JF/Sunley/MGM/UA. Directed by Nicolas Roeg. Produced by Jeremy Thomas. Screenplay by Paul Mayersberg. Photographed by Alex Thomson. Music by Stanley Myers. Cast: Gene Hackman, Theresa Russell, Rutger Hauer, Jane Lapotaire, Mickey Rourke, Ed Lauter, Joe Pesci. 129 minutes.

Misunderstood. 1983. Accent/Keith Barish. Directed by Jerry Schatzberg. Produced by Tarak Ben Ammar. Screenplay by Barra Grant, based on the novel by Florence Montgomery. Photographed by Pasqualino de Santis. Music by Michael Hope. Cast: Gene Hackman, Henry Thomas, Rip Torn, Huckleberry Fox, Maureen Kerwin, Susan Anspach, June Brown, Helen Ryan. 91 minutes.

Under Fire. 1983. Greenberg/Lion's Gate/Orion. Directed by Roger Spottiswoode. Produced by Jonathan Taplin. Screenplay Ron Shelton and Clayton Frohman. Photographed by John Alcott. Music by Jerry Goldsmith. Cast: Nick Nolte, Gene Hackman, Joanna Cassidy, Jean-Louis Trintignant, Ed Harris, Richard Masur, Hamilton Camp. 127 minutes.

Uncommon Valor. 1983. Paramount. Directed by Ted Kotcheff. Produced by John Milius and Buzz Feitshans. Screenplay by Joe Gayton. Photographed by Stephen H. Burum and Ric Waite. Music by James Horner. Cast: Gene Hackman, Robert Stack, Fred Ward, Red Brown, Randall 'Tex' Cobb, Patrick Swayze, Harold Sylvester. 105 minutes.

Twice in a Lifetime. 1985. Yorkin Company. Produced and directed by Bud Yorkin. Screenplay by Colin Welland. Photographed by Nick McLean. Music by Pat Metheny. Cast: Gene Hackman, Ann-Margret, Ellen Burstyn, Amy Madigan, Ally Sheedy, Stephen Lang, Darrell Larson, Brian Dennehy. 117 minutes.

Target. 1985. CBS. Directed by Arthur Penn. Produced by Richard D. Zanuck and David Brown. Screenplay by Howard Berk and Don Petersen, from a story by Leonard Stern. Photographed by Jean Tournier and Robert Jessup. Music by Michael Small. Cast: Gene Hackman, Matt Dillon, Gayle Hunnicutt, Victoria Fyodorova, Ilona Grubel, Herbert Berghof. 118 minutes.

Power. 1985. Lorimar/Polar. Directed by Sidney Lumet. Produced by Reene Schisgal and Mark Tarlov. Screenplay by David Himmelstein. Photographed by Andrzej Bartkowiak. Music by Cy Coleman. Cast: Richard Gere, Julie Christie, Gene Hackman, Kate Capshaw, Denzel Washington, E.G. Marshall, Beatrice Straight, Fritz Weaver, Michael Learned. 111 minutes.

Hoosiers (UK: *Best Shot*). 1986. Carter De Haven/Hemdale/Orion. Directed by David Anspaugh. Produced by Carter De Haven and Angelo Pizzo. Screenplay by Angelo Pizzo. Photographed by Fred Murphy. Music by Jerry Goldsmith. Cast: Gene Hackman, Barbara Hershey, Dennis Hopper, Sheb Wooley, Fern Parsons, Brad Doyle, Steve Hollar, Brad Long. 114 minutes.

No Way Out. 1987. Orion. Directed by Roger Donaldson. Produced by Laura Ziskin and Robert Garland. Screenplay by Robert Garland. Photographed by John Alcott. Music by Maurice Jarre. Cast: Kevin Costner, Gene Hackman, Sean Young, Will Patton, Howard Duff, George Dzundza. 106 minutes.

Superman IV. 1987. Cannon. Directed by Sidney J. Furie. Produced by Menahem Golan and Yoram Globus. Screenplay by Mark Rosenthal and Lawrence Konner, from a story by Christopher Reeve, Mark Rosenthal and Lawrence Konner. Photographed by Ernest Day. Cast: Christopher Reeve, Gene Hackman, Margot Kidder, Jackie Cooper, Marc McClure, Jon Cryer, Mariel Hemingway, Sam Wanamaker, Mark Pillow. 89 minutes.

BAT 21. 1988. Tri-Star. Directed by Peter Markle. Produced by Jerry Reed. Screenplay by William C. Anderson and George Gordon. Music by Jerry Reed. Cast: Gene Hackman, Danny Glover, Jerry Reed, David Marshall Grant, Clayton Rohner, Erich Anderson, Joe Dorsey. 105 minutes.

Full Moon in Blue Water. 1988. Transworld/Entertainment. Directed by Peter Masterson. Produced by Lawrence Turman, David Foster and John Turman. Screenplay by Bill Bozzone. Photographed by Fred Murphy. Music by Phil Marshall. Cast: Gene Hackman, Teri Garr, Burgess Meredith, Elias Koteas, Kevin Cooney, David Doty. 95 minutes.

Mississippi Burning. 1988. Rank/Orion. Directed by Alan Parker. Produced by Frederick Zollo and Robert F. Colseberry. Screenplay by Chris Gerolmo. Photographed by Peter Biziou. Music by Trevor Jones. Cast: Gene Hackman, Willem Dafoe, Frances McDormand,

Brad Dourif, R. Lee Ermey, Gailard Sartain, Stephen Tobolowsky, Michael Rooker, Pruitt Taylor Vince. 127 minutes.

Another Woman. 1988. Orion/Jack Rollins/Charles H. Joffe. Directed by Woody Allen. Produced by Robert Greenhut. Screenplay by Woody Allen. Photographed by Sven Nykvist. Cast: Gena Rowlands, Mia Farrow, Ian Holm, Blythe Danner, Gene Hackman, Betty Buckley, Martha Plimpton, John Houseman, Sandy Dennis, David Ogden Stiers. 84 minutes.

Loose Cannons. 1989. TriStar/RCA. Directed by Bob Clark. Produced by Aaron Spelling and Alan Greisman. Screenplay by Richard Christian Matheson, Richard Matheson and Bob Clark. Photographed by Reginald H. Morris. Music by Paul Zaza. Cast: Gene Hackman, Dan Aykroyd, Dom DeLuise, Ronny Cox, Nancy Travis, Robert Prosky, Paul Koslo, Dick O'Neill. 94 minutes.

The Package. 1989. Rank/Orion. Directed by Andrew Davis. Produced by Beverly J. Camhe and Tobie Haggerty. Screenplay by John Bishop. Photographed by Frank Tidy. Music by James Newton Howard. Cast: Gene Hackman, Joanna Cassidy, Tommy Lee Jones, Dennis Franz, Reni Santoni, Pam Grier, Chelcie Ross, Ron Dean, Kevin Crowley. 108 minutes.

Narrow Margin. 1990. Guild/Carolco. Directed and photographed by Peter Hyams. Produced by Jonathan A Zimbert. Screenplay by Earl Fenton Jnr. Music by Bruce Broughton. Cast: Gene Hackman, Anne Archer, James B. Sikking, J.T. Walsh, M. Emmet Walsh, Susan Hogan, Nigel Bennett, J.A. Preston. 97 minutes.

Postcards from the Edge. 1990. Columbia. Directed by Mike Nichols. Produced by Mike Nichols and John Calley. Screenplay by Carrie Fisher from her own book. Photographed by Michael Ballhaus. Music by Carly Simon. Cast: Meryl Streep, Shirley MacLaine, Dennis Quaid, Gene Hackman, Richard Dreyfuss, Rob Reiner, Mary Wickes, Conrad Bain, Annette Bening, Simon Callow. 101 minutes.

Class Action. 1991. Twentieth Century Fox. Directed by Michael Apted. Produced by Ted Field, Scott Kroopf and Robert W. Cort. Screenplay by Carolyn Shelby and Christopher Ames. Photographed by Conrad L. Hall. Music by James Horner. Cast: Gene Hackman, Mary Elizabeth Mastrantonio, Colin Friels, Joanna Marlin, Larry Fishburne, Donald Moffat. 109 minutes.

Company Business. 1991. Directed by Nicholas Meyer. Cast: Gene Hackman, Mikhail Baryshnikov, Kurtwood Smith, Terry O'Quinn, Daniel Von Bargen, Oleg Rudnick, Geraldine Danon, Nadim Sawalha, Michael Tomlinson. 98 minutes.

Unforgiven. 1992. Malpasso/Warner Brothers. Directed by Clint Eastwood. Produced by David Valdes. Screenplay by David Webb Peoples. Photographed by Jack N. Green. Music by Lennie Niehaus. Cast: Clint Eastwood, Gene Hackman, Morgan Freeman, Richard Harris, Jaimz Woolvet, Saul Rubinek, Frances Fisher, Anna Thomson. 125 minutes.

The Firm. 1993. Paramount/John Davis/Scott Rudin/Mirage. Directed by Sydney Pollack. Produced by Sydney Pollack, Scott Rudin and John Davis. Screenplay by David Rabe, Robert Towne and David Rayfiel, from the book by John Grisham. Photographed by John Seale. Music by Dave Grusin. Cast: Tom Cruise, Gene Hackman, Jeanne Tripplehorn, Ed Harris, Holly Hunter, Hal Holbrook, David Strathairn. 155 minutes.

Wyatt Earp. 1994. Warner Brothers/HG/Kasdan. Directed by Lawrence Kasdan. Produced by Jim Wilson, Kevin Costner and Lawrence Kasdan. Screenplay by Dan Gordon and Lawrence Kasdan. Photographed by Owen Roizman. Music by James Newton Howard. Cast: Kevin Costner, Dennis Quaid, Gene Hackman, Jeff Fahey, Mark Harmon, Michael Madden, Catherine O'Hara, Bill Pullman, Isabella Rossellini, Tom Sizemore, JoBeth Williams. 191 minutes.

Geronimo. 1994. Columbia. Directed by Walter Hill. Produced by Walter Hill and Neil Canton. Screenplay by John Milius. Photographed by Lloyd Ahern. Music by Ry Cooder. Cast: Jason Patrick, Robert Duvall, Gene Hackman, Wes Studi. 111 minutes.

The Quick and the Dead. 1994. Columbia/TriStar. Directed by Sam Raimi. Produced by Joshua Donen, Allen Shapiro and Patrick Markey. Screenplay by Simon Moore. Photographed by Dante Spinotti. Music by Alan Silvestri. Cast: Sharon Stone, Gene Hackman, Leonardo DiCaprio, Russell Crowe, Pat Hingle, Woody Strode, Michael Stone. 107 minutes.

Crimson Tide. 1995. Hollywood Pictures. Directed by Tony Scott. Produced by Don Simpson and Jerry Bruckheimer. Screenplay by Michael Schiffer. Photographed by Dariusz Wolski. Music by Hans

Zimmer. Cast: Denzel Washington, Gene Hackman, Matt Craven, George Dzundza, Viggo Mortensen, James Gandolfini, Rocky Carroll, Jaime P. Gomez. 116 minutes.

Get Shorty. 1995. MGM/Jersey. Directed by Barry Sonnenfeld. Produced by Danny DeVito. Screenplay by Scott Frank, from the novel by Elmore Leonard. Photographed by Don Peterman. Music by John Lurie. Cast: John Travolta, Gene Hackman, Rene Russo, Danny DeVito, Dennis Farian, Delroy Lindo, James Gandolfini, Jon Gries, Renee Props. 105 minutes.

The Birdcage. 1996. United Artists. Produced and directed by Mike Nichols. Screenplay by Elaine May, from the stage play *La Cage aux Folles* by Jean Poiret and the screenplay by Frances Verbier, Edouard Molinaro, Marcello Danon and Jean Poiret. Photographed by Emmanuel Lubezki. Music by Jonathan Tunick. Cast: Robin Williams, Gene Hackman, Nathan Lane, Dianne Wiest, Dan Futterman, Calista Flockhart, Hank Azaria, Christine Baranski, Tom McGowan. 119 minutes.

Extreme Measures. 1997. Rank-Castle Rock/Turner. Directed by Michael Apted. Produced by Elizabeth Hurley. Screenplay by Tony Gilroy, based on the book by Michael Palmer. Photographed by John Bailey. Music by Danny Elfman. Cast: Hugh Grant, Gene Hackman, Sarah Jessica Parker, David Morse, Bill Nunn, John Toles-Bey. Paul Guilfoyle. 117 minutes.

Index